COMMON
COMPUTER
ABBREVIATIONS

COMMON
COMPUTER
ABBREVIATIONS

John S. De Sousa, B.S.E.E., M.S.E.E.

(Stroke-Survivor)

iUniverse, Inc.

New York   Bloomington

Common Computer Abbreviations

iUniverse books may be ordered through booksellers or by contacting:

iUniverse
1663 Liberty Drive
Bloomington, IN 47403
www.iuniverse.com
1-800-Authors (1-800-288-4677)

ISBN: 978-0-595-48265-8 (pbk)
ISBN: 978-0-595-60352-7 (ebk)

Printed in the United States of America

iUniverse rev. date: 11/19/08

CONTENTS

PREFACE

Randomly use of abbreviations in the daily usage and communication has become a necessity. Lacking a universal forum to create these abbreviations has led to misinterpretation and frequent frustration on the part of many reviewers of technical records and essays. This book has been written with non-technical individuals in mind, and every effort has been made to collect the most frequently used abbreviations.

To explicate individually created abbreviations seems an appalling task. Similar abbreviations have different meanings and connotations in different technical areas, and for different individuals in the same field of specialty! They are more the result of habit and extensive use by different individuals and do not follow any specific and established form or order. Thus some may use a specific abbreviation all in capital letters with or without periods, others may use all lower case letters, and some even may combine capital and lower case letters. Variations in other foreign language letters may be used depending on the individual decision or technical specialty.

In general , this book consists of two parts: In first part, few hundreds of pages, are dedicated to comprehensive listings of abbreviations and acronyms commonly used in Computer and Internet.

(1) The abbreviations are arranged in alphabetical order.

(2) In some cases, alternate abbreviation(s) are enclosed in parenthesis.

(3) If applicable, an original foreign word is italicized.

(4) Emphasis on a needed word, is also italicized.

(5) Mostly, capital letters are used for abbreviations.

(6) Hyphens are used to show how a unique abbreviation is obtained.

In second part of this book, ten useful appendices are given:

1) Appendix A: "Table of Overseas Operating Voltages" — Valuable information to operate a computer or laptop in a foreign country.

2) Appendix B: "SI Electrical Characteristics Symbols" — An useful reference table for those who are interested in computers and Internet.

3) Appendix C: "Scientific Usage of Greek Alphabet" — Shows some Useful usage of Greek Alphabet in scientific area.

4) Appendix D: "Common Decimal SI Prefixes" — Listing of common decimal prefixes used in computers and Internet.

5) Appendix E: "Latin/Roman Numeral Symbols" — Gives listings of Latin and Roman Numeral Symbols used everywhere.

6) Appendix F: "E-mail and Newsgroup Smiley Faces" — "Smiley Faces" used in E-mails.

7) Appendix G: "E-mail Country Code" — Great tool to locate the origin of an E-mail.

8) Appendix H: "SI Weights and Measures" — Comprehensive guide to conversion of metric and non-metric system

9) Appendix I: "US spelled words versus International English" — Listing of some of the words converted to US and International English.

10) Appendix J: "Inspiring and Motivation words".

This collection is in no way a complete list of all the abbreviations in computer and Internet. Every attempt will be made to include more abbreviations hopefully in future editions.

John S, De Sousa, B.S.E.E., M.S.E.E.

(Stroke-Survivor)

ACKNOWLEDGEMENTS

My sincere thanks to my loving brothers and sister, and my whole family for all their support, patience, and help they provided me during my difficulties!

Special thanks to my Pulmonary Physician, for making me healthy again!

Thanks to Chaplain of Mercy General Hospital of Sacramento, California, for praying intensely for my recovery!

Gratitude to all the people of Pulmonary Department of Mercy General Hospital of Sacramento, California, for letting me have a bright life again. May all their students have beautiful lives ahead!

Many thanks to Don Bosco Salesian School, and its Past Rectors, Rev. F. Fedeli, S.D.B., and Rev. A. Picchioni, S.D.B., for leading me to achieve lifelong success in my education!

John S. DeSousa, B.S.E.E., M.S.E.E.
(Stroke-Survivor)

This book is dedicated to my deceased loving parents
who are always treasured in my memory!

Common Computer Abbreviations

A	acceleration; accumulator; ampere; amplitude; analog; angle; angstrom; anode; arc; area; assistant; audio; automatic; average
A+	CompTIA computer certificate
Å	Angstrom
a	are *(100 square metres)*; atto
AA	abbreviated addressing; absolute accuracy; absolute address; absolute assembler; accumulator address; adapter address; analog amplifier; anti-aliasing; archive attribute; auto answer; automatic answer
AAAS	American Association for the Advancement of Science
AAB	all-to-all broadcast
AAC	address automatic configuration; advanced audio coding; automatic aperture control
AAE	Academic American Encyclopedia
AAES	American Association of Engineering Societies
AAF	advanced authoring format
AAL	ATM adaptation layer
AALP	Adobe authorized learning provider
AAP	applications access point
AAS	all-to-all scatter
AASP	Apple authorized service provider; ASCII asynchronous support package

AAT	average access time
AB	accelerator board; adapter board; address book; address bus; alternate buffer; available block; avalanche break-down
A.B.	AB; B.A.; BA; *Artium Baccalaureus* (*Latin:* Bachelor of Arts)
ABA	absolute binary address
ABC	Atanasoff-Berry computer; audio-bass control; automatic balance (*or* bass *or* brightness) control; automatic bass (*or* brightness) compensation
ABD	avalanche break-down
ABEND	abnormal end
ABET	Accreditation Board of Engineering Training
ABI	application binary interface
ABID	answer back identification (*or* identifier)
ABIOS	advanced basic input-output system
ABIST	automatic built-in self-test
ABL	address book library
ABLE	activity balance line evaluation; adaptive battery life extender
ABM	asynchronous balanced mode
ABN	absolute binary number
ABR	available bit rate
ABROM	automatic boot read only memory
ABRS	automated book request system

ABS	abstract; address book synchronization; allocation block size
abs	*absolute* (*Latin:* absolute; completely; perfectly)
ABT	abort; attended bulk transfer
ABTS	ASCII block terminal services
AC	absolute coding; absorption circuit; absorption current; access code; access control; accumulator; acoustic coupler; acoustic coupling; adapter card; adaptive communication; adder accumulator; address connection; addressing capability; air conditioner; air conduction; alphabet code; alphabetic character; alphabetic coding; alternating current; ambient condition; analog channel; analog computer; animated curser; area chart; aspect card; assembly cause; asynchronous computer; attenuation characteristic; automatic check; automatic code; automatic computer; avalanche conduction
A/C	AC; air conditioner
Ac	actinium
a/c	A/C; AC; alternating current
ACA	asynchronous communications adapter; automatic cable (*or* circuit) analyzer
ACAP	application configuration access protocol
ACAS	automated cable analyzer system
ACB	access control byte
ACPI	advanced configuration and power interface
ACC	acceleration; accumulator; address computation circuitry; alternating charge characteristic; Apple compatible cable; automatic color compensation

ACCFF	alternating current coupled flip-flop
ACCMAIL	accessing electronic-**mail**
ACD	audio compact disc; automatic call distribution
ACDA	audio compact disc access
ACDI	asynchronous communications device interface
ACDS	audio compact disc support
ACE	access control encryption (*or* entry); advanced computing environment; automatic computing engine
ACF	access control field; advanced communication function; aural carrier frequency
ACFR	allocate cannot find route
ACH	automated clearing house
ACI	asynchronous communication interface
ACIA	asynchronous communication interface adapter
ACIAS	automated calibration interval analysis system
ACIS	American Committee for Interoperable Systems
ACK	acknowledge; acknowledgement
ACL	access control list
ACM	access control matrix (*or* memory); Association Computing Management; Association for Computing Machinery; audio compression manager
ACMS	application control management system
ACO	automatic check-out

ACORE	automatic check-out and readiness equipment; automatic check-out and readiness (*or* recording) equipment
ACP	ancillary control program; auxiliary control process
ACPI	advanced configuration and power interface
ACR	actual (*or* allowed) cell rate; advanced communication riser; audio cassette recorder
ACRC	A.C.R.C.; Advanced Cisco Router Configuration
ACRE	automatic checkout and readiness equipment
ACROSS	automated cargo release and operation service system
ACS	access (*or* automatic) control system; advanced computer system; anti-curl system; asynchronous channel splitter; asynchronous communication server (*or* system)
ACSS	analog computer sub-system; audio cascading style sheets
ACT	access control table; advanced computerized tomography; analog cellular telephone
ACTIS	advanced computerized tomography inspection system
ACTS	advanced communication technology satellite; automated computer time service
ACTT	advanced communication and time-keeping technology
ACTV	advanced compatible television
ACU	addressable control unit; anti-coincidence unit; array configuration utility; automatic calling unit
ACV	advanced common view

AD	absolute dimension; acoustic data; administrative domain; advantage disassembler; advertisement; aliasing distortion; alphanumeric display; alternative denial; amplitude distortion; application data; auctioneering device; audio device; audio driver; automatic dial; automatic dictionary; avalanche diode; average deviation; axis deviation
A/D	AD; analog-to-digital
ADA	airborne droplet analyzer; Augusta **Ada** Lovelace *(inventor of **ADA** programming language)*; automatic data acquisition
ADB	Apple desktop bus
ADC	adaptive data compression; add carry; analog-to-digital conversion (*or* converter)
ADCCP	advanced data communication control procedure
ADD	analog-digital data; automatic document detection
add	*adde* (*Latin:* add; addition)
ADDC	add carry
ADDT	analog-digital data transmission
ADF	adapter description file; automatic direction finder; automatic document feeder; automatically defined function
ADI	alternate digit inversion
ADL	address data latch
ADLAT	adaptive lattice *filter*
ADLC	asynchronous data link control
ADM	adaptive delta modulation; advanced data-base manager

ADMACS	Apple document management and control system
ADMD	administrative management domain
ADN	advanced digital network
ADNS	advanced digital network system
ADO	active data objects; ActiveX data objects
ADP	adaptive differential pulse; attach during processing; automatic data processing
ADPC	adaptive differential pulse code
ADPCM	adaptive differential pulse code modulation
ADR	adder; address; advanced digital recorder
ADS	AppleDesign speaker; application (*or* assembler) development system; asymmetric digital subscriber; automatic data switch; automatic distribution system; available directory slot
ADSC	Adobe document structuring convention
ADSI	active directory service interface; analog display service interface
ADSL	asymmetric digital subscriber line (*or* loop)
ADSP	Apple data-stream protocol
ADT	Apple's disk tool; application data types; asynchronous data transfer (*or* transmission)
ADU	automatic dialing unit
ADX	automatic data exchange
AE	absolute element; absolute error; active element; adaptive equalization; alignment error; ancillary equipment; asynchronous event; auxiliary equipment

AEB   analog expansion bus

AEBF   automatic executable batch file

AEC   automatic (*or* automotive) electronic control

AEL   average effectiveness level

AER   accumulator extension register

AERO   automated electrical retest operation

AES   advanced encryption standard; airborne emission
              spectrometer; audio editing software

AESA   ATM end system address

AF   abnormal frequency; abort flag; active file; active filter;
              address field; air force; application fit; audio frequency;
              automated factory; automatic file; auxiliary flag

aF   atto-farad

AFA   accelerated file access

AFB   analog feed-back

AFC   analog function circuit; application foundation class;
              automatic font change; automatic frequency control

AFD   automatic file distribution

AFE   Apple file exchange

AFF   asynchronous flip-flop

AFI   authority and format identifier

AFII   Association for Font Information Interchange

AFG   arbitrary function generator

AFIPS   American Federation of Information Processing
              Societies

AFIRM	automated fingerprint image reporting and match
AFIS	automated finger-print identification system
AFM	Adobe font metrics
AFP	advanced function presentation (*or* printing); analog flat panel; AppleShare file protocol; AppleTalk filing protocol
AFPC	automatic frequency phase control
AFPDP	AppleShare file protocol directory path; AppleTalk filing protocol directory path
AFPEID	AppleShare file protocol entry identification; AppleTalk filing protocol entry identification
AFR	annualized failure rate; audio frequency response; automatic forward reset
AFS	Andrew file system
AFSK	audio frequency shift key(ing)
AFT	anonymous file transfer
AFTP	anonymous file transfer protocol
AG	Adele-Goldstein; arithmetic game; asynchronous gateway
Ag	*argentum* (*Latin:* silver)
AGA	advanced graphics adapter
AGC	access grant channel; automatic gain control
AGP	accelerated (*or* advanced) graphic port
AGSGD	aluminum gate and silicon gate differences
AGU	address generation unit
AH	active hub; ampere-hour; automatic hold

Ah	ampere-hour
aH	atto-henry
AHA	advanced heuristic analysis
AHS	automated highway system
AI	accumaster integrator; active interrupt; Adobe Illustrator; alphanumeric instruction; analog interface; arithmetic instruction; armed interrupt; artificial intelligence; assembly instruction; automatic indexing; automatic intelligence; automatic interrupt; available inventory; average inventory; axis inhibit; axis interchange; axis inversion
AIA	application integration architecture
AIAA	American Institute of Aeronautics and Astronautics
AIC	AIX interface composer
AICK	Apple Internet connection kit
AIEE	American Institute of Electrical Engineers
AIER	average instruction execution rate
AIET	average instruction execution time
AIF	active (*or* attached *or* available) indexed file; audio interchangeable format
AIFF	audio interchangeable file format
AIIM	Association for Information and Image Management
AIM	AOL Instant Messenger; avalanche induced migration
AIN	advanced intelligent network
AIO	all-in-one
AI/O, AIO	analog input/output

AIP	American Institute of Physics
AIS	automated identification (*or* information) system
AISB	Association of Imaging Service Bureaus
AISP	Association of Information Systems Professionals
AIT	advanced information technology; advanced intelligent tape
AITP	Association of Information Technology Professionals
AIX	advanced interactive executive
AL	absolute loader; access line; address latch; AppleLink; application layer; artificial language; assembly language; assembly list; automatic loader; automatic log-on; average letter
Al	Aluminium; Aluminum
ALAP	AppleTalk link access protocol
ALAT	advanced load address table
ALB	analog loop-back
ALC	arithmetic logic circuit; automatic level control
ALD	automatic loader diagnostic
ALDC	adaptive lossless data compression
ALDT	automatic loader diagnostic test
ALE	address latch enable; application linking and embedding
ALF	adaptive lattice filter; allocation length field
ALGOL	algorithmic oriented language
ALINK	active link

ALIWEB	archived like indexing **Web**
ALL	assembly level language
ALN	asynchronous learning network
ALO	automatic log-on
ALP	assembly language processor (*or* programming)
ALPC	algorithmic language program conversion
ALRP	APT long range program
ALRS	arithmetic logic register stack
ALS	adjacent link station; advanced laser simulator
Alt	alternate; alternative; altitude; Apple local talk
ALU	arithmetic logic unit
ALVC	advanced low voltage CMOS
AM	access method; access mode; active matrix; active mode; active monitor; address modification; admissible mark; alphanumeric mode; amplitude; amplitude modulation; amplitude modulator; analog multiplier; angle modulation; arithmetic mean; asynchronous machine; attendant message; automatic mode; automatic monitoring; automatic manual; auxiliary memory
A.M.	AM; MA; MA; *Artium Magister* (*Latin:* Master of Arts)
Am	americium
a.m.	AM; A.M.; *ante meridiem* (*Latin:* morning; am)
AMA	actuated mirror array; automated message accounting
AMANDA	automated messaging and directory assistance

AMB	addressing mode byte
AMBA	advanced microcontroller bus architecture
AMBO	actual maximum binary objects
AMC	address mismatch count; associative memory condition; asynchronous memory capability; automatic modulation control
AMCD	active matrix color display
AMCC	associative memory condition code
AMD	active matrix display; Advanced Micro Devices
AME	asynchronous modem eliminator
AMG	Apple memory guide
AMI	alternate mark inversion; American Megatrends Incorporated
AMIC	alternate mark inversion coding
AMIF	actual maximum indexed file
AML	automatic mailing list
AMLCD	active matrix liquid crystal display
AMM	acoustic mechanical mice; Apple multi-media
AMMA	advanced memory management architecture
AMN	amplitude modulation noise
AMNL	amplitude modulation noise level
AMO	Apple menu options
AMOF	actual maximum open files
AMOV	advanced metal oxide varistor

AMP	active monitor present; advanced mobile phone; ampere; amplification; amplifier; amplitude; automatic message processor; average mean pressure
amp-hr	ampere hour
AMPS	advanced mobile phone service (*or* system); automatic message processing system
AMR	absolute maximum rating
AMS	angle modulated signal (*or* system)
AMSC	amplitude modulation suppressed carrier
AMST	actual maximum simultaneous transaction
AMT	amount; analog module testing; Apple modem tool; available machine time
amu	AMU; atomic mass unit
AMUD	actual maximum used directory
AMURD	actual maximum used routing buffer
AMUX	analog multiplexer
AMV	astable multi-vibrator
AN	acknowledged number; allocation number; alphabetic-numeric; ambient noise; answer; application note; avalanche noise
ANA	Apple network administrator
ANAT	Apple network administrator toolkit
ANC	alphabetic-numeric count
ANDF	architecture neutral distribution format
ANI	automatic number identification (*or* identifier)
ANL	automatic noise limiter

ANML	Australian National Measurements Laboratory
ANN	annotation; artificial neural network
ANOVA	analysis of variance
ANS	advanced network service; American National Standard; answer
ANSA	allocate no slots available
ANSI	American National Standards Institute
ANT	acoustic noise test; Aloha network; antenna; anterior
ANW	advanced NetWare; advantage network; analog network
ANX	automotive network exchange
AO	analog output; arithmetic operation; arithmetic overflow; Armstrong oscillator; audio output
AOC	automatic output control
AOCE	Apple open collaboration environment
AODI	always on dynamic ISDN
AOE	application operating environment
AOF	arithmetic over-flow
AOL	America On-Line
AOM	Apple omni microphone
AOP	amplifier output power; arithmetic operation
AOR	amplifier output rating
AOV	analysis of variance
AP	abnormal preamble; absolute path; absolute program; absolute programming; access priority; adapter plug;

adaptive packet; advantage premium; alignment pin; anomalous propagation; apparent power; application processor; application program; arithmetic progression; attendant phone; automatic programmer; auxiliary processor; available power

APA   adaptive packet assembly; all points addressable; Apple photo access; arithmetic processing accelerator; audio power amplifier

APAM   all points addressable mode

APAR   authorized program analysis report

APAREN   address parity enable

APC   American Power Conversion; automatic phase (*or* picture) control

APCUG   Association of Personal Computer User Groups

APD   avalanche photo diode

APDU   application protocol data units

APE   Apple phone extension

API   advanced programmable interrupt; application programming interface

APIC   advanced programmable interrupt controller

APIS   advanced passenger information system

APL   algorithmic programming language; analog phase lock; average picture level

APLD   auto program locate device

APLL   analog phase locked loop

APM   advanced power management; automated production management

APNIC	Asia-Pacific Network Information Center
APOH	average power-on-hours
APOP	authenticated post office protocol
APP	application; auxiliary power plant
APPC	advanced peer-to-peer communication; advanced program-to-program communication
APPL	application
AppleDOS	Apple disk operating system
APPN	advanced peer-to-peer network
APPN-EN	advanced peer-to-peer network end node
APPN-IR	advanced peer-to-peer network intermedia routing
APPN-IRN	advanced peer-to-peer network intermediate routing network
APPN-NN	advanced peer-to-peer network network node
APPN-NT	advanced peer-to-peer network network
APR	adaptive pattern recognition; April
APRAM	auxiliary programmable random access memory
APRP	adaptive pattern recognition processing
APS	advanced photo (*or* printing) system; active pixel sensor; asynchronous protocol specification
APSDC	active pixel sensor digital camera
APT	address pass through; advanced parallel technology; Apple PlainTalk; automatically programmed tools
APTM	Apple PlainTalk microphone
APU	automatic program unit

AQ	abstraction quotient; accomplishment quotient; achievement quotient; any quantity; automatic queue
AQA	accelerometer quartz array
AQL	acceptable quality level
AR	absolute readout; access rights; accumulator register; accuracy rating; achieved reliability; active ratio; adaptive routing; addend register; addition record; address resolution; alpha release; alternate routing; amplitude ratio; arithmetic register; aspect ratio; audio response; automatic reset; auxiliary routine
Ar	argon
ARA	AppleTalk remote access
A.R.A.	Associate of Royal Academy
ARAC	AppleTalk remote access client
ARAG	anti-reflective anti-glare
ARAP	AppleTalk remote access protocol
ARAS	anti-reflective anti-static
ARBF	all routes broadcast frame
ARC	archive; architecture; audio response calculator; automatic ratio control
ARCA	advanced RISC computing architecture
ARC-M	ARCM; automatic ratio control monitor
ARCnet	ARCNET; attached resource computer network
A.R.C.S.	Associate Royal Society of Science
ARE	alpha radiation error
A.R.I.C.	Associate of Royal Institute of Chemistry

ARJ	**arj**; archive Jung
ARK	automatic repeat key
ARL	adjacent (*or* adjusted) ring length
ARLL	advanced run length limited
ARM	advanced RISC machine; automatic regressive move; asynchronous response mode
ARMA	automatic regressive moving average
ARO	absolute read-out
AROM	active range of motion; automatic-boot read only memory
ARP	address resolution protocol
ARPA	Advance Research Projects Agency
ARPANET	Advance Research Projects Agency Network
ARPF	automatic restart power failure
ARQ	automatic request
ARRL	American Radio Relay League
ARPL	adjust requested privilege level
ARS	Amateur Radio Service; Amateur Radio Station; automatic remote switch; automatic route selection
ART	advanced real time; artificial; arts
ARTA	advanced real time architecture; Apple real time architecture
ARTIC	a real time interface co-processor
ARTS	advanced real time simulation; asynchronous remote take-over server

ARTT   asynchronous remote take-over terminal

ARU   audio response unit

AS   absolute syntax; absolute system; acknowledgement sent; active satellite; active session; active star; active storage; active system; address space; algebraic sum; allocated stock; alter switch; analog signal; analog switch; anti-streamer; AppleShare; application software; application study; application support; archive site; arithmetic section; arithmetic shift; assembly list; audio system; authentication server; automatic selector; automatic stop; automatic switch-over; autonomous system; auxiliary storage

A-S   A-s; ampere-second

As   arsenic

ASA   advanced systems analysis; American Standards Association

ASAI   adjunct switch application interface

ASAP   advanced systems analysis program; as soon as possible; automatic switching and processing

ASB   advanced system buffering

ASBF   all station broadcast frame

ASC   ASCII, active signal correction

ASCC   automatic sequence controlled calculator (*or* computer)

ASCII   American Standard Code for Information Interchange

ASCSI   advanced small computer system interface

ASD   anti-static device; automatic skip driver; automatic synchronized discriminator

ASF	active (*or* advanced) streaming format
ASI	asynchronous-synchronous interface
ASIC	application specific integrated circuit
ASID	allocate server is down
ASIT	advanced security and identification technology
ASK	amplitude shift key(ing)
ASL	adaptive session level; adaptive speed levelling
ASLP	adaptive session level pacing
ASLM	Apple shared library manager
ASM	assembler; assembly
ASME	American Society of Mechanical Engineers
ASMP	American Society of Media Photographers; asymmetric multi-processing
ASN	abstract syntax notation; autonomous system number; average sample number
ASN.1	abstract syntax notation 1
ASO	automatic switch-over
ASP	active server page; anti-static spray; Apple system profile; AppleTalk session protocol; Association of Shareware Professionals; authorized service provider
ASPI	advanced SCSI programming interface
ASPS	advanced signal processing system
ASPX	available sequenced packet exchange
ASPXC	available sequenced packet exchange connection

ASPXCC available sequenced packet exchange connection count

ASR address space register; amplitude slew rate; Apple speech recognition; associative storage register; automatic send-receive; automatic speech recognition; automatic stereophonic recorder

ASRA automatic stereophonic recording amplifier

ASRAM asynchronous static random access memory

ASS analog satellite system; automatic six shooter

AST add-subtract time; addressable synchronous transfer; Albert Wong, Safi Qureshey, Thomas Yuen *(AST Research, Inc.)*; Atlantic Standard Time

AS/U advanced server for UNIX

ASV adjustable shunt voltage

ASVR adjustable shunt voltage regulator

ASW anti-static wipe; Apple StyleWriter

ASYNC asynchronous; asynchronous communication

AT abort timer; acceleration time; acceptance test; access time; acquisition time; active transducer; add time; advanced technology; ambient temperature; analog transducer; analog transmission; AppleTalk; assembly testing; asynchronous timing; atom; attention; audit trail; automatic; automatic theory; automatic ticketing; Azores Time

At astatine

ATA advance technology attachment

ATAPI advanced technology attachment packet interface

ATBMK Asymetrix ToolBook Multimedia Kit

ATC	aspirated thermo-couple
ATDP	attention dial pulse
ATDT	attention dial tone
ATE	adaptive transversal equalizer; automatic test equipment
ATFP	AppleTalk filing protocol
ATG	Apple telecommunication guide
ATH	attention hang-up
ATL	active template library; Adobe type library
ATM	Adobe type manager; Apple telecommunication modem; asynchronous transfer mode; automatic teller machine
atm	atmosphere
ATN	attention
atn	atomic number
ATP	application transaction program; automatic test pattern (*or* program)
ATPG	automatic test pattern (*or* program) generation
ATR	anti transmit-receive; automatic terminal recognition; average transfer rate
ATS	advanced television standards
ATSC	advanced television standards committee; advanced television systems committee; American Television Standards Committee
ATSP	AppleTalk session protocol
ATSUI	Apple type services unicode imaging

ATT	American Telephone and Telegraph; automatic tape transmitter
AT&T	American Telephone *and* Telegraph
ATTN	attention
ATTP	AppleTalk transaction protocol
ATTRIB	attribute
ATV	amateur television; analog television
ATWP	adaptive tree walk protocol
atwt	atomic weight
ATX	advanced technology extended (*or* extension)
ATZ	attention zero
AU	access unit; addressing unit; allocation unit; arithmetic unit; assembly unit; astronomical unit; audio
Å.U	AU; Angstrom unit
Au	*aurum* (*Latin:* gold)
AUC	area under the curve
AUD	audio; audit
AUDI	automated data input
AUDIT	automated data input terminal
AUG	August
AUI	attachment (*or* autonomous) unit interface
AUP	acceptable use policy; arithmetic unit pipe-line
AUTO	automatic; automobile
AUTOEXEC	automatic execution

AUX	auxiliary
A/UX	Apple UNIX
AV	anti-virus
A/V	AV; av; analog video; audio-video; audio-visual
aV	atto-volt
AVA	audio visual authoring
AVC	Apple video compression; audio video compression; audio visual connection; automatic voltage control
AVG	average
AVI	analog video active; audio video (*or* visual) interleave
AVID	Apple video; Apple video display; automatic video display
AVIOS	American Voice Input/Output Society
AVM	absolute value machine; AppleVision monitor
AVP	Apple video-player
AVR	automatic voice recognition; automatic voltage regulation (*or* regulator)
AVT	absolute value transducer; applied video (*or* voice) technology
AVTK	anti-virus tool kit
AVU	anti-virus utility
AW	atomic weight; autonomous working; available work
aW	atto-watt
AWE	advanced wave effects
AWG	American wire gauge

AWGN	additive white Gaussian noise
AWI	automated window inspection
AWID	automated window inspection device
AWK	Al Aho, Peter Weinberger and Brian Kernighan *(famous in UNIX language)*
AWPA	attach while processing attachment
AWR	automatic word recall
AWT	abstract widows tool-kit
AX	architecture extended; architecture extension; automatic **transmission** *(where X→ transmission)*
AY	aramid yarn
AZ	azimuth
Az	*Azote (Greek:* nitrogen)
AZEL	azimuth elevation

~B~

B	back; balance; ballast; band; bandwidth; bank; bar; barrel; barrier; base; basic; bass; batch; battery; bel; bell, beta; big; binary; black; block; blue; book; boot; boron; boundary; bridge; bus; byte; *magnetic flux density*; *susceptance*
b	bit
BA	battery; base address; binary add; binary arithmetic; block access; Boolean algebra; bus available; byte address
B.A.	BA; A.B.; AB; Bachelor of Arts (*Latin* origin: *Artrium Baccalaures*)
Ba	barium
BAC	binary asymmetric channel
BACP	bandwidth allocation control protocol
BAK	backup; binary adaptation kit
BAL	balance; ballast; basic assembly language
BAPI	business application programming interface
BAR	barrel address register
bar	barn
BAS	basic
BASIC	beginners all-purpose symbolic instruction code
BASM	built-in assembler

BAT batch; battery; block address translation (*or* translator)

BB back-bone; bar-board; base bandwidth; base-band; battery backup; black box; blue book; bread-board; broad-band; bucket brigade; buffer box; building block

BBA bucket brigade attack

BBB back-bone bridge

BBBS base-band binary system

BBBT bit boundary block transfer

BBC back-bone circuit; bread-board construction; British Broadcasting Corporation

BBD back-to-back device; base-band data

BBDS base-band digital signal

BB-ISDN BBISDN; broad-band integrated services digital network

BBK bread-board kit

BB-LAN BBLAN; road-band local area network

BBN back-bone network; broad-band noise

BBP boot block programming

BBS Batcher-Banyan switch; bulletin board service (*or* system)

BBT base-band transmission

BBW base band-width; base-band width

BC back coupling; balanced configuration; balancing capacitor; balanced circuit; band center; bar code; barrel connector; barrier capacitance; basic course; bass control; batch control; battery charger; Bezier curve; bifurcated contact; binary cell; binary chain; binary code; binary counter; biphase code; biphase coding; biquinary code; biquinary coding; bistable circuit; bistable component; bit check; Boolean calculus; branch carry; branch circuit; bridge circuit; bridging connection; bridging contact; broad-cast; buffer capacitor; buffer circuit; buffer computer; bypass capacitor

BCC	blind carbon copy; block check character; broadcast control channel
BCD	binary coded decimal; binary count down; breakpoint condition diagnosis
BCFSK	binary coded frequency shift key(ing)
BCH	Bose-Chaudhuri-Hocquenhem
BCI	bar code library; Battery Council International; bit count integrity; broadcast interference
BCL	bar code label; batch command language; broadcast listener (*or* listening)
BCLM	bar code label maker
BCM	broadcast message
BCN	bad connection number
BCO	binary coded octal
BCP	broadcast packet; bulk copy program
BCPL	basic computer programming language
BCR	bar code reader; broadcast radio; byte count register
BCS	bar code sorter; basic control system; broadcast storm; bus control signal

BCT   binary counter transistor; broadcast television

BCW   buffer control word

BD   baby driver; backup data; backup date; bidirectional; binary data; binary digit; binary dump; bit density; block diagram; bode diagram; boot disk; bridge driver; bus driver

Bd   baud

BDA   base displacement address; bi-directional bus; bios data area

BDB   bi-directional buffer (*or* bus); British Digital Broadcasting

BDBD   bi-directional bus driver

BDC   backup domain controller; binary-decimal counter (*or* conversion)

BDI   break-down impedance

BDL   bi-directional line

BDLS   bi-directional loop switching

BDM   background debug mode

BDOS   basic disk operating system

BDP   bandwidth distance product; bi-directional printer (*or* pulse)

BDR   bus device request

BDS   bi-directional signal; branch delay slot

BDSL   broadband digital subscriber line

BDT   bi-directional transistor

BDU   basic display system

BDV	break-down voltage
BDW	background dirty writes; bi-directional waveform
BE	back end; below; big endian; branch equal; bulk encryption; burst error; bus expansion; bus extension
Be	beryllium
BEBO	binary exponential back-off
BECN	backward explicit congestion notification
BED	burst extended data
BEDO	burst extended data out(put)
BEDORAM	burst extended data out(put) random access memory
BEDS	best effort delivery service
BEE	band edge energy
BEF	band elimination filter
BEL	bell
BELLCORE	Bell Communications Research
BEM	boundary element method; bus extender module
BEMA	Business Equipment Manufacturers Association
BeOS	Be Operating System
BER	basic encoding rule; bit error rate (*or* ratio); block error rate
BERT	bit error rate test(er)
BESS	binary electromagnetic signal signature
BeV	billion electron volts (*or* BEV)

BF	back-fill; batch file; bipolar fabrication; blown fuse; bold- face
BFF	binary file format
BFO	beat frequency oscillator
BFR	Bellman-Ford routing
BFS	burst (*or* bunched) frame structure
BFT	binary file transfer
BFTP	batch file transfer protocol
BG	back-ground; balanced-to-ground; big; block gap
BGA	ball grid array
BGAA	ball grid array adapter
BGC	binary-Gray code
BGCC	binary-Gray code conversion
BGE	branch greater or equal
BGI	Borland graphic interface
BGL	burst grant line
BGN	back-ground noise
BGP	back-ground processing (*or* processor *or* program); border gateway protocol
BHE	bus high enable
BHI	branch higher
Bi	bismuth
BI	binary input; block input; branch impedance; branch instruction; burn-in; bus interface

BIA	**b**alanced **i**nstrumentation **a**mplifier
BIAS	**b**alanced **i**nstrumentation **a**mplifier **s**ystem
BIB	**bib**liograph(y)
BIC	**b**uild-**i**n **c**heck; **b**us **i**nterface **c**ircuit; **b**us **i**nterlocked **c**ommunication
BiCMOS	**BICMOS**; **bi**polar **c**omplimentary **m**etal **o**xide **s**emiconductor
BID	**b**iometric **id**entification; **b**lock **i**nteractive **d**ata
BIDA	**b**lock **i**nteractive **d**ata **a**pplication
BIDI	**bi-di**rectional
BIDP	**b**lock **i**nterleaved **d**istributed **p**arity
BIFET	**bi**polar **f**ield **e**ffect **t**ransistor
BIFF	**b**inary **i**nterchange **f**ile **f**ormat
BILE	**b**alanced **i**nductor **l**ogic **e**lement
Billi	**billi**on
BiMOS	**BIMOS**; **bi**polar and **m**etal **o**xide **s**emiconductor
BIN	**bin**ary; **b**inary **i**nput; **b**inary **i**nput **n**umber(s)
BINAC	**bin**ary **a**utomatic **c**omputer
BIND	**B**erkeley **I**nternet **n**ame **d**omain
binhex	**BinHex**; **BINHEX**; **bin**ary **hex**adecimal
BIOS	**b**asic **i**nput-**o**utput **s**ystem
BIP	**b**ad **i**ncoming **p**ackets; **b**inary **i**mage **p**rocessor; **b**lock (*or* **b**ut) **i**nterleaved **p**arity
BIPM	*Bureau International des Poids et Mesures* (*French:* International Bureau of Weights and Measures)

BIS	business information system
B-ISDN	BISDN; broadband integrated services digital network
BIST	built-in-self-test
BiSYNC	BISYNC; BSYNC; binary synchronous communication
BIT	built-in-test
bit	BIT; binary digit
BITE	built-in-test equipment
BITNET	because it's there network; because it's time network
BITNIC	BITNET network information center
bits	binary digits
BIU	bus interface unit
BIW	business intelligence warehouse
BIX	binary (*or* byte) information exchange
BJ	bubble jet
BJT	bipolar junction transistor
BK	back; backup; black; book; book-keeping
Bk	berkelium
BKP	back-up
BL	back lash; back-lit; back log; balanced line; bank link; barrier layer; base line; basic linkage; Bee Line; binary lookup; bit line; bit location; black line; black; blanking level; block length; blue; blue line; boot-strap loader; border line; bridge label; bridge limiter; buffer length; buried layer

BLAN	broadband local area network
BLAST	blocked asynchronous transmission
BLCN	bad logical connection number
BLD	Bold
BLERT	block error rate
BLI	beam-lead isolation
BLK	black; block
BLO	branch lower
BLOB	binary large object
BLOE	branch lower equal
BLS	balanced line system
BLT	branch less than
BLU	binary look-up
BM	backing memory; base material; base memory; base metal; batch mode; bench-mark; bio-medicine; bit-map; black mark; block marking; block mode; block move; branch minus; broadcast message; bubble memory; buffer module; bulk memory; burst mode; bus master; bus mastering; bus mouse; byte manipulation; byte mode; byte multiplexing
BMB	bipolar mask bus; bus mother-board
BMC	bench-mark comparison; bit-mapped character; block multiplexer channel; byte multiplexer channel
BME	bio-medical engineering
BMEWS	ballistic missile early warning system
BMF	bit-mapped font

BMG   bit-mapped graphic

BMIC   bus-master interface controller

BMO   bubble memory operation

BMP   batch message processing; bench-mark problem (*or* program); bipolar micro-program; bit-map; bit-mapped picture (*or* protocol)

BMR   barrel memory register

BMT   beginning of magnetic tape; burst mode transfer

BMV   bistable multi-vibrator

BN   background noise; balanced network; base notation; base number; bridge network; bridge number

BNC   Bayonet Neil-Concelman (*coaxial cable*)

BNE   branch not equal

BNF   Backus-Naur Form; Backus-Normal Form

BNS   backbone network service; binary number system

BNV   branch no overflow

BNZS   bipolar N-zero substitution

BO   back-order; balanced oscillation; balanced oscillator; binary operation; binary operator; binary output; block orientation; block output; blocking oscillator; blown-out; Boolean operator; branch-on; break-out; brown-out; burned-out

BOB   break-out box

BOC   basic operator console; Bell Operating Company

BOF   beginning of file; branch over-flow

BOI   branch output interrupt

BOM	basic online memory; beginning of message; block oriented memory
BOND	bandwidth on demand
BOOTP	boot-strap protocol
BOP	binary object program; bit oriented protocol
BOPS	billion operations per second
BORAM	block oriented random access memory
BOS	basic operating system; bus organized structure
BOT	beginning of table (*or* tape); brown-out detector
BP	back-plane; background processing; background program; backup path; band-pass; band printer; base pointer; batch processing; battery pack; bi-phase; bi-polar; binary pair; binary point; bistable point; bit parallel; bit parity; bit plane; bit position; block parity; Bode plot(ter); boiler plate; boiling point; branch point; break-point; bug patch; by-pass
BPA	bang path address; binary parallel adder; bridge protocol architecture
BPB	BIOS parameter block
BPC	being processed count; bi-phase coding; bi-polar coding; bus program counter; by-pass capacitor
Bpc	bytes per centimeter
bpc	bits per centimeter
BPCD	break-point condition diagnosis
BPCS	band-pass communication system
BPDU	bridge protocol data unit
BPE	back-porch effect

BPF	band-pass filter; bi-polar fabrication
BPI	break-point instruction (*or* interrupt); bus to peripheral interface
Bpi	bytes per inch
bpi	bits per inch
BPL	basic polling loop
BPM	bi-polar mask; blocked pointer mapping
BPMP	bi-polar mask bus; bi-polar micro-program
bpp	bits per pixel
BPR	by-pass register
BPRAM	bi-polar random access memory
BPROM	bi-polar read only memory
BPS	bent pipe satellite; bi-polar semiconductor; break-point switch
Bps	bytes per second
bps	bits per second
BPSI	buffered parallel-serial interface
BPSK	binary phase shift key(ed); binary phase shift keying
BPT	back-plane test(ing); bi-polar transistor
BPU	branch processing unit
BPV	bi-polar violation
BQC	bi-quinary code (*or* coding)
Bq	becquerel

BR	base register; baud rate; beta release; biased register; binary request; bistable relay; blocking rights; blue-ribbon; booster response; boot record; branch; break; break request; bridge; buffer register; byte rate; bytes read
Br	Bromine
bR	bit rate; bits read
BRC	baud rate clock
BREQ	bus request
BRGC	binary reflected gray code
BRI	basic rate interface
BRISC	Berkeley reduced instruction set computer
BRL	burst request line
BROM	blastable read only memory
BRP	blue ribbon program
BRS	bibliographic retrieval service; break (*or* burst) request signal
BS	back-space; backup schedule; backup scheduling; backup server; backup system; balanced system; band splitter; bank select; bank switching; base station; batch system; Batten system; battery system; bipolar semiconductor; bi-stable; binary search; binary signal; binary synchronous; bio-sensor; bit serial; bit sign; bit slice; bit stream; bit string; bit stuffing; block sort; blue sheet; book search; boot sector; boot-strap; breakpoint switch; bubble sort; bus slave
B.S.	BS; B.Sc.; BSc; *Baccalaureus Scientiae* (*Latin*: Bachelor of Science)
BSAM	basic sequential access method

BSC   back-space code; binary synchronous communication; bi-stable circuit (*or* component); boundary scan cell

B.S.C.   BSC; Bachelor of Science in Computers

B.Sc.   *Baccalaureus Scientiae* (*Latin*: Bachelor of Science; BSc; B.S.; BS)

B.Sc.(E.E.)   Bachelor of Science in Electrical Engineering

B.S.C.S.   BSCS; Bachelor Science in Computer Science

BSD   Berkeley source code; bit-slice device

B.S.E.E.   B.S.E.E.; B.Sc.E.E.; Bachelor Science in Electrical Engineering

BSG   Brown-Sharpe gauge

BSI   basic rate interface; British Standards Institute

B.S.I.E.   BSIE; Bachelor Science in Industrial Engineering

BSL   bi-stable latch; boot-strap loader

BSM   basic storage module

BSNP   bad sequence number packets

BSO   bit serial operation

BSP   bi-stable point; bit-slice processor; Burroughs scientific processor

BSPI   buffered serial-to-interface

BSR   bad send request; bank select register; bit scan reverse; blip scan ratio; bi-stable relay; boundary scan register; bubble shift register

BS-RAM   BSRAM; burst static random access memory

BST   bi-stable trigger; boundary scan test; British Summer Time

BSTC	bi-stable trigger circuit
BSTP	bit-stream scaleable type-face package
BSW	bank street writer
BSY	busy
B-SYNC	BSYNC; binary synchronous communication
BT	backup time; balanced transmission; banner text; base time; BASIC tutor; batch total; begin time; bipolar transistor; binary tree; bit test; bit time; block transfer; body text; bold type; bridge tap; buffered timing; burst tolerance; bus token; bus topology; bus transceiver
BTA	basic telecommunication access
BTAM	basic telecommunication access method
BTB	branch target buffer
BTC	bistable trigger circuit; bit test and complement; byte transfer control
bTC	bit transfer control
BTG	balanced-to-ground
BTI	branch target instruction
BTO	build-to-order
BTP	batch transfer program
BTR	bit test and reset
BTREE	binary tree
BTS	bit test and set
BTU	British thermal unit *(large)*
Btu	British thermal unit *(small)*

BTV	broadcast television
BTW	by the way
BU	back-up; backup utility; bus unit
BUBL	bulletin board for libraries
BUC	build-up chart
BUD	back-up date
BUF	buffer
BUP	back-up path
BUS	back-up schedule (*or* server *or* system); boot-up system; broadcast and unknown server; business
BUSS	boot-up system speed
BUT	back-up time
BV	balanced voltage; base video; base voltage; bipolar violation; Boolean variable; breakdown voltage
BVD	boot virus detection
BVM	build-virtual machine
BVP	binary voltage pulse
BW	bytes written
BW	B/W; band-width
B/W	BW; B&W; black-white
BWA	backward wave amplifier
BWC	balanced wire circuit
BWG	Birmingham wire gauge
BWM	block-write mode

BWO	backward wave oscillator
BWS	broken work-station
BWT	black-white television
BW/TV	BWTV; black-white television
BX	box; bus *speed (where X→ speed); **insulated electrical cable***
B2X	binary *to* hexadecimal
BYO	build your own
BZ	branch zero; bu*sy*
B8ZS	bi-polar with 8 zeros substitution

~C~

C	cabinet; cable; call; caller; camera; candle; capacitance; capacitor; capacity; capital; carbon; card; carrier; carry; case; casting; cathode; cell; cellular; Celsius; center; centigrade; centimeter; character; charge; chemistry; chime; chip; circle; circuit; clamp; class; clock; clone; code; cold; collector; color; comment; communication; compact; compare; complement; complete; compound; computation; computer; connection; contact; control; convex; convolution; copper; core; correct; correction; coulomb; count; course; credit; cross; crystal; cube; cubic; Curie; current; cycle; cylinder
c	*celeritas* (*Latin:* speed); centi-; *centum* (*Latin:* hundred)
C^{14}	**carbon radio-active**
CA	calendar age; cathode; character amount; chassis assembly; chip architecture; circuit analyzer; clean area; clear area; clip art; closed architecture; collision avoidance; composition analyzer; computer architecture; constant area; contract alignment; core allocation; cross assembler; current attenuation; cycle availability
CAB	cabinet; compressed application binary
CAD	computer aided design
CADD	computer aided design and drafting
CADE	client application development environment
CADIC	computer aided design of integrated circuit

CAE	client application enabler; computer aided engineering
CAEX	computer aided exploration
CAG	column address generator
CAHS	computer aided hand-scoring
CAI	computer aided instruction
CAIDI	customer average interruption duration index
CAIRN	collaborative advanced inter-agency research network
CAL	calculator; calendar; calibration; calorie *(large)*; client access licence; computer aided language *(or* learning); conversional algebraic language; Cornell Aeronautical Laboratory
cal	calendar; calorie *(small)*; calculation; calculator
calc	calculation; calculator
CALS	computer aided acquisition in logistic support
CAM	common access method *(or* mode); computer aided manufacturing; computer automated measurement; content addressable memory
CAMAC	computer automated measurement and control
CAMC	connection address mismatch count *(or* C/AMC)
CAN	Canada; cancel; controller area network
CANBUS	conroller area network bus
CANCL	cancel
CAP	capacitance; capacitor; capacity; capital; capture; carrier amplitude phase; communication application platform; competitive access provider; computer aided

programming (*or* publishing); configurable array processor; cut and paste

CAPS   capitals

CAR   control address register

CARO   Computer Anti-virus Research Organization

CAS   channel associated signalling; code activated switch; color adapter signal; column address select (*or* strobe); computer aided styling

CASE   computer aided software (*or* system) engineering

CASL   cross-talk application scripting language

CASP   communication application specific processor

CASS   computer assisted search service

CASSIS   classified and search support information system

CAT   cable analyzer-tester; catalog; Central Alaska Time; computer adaptive test; computer aided technology (*or* testing *or* tomography *or* transcription); computer assisted tomography; computer of average transients; computerized axial tomography

CATH   cathode

CATS   computer assisted training system

CATV   cable (*or* community) antenna television; cable television

CAU   controlled access unit

CAV   constant angular velocity

CAVE   computer automatic virtual environment

CAW   channel address word

CB	cable box; call-back; call box; change bank; character boundary; chart box; chatter box; check bit; circuit breaker; clip-board; clock battery; clock bit; code book; cold boot; color balance; color bars; command buffer; command button; computed bound; connection box; control block; control bus; copy back; current balance
C$_B$	capacitance of base *(base capacitance)*
Cb	Columbium
CBC	cache buffer count; Centronics busy condition; cipher block chaining; cyclic binary code
CBCR	channel byte count register
CBD	complete binary decoder
CBDS	connection-less broadband data service
CBEMA	Computer and Business Equipment Manufacturers Association
CBGA	ceramic ball grid array
CBI	channel based interface; computer-based instruction
CBIOS	conventional basic input-output system
CBL	cable bend radius; computer-based learning
CBMS	computer-based mail system
CBP	complex bi-polar; conditional break-point
CBR	circuit board retainer; constant bit rate
CBS	cache block scrapping; cache buffer size; committed burst size; cycle-based simulation
CBT	computer-based training
CBTV	cable television

CBX   call-box; controlled branch exchange

CC   calling card; canned cycle; carbon copy; card cage; card chassis; carriage control; cascade control; change capacity; character check; chroma crawl; circuit capacity; circuit component(s); cleared condition; clock counter; closed caption; closed circuit; cluster controller; coaxial cable; code conversion; code converter; coincidence circuit; collector capacitance; color corrector; column chart; combinational circuit; command control; common carrier; comparator check; complete carry; composite cable; composite conductor; computer circuit; computer clock; computer code; computer configuration; concurrency control; condition code; congestion control; connection control; connection count; continuity checker; control character; control circuit; control code; control counter; correspondence center; coupled circuit; crimp; connection; cross compiler; cross coupling; crossover cable; current changes; cycle counter; cycle criterion; cyclic check; cyclic code; cycling control

C_c capacitance of collector *(collector capacitance)*

c.c   cubic centimeter

CCA   current controlled amplifier

CCC   common capacitor coupling; common control channel; communication control character; counter comparator conversion

CCCL   complementary constant current logic *(or* C^3L*)*

C.C.C.T.   CCCT; CompTIA Certified Computer Technician

CCD   charge-coupled device

CCDA   C.C.D.A.; Cisco Certified Design Associate

CCDP   C.C.D.P.; Cisco Certified Design Professional

CCFL   cold cathode fluorescent

CCFT   cold cathode fluorescent tube

CCGF   collectible card games forum

CCI   common client interface; computer currents interactive

CCIE   C.C.I.E.; Cisco Certified Internet Expert

CCIR   *Comité Consultatif International Radio* (*French:* International Consultative Committee on Radio)

CCIRN   Coordinating Committee for Intercontinental Research Networks

CCIS   common channel interface signalling

CCITT   *Comité Consultatif International Télégraphique et Téléphonique* (*French:* Consultative Committee for International Telegraph and Telephone)

CCL   communication command language; communication control link; connection (*or* cursor) control language

CCM   computer controlled machine; CPU clock multiplier; credit card memory

C/CM   CCM; clock-calendar module

ccm   cubic centimeter per minute

CCM/DAC   CCMDAC; CCM-DAC; capacitively coupled multiplying digital-to-analog converter

CCN   California Computer News

CCNA   C.C.N.A.; Cisco Certified Network Associate

CCNP   C.C.N.P.; Cisco Certified Network Professional

CCP	Certified Computing Professional; chip carrier package; console command processor; communication control program
CCR	central control room; channel control register; condition code register; current charge rate
CCRD	current charge rate divisor
CCRM	current charge rate multiplier
CCS	color calibration system; common channel signalling; common command set; current-controlled switch
CCSD	cellular circuit-switched data
CCSDS	consultative committee for space data system
CCSM	common channel signalling mode
CCT	China Coast Time; clear channel transmission; clock cycle time; congestion controlled traffic; controller card test
CCTU	calculator circuit test unit
CCTV	closed circuit television
CCU	central control unit
CCVT	cold cathode vacuum tube
CCW	channel control word; counter clock-wise
CD	card deck; carrier detect; change directory; change dump; character device; character display; character duration; check digit; chemical deposition; coherent detection; collision detection; collision domain; color depth; color display; compact disc; compact disk; component density; conduction defect; configuration description; connection duration; console debugging; control data; conversion device; coordinating

dimensioning; creation date; critical date; current density; current directory

C2D   character *to* decimal

Cd   cadmium

cd   candela

cd/m²   candelas/meter square; candelas/metre square

CDA   compound document architecture; computerized data acquisition

CDAS   computerized data acquisition system

CDBT   compact disc based training

CDC   code directing character; command and data-handling console; Control Data Corporation; current diameter compensation; cyclic decimal code

CDCE   central data conversion equipment

CDCS   cellular data communication system

CDDI   copper-distributed data interface

CDD   color display device

CD-DA   **CD/DA; CDDA;** compact disc digital audio

CDDI   copper distributed data interface

CD-E   **CD/E; CDE;** compact disc erasable

CDE   common desktop environment

cdev   **CDEV;** control-panel device

CDF   channel definition format; clear direction flag; coma delimited format; common data format

CDFS   compact disc file system

CD+G   compact disc *plus* graphics

CDHC   command and data-handling console

CD-I   CD/I; CDI; compact disc interactive

CDIA   C.D.I.A ; Certified Document Imaging Architect

CDL   computer design language

CDM   corrugated diskette mailer

CDMA   code division multiple access

CD-MO   CD/MO; CDMO; compact disc magneto-optical

CDN   controller drive number

CDOS   current disk operating system

CDP   cellular digital packet (*or* phone); checkout data processor; computer dependent program

CDPD   cellular digital packet data

CDR   critical damping resistance (*or* resistor)

CD-R   CD/R; CDR; compact disc recordable

CD-RAM   CD/RAM; CDRAM; cached dynamic random access memory

CD-RDx   compact disc ROM data exchange standard (*or* CD/RDx)

CD-ROM   CDROM; compact disc read only memory

CD-ROM/XA compact disc read only memory extended architecture

CD-RTOS   CD/RTOS; compact disc real time operating system

CD-RW   CD-R/W; CD/RW; compact disc re-writable

CDS   clock data separator; current directory structure

CDSA   common data security architecture

CDSL   consumer digital subscriber line

CDT   Central Daylight Time; co-directional timing; concentrated data transmission; contra-directional timing; Corel Draw template

CDTP   compelled data transfer protocol

CD-TV   CD/TV; CDTV; compact disc television

CD-V   CD/V; CDV; compact disc video

CDV   cell delay variation

CDW   coordinate dimension word

CD-WO   CD/WO; CDWO; compact disc write once

CD-XA   CD/XA; CDXA; compact disc extended architecture

CE   character element; check error; chemical etching; collision elimination; communication electronics; component error; computer error; consumer electronics; continuing education; contrast enhancement; cryptographic equipment; current entry

C_E capacitance of emitter (*emitter capacitance*)

Ce   cerium

CEC   check error count; coded extension character

CEG   color electron gun

CEI   communication electronics implementation; conducted electromagnetic interference

CEIP   communication electronics implementation plan

CELP   card edge low-profile-socket

CEMA   Consumer Electronics Manufacturers Association

CEMCAN	ceramic matrix composite analyzer
CEMS	constituent electronic mail system
cent	centiare
CEO	Chief Executive Officer
CEOP	conditional end of page
CEPT	Conference of European-administration on Postal and Telecommunication
CER	cell error ratio; certification; certificate; certify
CERT	certification; certificate; certify; computer emergency response team
CET	Central European Time
CF	centrifugal force; character fill; clock frequency; color filter; comb filter; command field; composite filter; connection flag
Cf	californium
CFA	color filter array
CFB	cipher feed-back
CFBM	cipher feed-back mode
CFD	computational fluid dynamics
CFG	configuration
CFI	common flash interface
CFM	cipher feed-back mode; code fragment manager; color fidelity module
cfm	cubic feet per minute
CFP	color flat panel

CFPB	color flat panel board
CFR	Code of Federal Regulations; computerized facial recognition
CFS	common file system; continuous field simulation
CFT	continuous Fourier transform
CFV	call for votes
CFW	cache full write; channel find window
CFWR	cache full write request
CG	character generator; clock Generator; code generator; color graphics; control gate; cumulative graph; current gain
cg	centi-gram
CGA	color graphics adapter
CGB	conversion of Gray to binary
CGCT	*Compagnie Générale des Communications Téléphoniques* (*French:* General Company of the Telephonic Communications)
CGE	common graphics environment
CGF	computer generated force
CGI	common gateway interface; computer generated images computer graphics interface
CGIB	common gateway interface binary
cgi-bin	common gateway interface binary
C_{GK}	capacitance of grid-*kathodos* (*kathodos*→*Greek:* cathode)
CGM	computer graphics meta-file

CGN	colored Gaussian noise
C$_{GP}$	capacitance of grid-plate *(grid-plate capacitance)*
CGQ	channel gain queuing
CGQ-RAM	channel gain queuing random access memory
CGR	cache get request
CG-RAM	**CG/RAM**; **CGRAM**; character generator random access memory
CGS	centimeter-gram-second; clock signal generator
CH	circuit hole; compatible hardware; computer hardware; copy holder
CHAMPION	compatible hardware and milestone program for integrating organized needs
CHAP	challenge handshake authentication protocol
CHAR	character
CHAT	conversational hypertext access technology
CHCK	Check
CHCP	change code page
CHDIR	change directory
CHFN	change finger
CHGRP	change group
CHIL	current hogging injection logic
CHK	Check
CHKCOP	check co-processor
CHKDSK	check disk

CHMOD   change mode

ChLCD   cholesteric liquid crystal display

CHP   chapter

CHR   character; common hardware reference

CHRP   common hardware reference platform

CHS   Centronics handshaking sequence; cylinder head sector

CI   call indicator; character interleave; check indicator; circular interpolation; color information; component interface; computer instruction; computer interface; conditional implication; confidence interval; contingency interrupt; control instruction; coordinate indexing; cycle index; cycle interrupt

C_i   capacitance of input *(input capacitance)*

Ci   curie

CIA   communication (*or* complex) interface adapter; current instruction address

CIAC   computer incident advisory capability

CIC   communication (*or* complex) interface circuit; cycle index counter

CICS   customer information control system

CID   C.I.D.; caller identifier display; caller identifier; charge-injection device; Cisco Internet-work Design; connection identification (*or* identifier)

CIDR   classless inter-domain routing

CIF   clear interrupt flag; common interchange format; customer information feed

CIFS	common Internet file system
CIM	check idle mode; computer integrated manufacturing; constant impedance multiplexer
C$_{in}$	capacitance of input (*input capacitance*)
CIO	Chief Information Officer
CIOCS	communication input-output control system
CIP	capture in progress; commercial instruction processor; command interface port; common indexing protocol
CIPM	*Comité International des Poids et Mesures* (*French:* International Committee for Weights and Measures)
CIR	circle; circular; circulation; committed information rate; current instruction register
CIRC	circle; circular; circulation
CI/RC	circular reference
CIS	client (*or* computer *or* customer) information system; contact image sensor
CISC	complex instruction set chip (*or* computer); customer information control system
Cisco	*Cisco Systems, Inc.*
CIT	C.I.T.; cell insertion time; character interactive traffic Cisco Internet-work Troubleshooting; computer-integrated telephony
CIVR	computer and interactive voice response
CIW	C.I.W.; Certified Internet Webmaster
CIX	commercial information (*or* Internet) exchange; computer-link information exchange
CJ	conditional jump

CJLI	command job language interpreter
CK	command key
CL	calendar life; channel logic; check-list; circuit limiter; circuit load; client layer; closed loop; coding line; combinatorial logic; command language; common link; communication link; composite link; compound logic; condition line; confidence level; connection line; connection link; connection list; control logic; control loop; conversational language; credit limit; current loop; cutter location
C^3L	CCCL; complementary constant current logic
Cl	chloride; chlorine
cL	cl; centi-liter; centi-litre
cl	cutter location
CLAR	channel local address register
CLASS	cables, labels, alignment, screws, sight; custom local area signalling (*or* switching) service
CLC	clear carry flag; current loop cable
CLCK	clock
CLD	cld; cold; cutter location data
CLEC	competitive local exchange carrier
CLF	cross linked file
CLI	clear interrupt flag; client library (*or* loop) interface
CLIC	current loop interface converter
CLID	calling line identification
CLIDR	class-less inter-domain routing

CLK	clock
CLKMUL	CLK/MUL; CLK-MUL; clock multiplier
CLL	compiler level language
CLM	Clarion LEM maker; client-server model;
CLN	connection-less network
CLNP	connection-less network protocol
CLNPP	certified lotus notes peripheral programming
CLO	connection-less operation
CLP	cell loss priority; cellular lightning protector; clip; closed loop program; connection-less packet; constant luminance principle; cord-less phone; cylinder line printer
CLR	cell loss ratio; clear
CLRC	clear carry
CLS	clear screen; combination lock system; communication line speed
CLSC	C.L.S.C.; Cisco LAN Switch Configuration
CLSID	class identifier
CLTP	connection-less transport protocol
CLTV	constant linear time velocity
CLUI	command line user interface
CLUT	color look-up table
CLV	constant linear velocity
CM	calendar module; calling macro; check-mark; check-mate; chip material; color mark; color monitor; common memory; compound modulation; computer

module; connection machine; conventional memory; conversional mode; core memory; corrective maintenance; cross modulation; cyclic memory

Cm	Curium
cm	centimeter; centimetre
cm^2	centimeter (*or* centimetre) **square** *(area)*
cm^3	centimeter (*or* centimetre) **cubic** *(volume)*
c.m.	circular mil
C_{max}	capacitance of **max**imum *(**max**imum capacitance)*
CMB	conventional memory barrier
CMBO	configured maximum bindery objects
CMC	capacitance measuring circuit; ceramic matrix composite; common mail (*or* messaging) calls; communication management configuration; computer-mediated communication
CMD	command
CME	contextual menu extension
CMF	creative music format
CMI	coded mark inversion
C_{min}	capacitance of **min**imum *(**min**imum capacitance)*
CMIP	common management information protocol
CMIR	cell mis-insertion rate
CMIS	common management information service (*or* system)
CML	conceptual modelling language; current mode logic
cm/m	**cmm**; cubic meter (*or* metre) *per* minute

CMMS	computerized maintenance management software
CMMU	cache-memory management unit
CMOF	configured maximum open files
CMOS	complementary metal oxide semiconductor
CMP	compare
CMR	cell misinsertion rate; common mode range (*or* rejection)
CMRR	common mode rejection ratio
CMS	code management settings (*or* system); common mode shielding
CMST	configured maximum simultaneous transaction
CMTD	**C.M.T.D.**; Configuring, Monitoring & Troubleshooting Dial-up Services
CMUL	current multiplexer
CMVC	configuration management version control
CMW	cache memory write
CMWO	cache memory write operation
CMY	cyan-magenta-yellow
CMYK	cyan-magenta-yellow-black
CN	channel number; chart name; chart number; check number; circuit noise; circuit number; class number; color noise; computer network; connection number; control number
CNA	**C.N.A.**; Certified NetWare Administrator
CNAPS	co-processing node architecture for parallel system
CNC	computerized numerical control

C.N.E.   CNE; Certified NetWare (*or* Network) Engineer

CNF   configuration

CNI   C.N.I.; Certified NetWare (*or* Novell) Instructor

CNIDR   clearing-house for network information and discovery and retrieval

CNMAT   Center for New Music and Audio Technology

CNN   composite network node; computer news network

CNP   customized networking platform

CNR   carrier-noise ratio

CNRZ   conditioned non-return to zero

CNSS   core nodal switching sub-system

CNX   certified network expert

CO   central office; check-out; collation operation; command output; complementary operator; complete operation; conditional operator; control operation

Co   Cobalt

C_o capacitance of output

COAST   card-on-a-stick (*module*)

COAX   coaxial

COB   chip-on-board

COBOL   common business oriented language

COC   calendar of conversion; concurrent operating control; cross-over cable

COD   check-out date

CODAS	computer-based oscillograph and data acquisition system
CODASYL	conference on data system languages
CODEC	coder-decoder; compression-decompression
COEM	commercial original equipment manufacturer
COF	current open file
COFF	common object file format
COFDM	coded orthogonal frequency division multiplexing
COGO	co-ordinate geometry
COHO	coherent oscillator
COL	color; column; collision; computer oriented language
COLD	computer output to laser disc
COLORSYNC	color synchronization
COM	center of mass; command; commercial; common; communication; complement; component object model; computer; computer output microfilm
COMA	cache optimization memory architecture
3COM	computer-communications-compatibility
COMC	complement carry
COMDEX	Computer Dealers Exposition
COMF	computer output micro-film
COMM	communication
COMP	computation; computer
CompTIA	Computing Technology Industry Association

COMSAT   communication satellite

COND   condition

CONFIG   configuration

CONS   connection-oriented network service

CONT   continuation; continue; continued

COP   character oriented protocol

COPICS   communication oriented production information and control system

COR   common object runtime

CORBA   common object request broker architecture

COREN   corporation for research and enterprise network

COS   compatible operating system; complementary symmetry; connection oriented service; cosine

COSE   common open software (*or* system) environment

COSMIC   computer software management and information center

COSMOS   computer system for mainframe operations

COSS   code operated six shooter; common object service specification

COTS   commercial-off-the-shelf

COZI   communications zone indicator

CP   central processing; central processor; ceramic package; character parity; character printer; check-point; check problem; circuit parameter; clock pulse; co-processor; coded program; color palette; color processor; column parity; command processor; common program; communication processor; communication protocol;

commutator pulse; compiling program; component position; computer program; concurrent processor; control packet; control panel; control point; control program; controlling process; convex programming; copy protected; copy protection; cordless phone; core patch; critical path; cross point; cutter path; cyclic polynomial

cp	candle power
CPC	ceramic printed circuit
cpc	characters per centimeter
cPCI	CPCI; compact peripheral component interface
CPCS	check processing control system; common part convergence sublayer
CPD	capacitive pressure device; color plasma display; control panel device
CPE	central processing element
CPG	clock pulse generator
CPGA	ceramic pin grid array
CPI	Centronics parallel (*or* printer) interface; checkpoint information; clocks per instruction; code page information
cpi	characters per inch
CPIC	common programming interface for communication
CPIO	CP/IO; copy in and out
CPKP	command-patch, key-patch
CPL	characters per line; control panel; current privilege level

CPLD	complex programmable logic device
CPM	check-point message; check power mode; communication processor module
CP/M	control program for microprocessor
cpm	centimeters per minute
CPP	cross platform parity
CPS	characters per second
cps	cycles per second
CPSI	configurable PostScript interpreter
cpt	compact; compact-pro *(extension)*
CPU	central processing unit
CPW	cache partial write; commercial processing workload
CPWR	cache partial write request
CR	call reference; carriage return; cathode ray; cell relay; character reader; character recognition; check register; check routine; chroma resolution; circuit reliability; circulating register; clock rate; computer run; contrast ratio; control ratio; control register; control routine; correction routine; cyclic redundancy; cylinder register
Cr	chromium
CRAM	cyberspatial reality advancement movement
CRC	cyclic redundancy check; cyclic redundancy code
CRC-12	cyclic redundancy check 12-bits
CRC-16	cyclic redundancy check 16-bits
CRCC	cyclic redundancy check character

CRD	**card**; **c**omputer **r**elated **d**isorder
CREF	**c**ross-**ref**erence
CREN	**c**omputer **r**esearch and **e**ducation **n**etwork
CRF	**c**able **r**etransmission **f**acility; **c**ross **r**eference **f**ile
CRI	**c**olor **r**eproduction **i**ndice
CRO	**c**athode **r**ay **o**scillograph (*or* **o**scilloscope); **c**utter **r**adius **o**ffset
C-ROM	**CROM**; **c**ontrol (*or* **c**ustom) **r**ead **o**nly **m**emory
CROS	**c**utter **r**adius **o**ff-**s**et
CRP	**c**hallenge **r**esponse **p**rotocol
CRR	**c**ache **r**ead **r**equest
CRT	**c**athode **r**ay **t**ube
CRTC	**c**athode **r**ay **t**ube **c**ontroller
CRT-DM	**CRT/DM**; **c**athode **r**ay **t**ube **d**isplay **m**icroprocessor
CRUD	**c**reate-**r**etrieve-**u**pdate-**d**elete
CS	**c**able **s**elect; **c**all **s**creen; **c**alling **s**cheduling; **c**alling **s**equence; **c**apacitor **s**torage; **c**arrier **s**ense; **c**arrier **s**ystem; **c**hange **s**ize; **c**hannel **s**tate; **c**hannel **s**tatus; **c**hannel **s**ynchronization; **c**hannel **s**ynchronizer; **c**haracter **s**et; **c**haracter **s**hift; **c**haracter **s**tring; **c**haracter **s**ubset; **c**hip **s**elect; **c**hip **s**equence; **c**hip **s**ystem; **c**ircuit **s**witching; **c**ircular **s**hift; **c**irculating **s**torage; **c**leaning **s**olution; **c**lear **t**o **s**end; **c**lient **s**tation; **c**lock **s**ignal; **c**lock **s**peed; **c**losed **s**et; **c**losed **s**ubroutine; **c**losed **s**ystem; **c**ode **s**egment; **c**ode **s**et; **c**oding **s**cheme; **c**old **s**tart; **c**ollating **s**equence; **c**olor **s**canner; **c**olor **s**ynchronization; **c**ombined **s**et; **c**ombined **s**tation; **c**ommunications **s**erver; **c**ommunications **s**oftware; **c**ommunication **s**tatement; **c**omplementary **s**ymmetry;

component stress; composite signal; computer science; concentric stranding; condenser storage; conditional stop; conditioning signal; connection state; contact sensing; contact switch; context switching; continuous simulation; control cycle; control section; control sequence; control statement; control store; control strip; control system; coordinate storage; correspondence study; current cycle; current server; current shift; current switching; cyber-scoring; cyber-space; cycle stealing; cyclic shift; cyclic storage

Cs   Cesium

CSA   cable scanner adapter; Canadian Standard Agency; common scrambling algorithm; cyclic storage access

CSAR   channel system address register

CSC   color sub-carrier; common signalling channel; complementary symmetry circuit; consecutive sequence computer

CS/CDPD   **CSCDPD**; circuit switched cellular digital packet data

C-SCR   **CSCR**; complementary silicon controlled rectifier (*or* **CSCR**)

CSCW   computer supported cooperative work

CSD   circuit-switched data; computer service department

CSDS   circuit-switched data service

CS/DAC   current switching digital-to-analog converter (*or* **CSDAC**)

CSDC   chip select decode couple; circuit switched data service

CSE   **C.S.E.** ; Certified Software (*or* System) Engineer (*or* **C/SE**)

CSF	chrominance subcarrier frequency; contact separating force
CSFI	communication subsystem for interconnection
CSG	clock signal generator
CSI	character string instruction; command sequence introducer
CSIA	current shunt instrumentation amplifier
CSID	call subscriber identification
CSL	computer sensitive language
CSLIP	compressed serial line interface protocol (*or* provider)
CSM	central (*or* client) server model; code set map; communication service manager (*or* module)
CSMA	carrier sense multiple access
CSMA/CA	carrier sense multiple access with collision avoidance
CSMA/CD	carrier sense multiple access with collision detection
CSMAP	carrier sense multiple access protocol
CSMS	customer support management system
CSNET	computer science network
CSP	certified systems professional; carrier sense protocol; chip scale package (*or* packaging); communicating sequential processes
CS-PDN	CSPDN; circuit-switched public data network
CSR	circuit-switched routing; closed sub-routine
CSRAM	CS-RAM; custom static random access memory
CSS	cascading styling sheets; contact start-stop; content scrambling system; continuous system simulator

CS/SH current switching—sample hold

CSSM client-server system management

CSSP color synchronization system profile

CST Central Standard Time

CSTA computer-supported telephony application

CSU channel service (*or* switching) unit

CSU/DSU CSU-DSU; channel service unit—data service unit

CSV circuit-switched voice

CT calculator terminal; capacitor transducer; carrier transmission; cipher text; circuit tune; claim token; clock track; coding table; coding tool; co-directional timing; color table; communication terminal; compilation time; complimentary tracking; computation time; computed tomography; computerized tomography conditional transfer; connection time; control transfer; control type; conversion time; cross-talk; current test; current tracer; current tracker; cyber train; cycle time

Ct capacitance terminal (*terminal capacitance*)

CTAT computerized transaxial tomography

CTB cipher type byte

CTC channel-to-channel; current transaction count

CTCP client-to-client protocol

CTD cell transfer delay; charge transfer device; cumulative trauma disorder

CTE coefficient of thermal expansion

C-terp C interpreter

CTG computed (*or* computerized) tomography

CTI	computer telephony integration
CTIB	counter timer interface board
CTL	complementary transistor logic
CTM	close talk microphone
CTN	client task number
CTOS	computerized tomography operating system
CTP	configuration testing protocol
CTPA	coax-to-twisted-pair adapter
CTR	counter
CTRCO	Calculating, Tabulating, Recording Company *(former name of IBM Co.)*
CTRL	control
CTS	clear-to-send; computer telephony solution; customer telephone system
CTS-10	clear-to-send 10-MHz
CTSS	compatible time sharing system
CTT	communication test set
CU	central unit; close-up; comparing unit; communication unit; control unit; credit unit
Cu	*Cuprum (Latin:* copper*)*
cu	cubic
cu/cm	cubic/centimeter; cubic/centimetre
cu/ft	cubic/foot
CUA	common user access

CUB	cursor backward
CUBO	current used binary object
CUD	cursor down
CUDS	current used dynamic space
CUF	cursor forward
CUI	common user interface
CUP	cursor position
CUPID	completely universal processor input-output design
CUR	cursor
CURB	currently used routing buffer
CUSIP	Committee for Uniform Security Identification Procedures
CUT	control unit terminal
CUU	cursor up
CV	channel vocoder; circuit video; clamping voltage; color value; color video; common virus; compliance voltage; component video; composite video; computer virus; cross validation; custom variable
c.v.	*curriculum vitae* (*Latin:* resumé; bio-data)
CVC	channel voice coder *(channel vocoder)*; color video controller; concatenated virtual circuit
C/VC	CVC; current-to-voltage converter
CVCB	color video controller board
CVD	chemical vapor deposition
CVDT	cell variation delay tolerance

CVF	compressed volume file
CVGA	color video graphics adapter (*or* array); color visual graphics adapter
CVIA	Computer Virus Industry Association
CVRAM	CV-RAM; cached video random access memory
CVS	composite video signal
CVSD	continuously variable slope delta
CVSDM	continuously variable slope delta modulation
CW	check-write; clock-wise; command word; communication word; computer word; congestion window; continuous wave; counter-wave
CWD	change working directory
CWIS	campus wide Information service (*or* system); community wide Information service (*or* system)
C2X	character *to* hexadecimal
CXR	*carrier*
CYC	cycle
CYL	cylinder
CYMK	cyan-yellow-magenta-black
CZT	chirp z-transform

~D~

D	**d**ata; **d**ate; **d**ay; **d**egree; **d**elete; **d**ensity; **d**epth; **d**esign; **d**esigner; **d**ial; **d**iameter; **d**igit; **d**igital; **d**imension; **d**iode; **d**iopter; **d**irection; **d**irector; *discus* (*Latin:* disk; disc); *diskos* (*Greek:* disc; disk); **d**istance; **d**omain; **d**uration
3D	**3-D**; **3 d**imensions
2D	**2-D**; **2 d**imensions
d	**d**eci
DA	**D/A**; **d**amping **a**ction; **d**ata **a**ccess; **d**ata **a**cquisition; **d**eferred **a**ddress; **d**elayed **a**ccess; **d**erivative **a**ction; **d**esign **a**id; **d**esk **a**ccessory; **d**estination **a**ddress; **d**ial **a**ssist; **d**ielectric **a**mplifier; **d**ifferential **a**nalyzer; **d**ifferentiating **a**mplifier; **d**igital **a**ddition; **d**igital **a**udio; **d**igital-to-**a**nalog; **d**iode **a**mplifier; **d**iode **a**rray; **d**irect **a**ccess; **d**irect **a**cting; **d**irect **a**ddress; **d**iscrete **a**ddress; **d**isk **a**ccess; **d**isplay **a**dapter; **d**ope **a**dditive; **d**ummy **a**rgument
D/A	**d**ata **a**cquisition; **d**igital-to-**a**nalog; **d**iscrete **a**ddress
Da	**d**a**l**ton
da	**D**e**k**a; **d**e**c**a
DAA	**d**ata **a**ccess **a**rrangement; **d**irect **a**ccess-**a**rchitecture **p**rogramming
DAB	**d**igital **a**udio **b**roadcasting
DAC	**d**ata **a**cquisition **a**nd **c**ontrol; **d**igital-to-**a**nalog **c**onverter; **d**ual **a**ttachment **c**oncentrator
DACB	**d**ata **a**cquisition **a**nd **c**ontrol **b**oard

DAD   desktop application director; digital audio device; direct access device; drag and drop

DAE   digital audio extraction

DAF   digital audio file

dag   deca-gram; deka-gram

DAI   distributed artificial intelligence

DAL   data access language; disk access lockout

dal   daL; deka-liter; deca-liter; deka-litre; deca-litre

DAM   data acquisition and monitoring; data acquisition module; data address modification

dam   deca-meter; deka-meter; deca-metre; deka-metre

DAMA   demand assigned multiple access

DAMPS   digital advanced mobile phone service

DAN   dedicated advanced NetWare

DAO   data access object; disk-at-once

DAP   data access protocol; developer assistance program; digital approximation pre-modulation

DAPIE   developer application programming interface extension

DAPM   digital approximation pre-modulation

DAQ   direct access queue

DAR   data access register; dump and restart; dynamic adaptive routing

DARI   data-base application remote interface

DARMS   digital alternate realization of musical symbol

DARPA	Defense Advance Research Projects Agency
DART	data analysis recording tape; digital audio reconstruction technology
DARTS	dynamics algorithms for real time simulation
DAS	data acquisition system; digital audio system; display adapter slot
DASB	data acquisition system board
DASD	direct access storage device
DAST	division for advanced system technology
DAT	data; diffused alloy transistor; digital audio tape; disk access time; disk array technology
DATACOM	data communications
DATS	diode automatic test system
DAV	data above voice; digital audio-video
DAVIC	Digital Audio-Visual Council
DB	data bank; data base; data bit; data broadcast; data buffer; data buffering; data bus; daughter-board; dead band; decision box; device bay; dial backup dialog box
dB	decibel
D.B.A.	DBA; Doctor of Business Administration
DBA	doing business as
dBA	decibel adjusted *(adjusted decibel)*
dBase	data base
DBC	data broadcast; decimal-binary conversion; device bay controller

DBCN	detach for bad connection number
DBCS	delivery bar code sorter; double byte character set
dbcs	double bit character set
DBE	data byte exchange; data bus enable
DbE	data bit exchange
DBF	data-base file
dbGE	data-base graphics enhancement
DBL	data (*or* double) byte link; double
DBM	data base management
dBm	decibel meter; decibel metre
DBMS	data base management system
DBO	dyadic Boolean operation
DBP	data-base protocol; digital bit pipe; direct binary programming
DBR	dead band range; DOS boot record
DBS	data base server (*or* system); data bit stream; digital broadcasting system; direct broadcast satellite (*or* system)
DBU	dial back-up; dial backup unit
DBV	digital broadcast video
DBW	data band-width
DBX	data byte exchange
DbX	data bit exchange
DBZ	divide by zero

DC   daisy chain; data chain; data collection; data code; data communication; data compaction; data compression; data contester; data control; data converter; data count; decimal correction; dedicated channel; dedicated circuit; dedicated computer; delay circuit; delay counter; delta clock; design check; design cycle; device control; dialog coder; dielectric current; differentiating circuit; diffusion capacitor; digital circuit; digital clock; digital code; digital computer; digital control; digital controller; DIN cable; direct code; direct coding; direct count; direct coupling; direct control; direct current; direct cycle; directive command; directory caching; discontinue; discontinued; discrete circuit; disk cache; disk card; disk case; disk controller; disk crash; distributed control; division circuit; drive cluster; drive cylinder; drop cable; dry contact; dump check; duplex cable; duplex channel; duplication check; duty cycle; dynamic check

D/C   direct connection; discontinue; discontinued

dc   d/c; DC; D/C; direct current

DCA   Defense Communications Agency; destination computer address; Digital Computer Association; direct control amplifier; document content architecture; drift corrected amplifier

DCAM   digital camera; direct chip attach module

DCB   device control block; digital channel bank; direct current balance(r); dirty cache buffer; disk co-processor board

DCC   data control clerk; dedicated control channel; device control character; digital command control; digital compact cassette; direct client connection; direct current coupling

DCD   data carrier detect; direct current dump; disorderly close-down; duty cycle distortion

DCE   data communication equipment; distributed computing environment (*or* equipment)

DCED   distributed computing environment Daemon

DCF   data communication (*or* compression) facility; data count field; driver configuration file

DCFEM   dynamic crossed field electron multiplication

DCI   data communication interface; display control interface

DCID   destination connection identification (*or* identifier)

DCL   data control language; data conversion line; digital control logic; digital command language

DCLT   digital cord-less telephone

DCM   digital counter module; direct connect modem

DCMD   debugger command

DCMP   digital communication message protocol

DCN   disk channel NetWare

DCO   direct cut-over

DCOM   days charge occurrings mask; distributed component object model

DCP   daisy chain polling; device control protocol

DCR   digital cellular radio

DCS   daisy chain structure; data collection station (*or* system); data control system; desktop color separation; digital carrier system; digital cinema sound; digital communication system; distributed computer (*or* control) system; dual channel sampling

DCSH   dual channel sampling head

DCT   daisy chain topology; dictionary; digital camcorder tape; digital carrier trunk; digital cellular technology; digital cordless telephone; discrete cosine transform

DCTE   data circuit terminating equipment

DCTL   direct coupled transistor logic

DCU   data cache unit

DD   data delimiter; data description; data dictionary; data distribution; data document; data dump; default drive; delay distortion; delayed dialing; delta decoding; detail diagram; device dependence; device driver; dielectric diode; dielectric dispersion; differential delay; digital data; digital decoder; digital decoding; digital delay; digital display; diode detector; direct dial; disaster dump; disk density; disk directory; disk doubler; disk drive; distortion delay; distributed data; double density; double drive; dual diode; duo-decimal; dynamic data; dynamic debugging; dynamic dump(ing)

DDA   distributed data access; digital data acquisition; digital differential analyzer; disk drive array; domain defined attribute

DDAC   disk drive array connector

DDAS   digital data acquisition system

DDB   device descriptor block; distributed data base

DDBCS   distributed data base connection service

DDC   digital (*or* display) data channel; direct data capture; direct digital connection (*or* control); display data channel

DDCMP   digital data communication message protocol

DDCS   distributed data-base connection service

DDD   digit(al) delay device; direct distance dialing

DDE   direct data entry; dynamic data exchange

DDEML   dynamic data exchange manager library

DDF   dirac delta function; dynamic data formatting

DDH   drop-dead halt

DDI   device driver interface; digital document interchange; direct dial-in

DDJ   data dependent jitter

DDK   device driver kit

DDL   data definition (*or* description) language; disk data layout

DDM   distributed data management; dynamic data manager

DDMMYY   day-day, month-month, year-year

DDN   defense data network; dotted decimal notation

DDNS   dynamic domain naming system

DDO   dynamic drive overlay

DDP   datagram delivery protocol; detach during processing; digital data processing (*or* processor); distributed data processing (*or* processor)

DDPS   distributed data processing system

DDR   data direction register; directional discontinuity ring; double date rate; double density recording

DDR DIMM   double data rate dual inline memory module

DDR-SDRAM   DDR/SDRAM; double date rate synchronous dynamic random access memory

DDRR   directional discontinuity ring radiator

DDS   design data sheet; digital data-phone service; digital data storage; disk drive system; distributed data-base service drive definition string; dynamic digital sound

DDT   decimal data type; direct data transmission; double doped transistor; dynamic debugging technique

DDX   digital (*or* dynamic) data exchange

DE   data element; data encoding; data encryption; data entry; data error; data exchange; dead end; deflection electrode; delayed element; delta encoder; delta encoding; device end; diced element; digital element; digital encoder; digital encoding; digital equipment; directory entry; distributed environment; divide exception; double error

DEA   data encryption algorithm

DEC   data exchange control; deceleration; December; decrement; Digital Equipment Corporation

DECNET   DECnet; Digital Equipment Corporation network

DECT   digitally enhanced cordless telephony

DED   data element dictionary; delta encoder-decoder; delta encoding-decoding; double error detection

DEDSEC   double-error detection, single-error correction

DEF   default; definition; di-electric fatigue; double error flag; dynamic exchange format

DEFRAG   defragment; defragmentation

DEG   di-electric guide

DEH	di-electric heating
DEI	di-electric isolation
DEK	data encryption key
DEL	delete
DEM	demonstration; digital echo modulation
DEMO	demonstration
DEMUX	demultiplexer
DEN	Denmark; document enabled network(ing)
DEP	data entry procedure; data exchange protocol; di-electric polarization
DEPC	double entry polyethylene container
DER	di-electric relaxation
DES	data encryption standard; data entry sheet; description; di-electric strength; digital expansion system; discrete event simulation
DES-CBC	data encryption standard cipher block chaining
DET	device execute trigger
DEU	data exchange unit
DEV	device; di-electric velocity
DF	damaged file; damaged frame; data field; data file; data flow; data fork; data format; data frame; dead front; degenerative feedback; degradation factor; delay factor; delay flop; demand fetching; departure frequency; describing function; destination field; device flag; dielectric fatigue; digital field; digital filter; disk format; direct flow; direct formatting; display

font; distributed frame; double flag; double frame; dual frequency

DFA	data flow architecture; disk first aid
DFB	degenerative feed-back
DFBE	decision feed-back equalizer
DFBEEL	distributed feed-back edge emitting laser
DFC	data flow control
DFDR	digital flight data recorder
DFE	decision feedback equalizer
DFEEL	distributed feedback edge emitting laser
D-FF	D-type flip-flop
DFG	data flow graph; diagnostic (*or* diode) function generator
DFM	dual frequency monitor
DFOC	duplex fiber-optic cable; duplex fibre-optic cable
DFOM	duplex fiber-optic modem; duplex fibre-optic modem
DFP	digital flat panel
DFS	data fork size; de facto standard; digital frequency synthesizer; distributed file service (*or* system); distributed frame structure
DFSMS	data facility storage management sub-system
DFT	design for testability; diagnostic function test; discrete Fourier transform
DFTT	diagnostic function test table; discrete Fourier transform table
DFU	data file utility

DFWMAC   distributed foundation wireless medium access protocol

DG   data grade; data-gram; decision gate; dielectric guide; disc generator; drain gate; dual gate; dynamic gain

dg   deci-gram

DGBV   drain gate breakdown voltage

DGDP   data-gram delivery protocol

dGE   data-base graphics enhancement

DGFET   dual gate field-effect transistor

DGIS   direct graphics interface standard

DGL   data grade line

DGSOSV   drain gate source on-state voltage

DGSOV   drain gate source on-state voltage

DGR   dynamic growth and reconfiguration

DGV   drain gate voltage

DH   data handling; data hierarchy; dielectric heating; direct handling; directory hashing; drive head; dynamic host

DHC   decimal-hexadecimal conversion; dynamic host configuration

DHCP   dynamic host configuration protocol

DHKE   Diffie-Hellman key exchange

DHL   display high-lighting; dynamic head loading

DHS   data-handling system

DHTML   dynamic hyper-text markup language

DI	data inspection; data input; data integrity; data item; decision instruction; decision integrator; destination index; device independence; dielectric isolation; digital input; digital integrator; direct impression; direct instruction; disabled interrupt; donor ion; dopand impurity; drop-in; dummy instruction; durability index
DIA	diameter; differential instrumentation amplifier; document interchange architecture
DIAG	diagnosis; diagnostic; diagonal; diagram
DIB	data input bus; directory information base; dual independent bus
DIC	dictionary; digital inter-connection; digital intercontinental conversion;
DICE	digital intercontinental conversion equipment
DIDS	distributed intrusion detection system
DIF	data inspection function; data interchange format; distributed inter-frame
DIFS	distributed inter-frame scheme
DIIP	drect interrupt identification port
DIL	dual in-line
DIM	dimension; disk image mounter; dual in-line memory
DIMC	distributed intelligence micro-computer
DIMM	dual in-line memory module
DIMS	distributed intelligence microcomputer system
DIN	Deutsche Industrie Normenausschufs *(German)*
D/IO	DIO; data input-output

DIP   dial-up Internet protocol; digital image processing; dual in-line package; dual in-line pin

DIPS   distributed information processing system; dual in-line package switch

DIPSA   distributed information processing systems application (*or* architecture)

DIR   device identifier register; direction; director; directory

DIS   direct insert subroutine; distributed interactive simulation; draft international standard

DISA   Data Interchange Standards Association; direct inward system access; distributed information-processing systems-application architecture

DISC   disconnect; disconnection; discontinued; discount

disc   *discus* (*Latin:* disc; disk)

disk   *diskos* (*Greek:* disc; disk)

DISP   displacement

DISR   direct insert sub-routine

DIT   directory information tree; digital (*or* direct) imaging technology

DIV   divide; division; divisor

DIVE   direct interface video extension

DIVX   digital video express

DIZ   description in zip

DJ   deterministic jitter; divided junction; doped junction

DJS   De June standards

DK   development kit; direct key

DL	data length; data librarian; data library; data link; data log; data look-up; dead-lock; decision level; dedicated line; delay line; diffusion length; digital library; digital line; digital link; digital lock; digital logic; digital loop; direct line; direct link; dot leader; double length; double line; down-link; down-load; dummy load
dl	dL; deci-liter (or deciliter)
DLB	digital loop-back
DLC	Data-layer (*or* line) control; data-link connection (*or* control); distributed loop carrier
DLCI	data link connection identifier
DLE	data link escape
DLEC	data link escape character
DLF	down-loadable font
DLI	digital library initiative
DLL	data link layer; digital locked loop; dynamic link library
DLM	data line monitor; dynamic link module
DLN	double length numeral
DLP	delta link protocol; digital light (*or* list) processing; display list processing
DLPI	data link provider interface
DLPS	double level poly-silicon
DLR	DOS LAN requester
DLS	data link switching
DLT	digital linear tape

DLTL   dedicated leased telephone line

DLU   data look-up; dependent logic unit

DLV   dependent logic value

DLY   delay

DM   data management; data medium; data migration; data model; data name; delta modulation; differed maintenance; differential multiplexer; digital modem; digital multiplexing; digital multiplication; digital multiplier; dipole modulation; disconnect mode; discrete media; diskette mailer; display microprocessor; display mode; display model; distributed memory; drive model; drive module; dual media; dynamic memory

dm   deci-meter

DMA   direct memory access; direct memory addressing

DMAB   direct memory access board

DMAC   direct memory access controller

DMACS   distributed manufacturing automation and control software

DMA/CS   DMA-CS; direct memory access cycle stealing

DMAL   direct memory access line

DMARQ   direct memory access request

DMC   direct memory cache; distributed memory computer

DMD   digital micro-mirror device; digital mirror device

DME   digital message entry; direct memory execution; distance measuring equipment; distributed management environment

DMED	digital message entry device
DMF	dimension meta-file; distribution media format
DMI	desktop management interface
DML	data manipulation language; dedicated modem line
DMM	digital multi-meter
DMMD	digital micro-mirror device
DMMS	dynamic memory management system
DMOS	diffused metal oxide semiconductor
DMOSFET	diffused metal oxide semiconductor field effect transistor
DMOSRAM	dynamic metal oxide semiconductor random access memory
DMP	dot matrix printer; dynamic micro-programming
DMPC	distributed memory parallel computer
DMPP	distributed memory parallel processor
DMR	digital magnetic recorder (*or* recording)
DMS	data management software; draft mode speed
DMSD	digital multi-standard decoding
DMSP	distributed mail system protocol
DMSS	distributed mass storage system
DMT	dead mirror table; dedicated microprocessor technique; digital multi-tone; discrete multi-tone; drive mapping (*or* mirror) table
DMTF	desktop management task force
DMX	digital music express

DMY	day-month-year
DN	delta noise; destination node; device number; dial network; digital number; direct number; distributed network; down; drive number; drive name
DNA	digital network architecture; direct network access
DNAL	direct network access line
DNC	digital (*or* direct) network connection; direct numerical control
DNHR	dynamic non-hierarchical routing
DNIC	data network identification code
DNIS	dialed number identification service
DNS	digital networking system; domain name server; domain naming system
DNW	destination (*or* dial *or* digital *or* distributed) network; does not work
DO	data out; descending order; digital operation; digital output; direct operation; direct order; disk optimizer; drop-out; dual operation; duplex operation; dyadic operator
DOA	date of adjustment
DOC	date of cause; document; documentation; dynamic output control
DOCSV	data over circuit-switched voice
DOE	Department of Energy
DOM	discretionary overlay matrix; document object model
DOMF	distributed object management facility
DOP	difference of potential

DOS	Disk Operating System
DOSEM	Disk Operating System emulation
DOV	data-over-voice
DP	data packet; data processing; data purification; database protocol; delayed page; delayed pulse; design proof; desktop picture; di-phase; diagnosis program; diagnostic program; dielectric polarization; differential pulse; digit place; digital path; digital plot; digital plotter; digital processor; digital pulse; directory path; dirty power; discrete programming; disk pack; disk partition; distributed processing; dot pitch; double pole; double precision; draft proposal; draw program; drum plotter; dual phase; dual port; dual processor; dump point; duplicate packet; duplicate program; dynamic password; dynamic program; dynamic programming
DPA	demand protocol architecture; differential pulse amplitude; document printing architecture
DPAM	demand priority access method; differential pulse amplitude modulation
DPAREN	data parity enable
DPB	drive parameter block
DPC	differential pulse code; direct program control
dpc	dots per centimeter
DPCM	differential pulse code modulation
DPDN	digital packet data network
DPDS	data-phone digital service
DPDT	double-pole double-throw
DPF	delayed page fault

DPI	distributed protocol interface
dpi	dots per inch
DPL	descriptor privilege level; digital phase lock
DPLL	digital phase locked loop
DPM	desktop PrintMonitor; development processor module; digital panel meter; di-pole modulation; direct (*or* display) power management
dpm	dots per millimeter
DPMA	Data Processing Management Association
DPMI	DOS protected mode interface
DPMS	display power management signal (*or* support)
DPO	data phase optimization
DPR	double pulse recording
DPS	data (*or* document) processing system; desktop printer spooler; dual power supply; dual protocol stack
DPSK	differential phase shift key(ing)
DPT	design proof test; digital pressure transducer; disk partition table
DPU	data processing unit
DPVM	demand paged virtual memory
DQDB	distributed queue dual bus
DQL	data query language
DR	data range; data rate; data read; data received; data record; data reduction; data reliability; decode range; derivation ratio; destructive read; detail report; diagnosis routine; dielectric relaxation; digital radio;

digital receiver; digital route; digital routing; direct route; discretionary replace; display register; doctor; document reference; door; double rail; drive; driver; dry run; dual ramp; dumping resistor; dynamic range; dynamic relocation; dynamic response

DRA   dead reckoning analyzer; direct reference address; dual reflector antenna

DRADC   dual ramp analog-to-digital conversion

DRAM   dynamic random access memory

DRAW   direct read after write

DR-BOND   dial-up router bandwidth on demand; DR/BOND

DRC   deny read count; digital reality creation; diminished radix complement; dry read contact; dual ramp conversion

DRCI   dual ramp conversion interface

DRCP   dual ramp conversion program

DRCPSC   double resistance-capacitance phase shift converter

DRDA   distributed relational data-base architecture

DR-DOS   Digital Research Disk Operating System

DRDW   direct read during write

DRE   document reference edge

DRF   drive removable flag

DRI   data reduction interpreter

DRM   destructive read memory

DRO   data request output; destructive read-out

DROM   diode read only memory

DRP	digital routing protocol
DRQ	data request
DRS	document registration system; duplicate reply sent
DRT	dynamic range tester
DRV	drive; driver
DRW	draw; digital radio wave
DS	data seek; data segment; data send; data server; data set; data sink; data source; data storage; data stream; data switch; data system; data-speak; decision symbol; description strings; destination socket; destination system; deterministic simulation; development system; diagnostic software; dielectric strength; differential signalling; digital signal; digital signature; digital storage; digital subtraction; digital system; directive statement; directory server; discrete simulation; display switch; double sided; down-size; drift stabilization; drive sector; drive size; drive slot; dual system; duplex system; dye sublimation; dynamic scattering; dynamic storage; dynamic subroutine
D/S	DS; digital switch; display switch
DSA	destination service access; digital signature algorithm; digital spectrum analysis; digital subtraction angiography; disk speed adjustment
DSAP	destination service access point
DSB	double side-band
DSBS	double side-band signal
DSBSC	double side-band suppressed carrier
DSBTC	double side-band transmitted carrier

DSC	device selection check; digital still camera; document structuring convention
D.Sc.	DSc; Doctor of Science
DSD	direct stream digital; double sided disk
DSDD	double sided, double density
DSE	data storage equipment; data switching exchange
DSEA	display station emulation adapter
DSECT	direct section
DSFD	double sided floppy diskette
DSH	digital sample-hold
DSHD	double sided, high density
DSI	digital speech interpolation; digital subtraction imaging
DSIS	distributed support information standard
DSK	desk; diskette; Dvorak simplified keyboard
DSL	deep scattering layer; digital subscriber line; digital subscription line; dynamic simulation language
DSLAM	digital subscriber line access multiplexer; digital subscription line access multiplexer
DSMA	digital sense multiple access
DSN	deep space network; delivery service notification
DSNW	deep space network
DSO	data source object
DSOM	distributed system object model

DSP   de-spiking; digital signal processing (*or* processor); directory synchronization protocol; discretionary security policy

DSR   data set ready; data signal rate; device status register; dynamic sub-routine

DSQD   double sided, quad density

DSS   digital signalling system; digital signature standard; digital spread spectrum; display slide switch; distributed sniffer system; double side-band signal

DSSG   diffused semiconductor strain gauge

DSSI   digital standard systems interconnect

DSSS   direct sequence spread spectrum

DSSSL   document style semantics and specifications language

DST   data stream type

DSTN   double super-twisted nematic

DSU   data service (*or* switching) unit; digital service unit

DSV   drain substrate voltage

DSVD   digital simultaneous voice—data

DSVM   demand segmented virtual memory

DSW   data (*or* device) status word; device selection word

DSX   data switching exchange; digital signals *cross-connect* (*where X→ cross-connect*)

DT   data terminal; data through; data through-put; data transfer; data transmission; data transparency; data type; date/time; day time; dead time; decay time; decision table; decision threshold; delay time; depletion type; desk-top; destructive test; destructive testing;

development time; diagnostic test; diagnostic trace; diffusion theory; digital technique; digital television; digital test; digital time; digital transducer; disk track; displacement transducer; display time; display tube; documentation technique; domain tip; double time; down-time; drive type; dual timing; dumb terminal; duplex transmission

DTA   data; differential thermal analysis; disk transfer area

DTC   desk-top conferencing

DTCS   desk-top color separation

DTD   document type definition

DTE   data terminal equipment

DTFET   depletion type field effect transistor

DTG   dual timing gate

DTI   data transfer instruction; digital transducer input; digital transducer interface

DTII   digital transducer input interface

DTIP   digital transducer interface program

DTL   diode-transistor logic

DTM   data transfer mode; dynamic traffic management

DTMF   data (*or* direct; *or* dual) tone multi-frequency

DTMFS   dual tone multi-frequency signalling

DTMI   desk-top management interface

DTP   data through-put; desk-top picture-publishing; desk-top picture-publisher

DTPS   desk-top printer spooler

DTR   data terminal ready; data transfer rate; dwell time reset

DTS   digital termination system; digital true sound

DTTB   digital terrestrial television broadcasting

DTTV   digital terrestrial television

DTUS   desk-top utility software

DTV   desk-top video; digital television

DTVC   desk-top video conferencing

DTV-R/D   digital television receiver-decoder

DU   delay unit; dial-up; delni unit; digital unit; disk unit; disk usage; ; disk user; dorfed-up

DUA   dial-up access; directory user agent

DUAT   direct user access terminal

DUI   data unit identifier

DUL   dial-up line

DUN   dial-up network(ing)

DUNC   dial-up network connection

DUNCE   dial-up network connection enhancement

DUP   duplicate; duplication

DUS   desktop utility software

DUT   device under test

DUV   data under voice

DV   data valid; data validation; dielectric velocity; digital video; direct-view

DVA	digital video active
DVB	digital video broadcast(ing)
DVC	desktop video communication (*or* conferencing); digital video camera (*or* control *or* controller)
DVCAM	digital video camera
DVD	digital versatile (*or* video) disc
DVD-R	digital versatile (*or* video) disc recordable
DVD+RW	digital versatile (*or* video) disc *plus* re-writable
DVD-R/W	DVD-RW; digital versatile (*or* video) disc re-writable
DVD-RAM	digital versatile (*or* video) disc random access memory
DVD-ROM	digital versatile (*or* video) disc read only memory;
DVE	digital video effect; digital video express; distributed virtual environment; drift voltage equivalent
DVI	digital video interactive; digital visual interface; device independent; dual vascular imaging
DVM	digital volt-meter
DVMRP	distance vector multicast routing protocol
DVR	distance vector routing; driver
DVS	direct view storage
DVST	direct view storage tube
DVT	digital video transmission (*or* transmitter)
DVX	digital video express
DW	data word; double word; driver workspace; dynamic worksheet
DWC	deny write count

DWDM	dense wavelength division multiplexer
DWG	drawing
DWL	double word length
DWMT	discrete wavelength multi-tone
DWP	daisy wheel printer
DWS	diskless work-station; driver work-space; dynamic work-sheet
DX	digital *receiver*; double *speed*
DXA	dual X-axis
DXB	drawing **interchange** binary *(where X→ interchange)*
DXC	data exchange control
DXF	drawing *(or* dynamic) exchange format
DXI	data exchange interface
DXPERT	diagnostic **expert**
DXU	data exchange unit
DY	deflection yoke
Dy	dysprosium
DYA	dual Y-axis
DZ	Dead Zone
DZA	dual Z-axis

~E~

E	ear; earth; easy; Einstein; electric; electrical; electricity; electrode; electronics; emergency; emitter; empty; end; energy; engineer; engineering; enter; entrance; erlang; error; exa; expansion; extension; extra
e	2.7182818284...*(natural logarithm base)*; electric-charge; electron
EA	each; effective address; effective area; electric axis; electrode admittance; electron affinity; electron avalanche; electronic ear; embedded application; error ambiguity; explicit address; extended address; extended area; extended attribute
EAA	Electric Auto Association
EAB	European Air Bus
EABI	embedded application binary interface
EAC	end around carry
EAD	East Australian Daylight
EAE	extended arithmetic element
EAF	extended attribute file
EAR	entertainment area resource; external access register
EARN	European Academic Research Network
EAROM	electrically alterable read only memory
EARS	electronic access to reference services; electronic authoring and routing system

EAS   East Australian Standard; emergency alert system; extended area service

EASI   elastic asynchronous-synchronous interface

EASY   efficient assembly system

EATA   enhanced advanced technology attachment

EAX   electric automatic exchange; environmental audio extension

EB   echo box; elastic buffer; electron beam; electron bombardment; embedded board; emitter bias; energy band; equivalent binary; error budget; error burst; Exa-byte; expansion board; extension bay

EBB   EISA bus controller; electronic bulletin board

EBC   extended binary code

EBCDIC   extended binary coded decimal interchange code

EBCT   electron beam computed tomography

EBD   equivalent binary digit

EBICON   electron bombardment induced conductivity

EBNF   extended Backus-Naur form

e-book   **E-book; ebook; EBOOK; E-BOOK); electronic book**

EBR   electron beam recording

EBS   emergency broadcast system; excessive burst size

EBW   effective band-width

EBX   embedded board expandable (*or* extension)

EC   echo check; edit command; electric car; electric charge; electrical circuit; electrical code; electrical contact;

electrical control; electrode conductance; electrode current; electron charge; electron conduction; electron control; electronic camera; electronic circuit; electronic configuration; electronic control; embedded command; embedded computer; emitter current; empty case; entry code; entry condition; entry counts; environmental condition; error checking; error condition; error control; error controller; error corrected; error correcting; error correction; escape character; escape code; essential communication; etched circuit; European Community; exalted carrier; execute cycle; execution cycle; executive cycle; exit block; exit condition; express calculation; extended character; external checking; external clock; external clocking; external code; external copy; extra code

ECA   electronic circuit analysis

ECAC   Electromagnetic Compatibility Analysis Center

ECAL   enjoy computing and learn

ECAP   electronic circuit analysis program

ECAT   electronic card assembly and test

ECB   electronic code book; event control block

ECBA   event control block address

ECBM   electronic code book mode

ECC   error checking and correcting; error checking code; error correcting code

ECCM   electronic counter counter-measure

ECD   elecrtro-chromeric display; enhanced color display; enhanced compact disc

EC/ER   error correction, error rate

ECF   establish connection failure

ECHO   European Commission Host Organisation (*or* Organization)

ECI   external call interface

ECK   extender card kit

ECL   emitter coupled logic

ECLM   emitter coupled logic microprocessor

ECM   electronic cipher machine; electronic control module; electronic counter-measure; error correction mode

ECMA   European Computer Manufacturers' Association

ECNE   E.C.N.E.; Enterprise Certified NetWare

ECO   engineering change order

ECONFIG   EtherNet configuration

ECP   enhanced (*or* extended) capability port

ECR   establish connection request

ECS   enhanced chip set; extended character set

ECU   EISA configuration utility

ED   edit; edition; editor; education; elective data; electric delay; electric desk; electric doublet; electrical degree; electricity discharge; electro-dynamics; electrolytic dissociation; electron device; electron discharge; electron drift; electronic data; electronic design; electronic desk; electronics degree; end delimiter; engineering data; engineering degree; envelope delay; envelope detection; error detection; error diagnostic; error dump; executive diagnostics; extended definition; external data; external delay; external device; external disk; external drive; eye diagram

EDA	electronic design automation; electronic differential analyzer; embedded document architecture
EDB	embedded data-base; extended definition Betamax; external data bus
ED-Beta	extended definition Betamax
EDC	elective data compression; electrical (*or* electronic) digital circuit; enhanced data correction; error detecting code; error detection and correction
EDD	extended distance data
EDDC	extended distance data cable
EDF	erbium-doped fiber; erbium-doped fibre
EDFA	erbium-doped fiber amplifier; erbium-doped fibre amplifier
EDG	electronic data gathering
EDGAR	electronic data gathering, analysis and retrieval
EDGE	electronic data gathering equipment
EDGS	external data-gram service
EDI	electronic data (*or* design *or* document) interchange
EDIF	electronic design interchange format
EDL	edit decision list; electric delay line
EDLC	EtherNet data link control
EDLIN	edit line; editor line
EDM	end data marker; exponential delta modulator
EDMS	electronic document management system
EDO	extended data out(put)

EDODRAM   extended data out(put) dynamic random access memory

EDORAM   extended data out(put) random access memory

EDOS   enhanced Disk Operating System

EDP   electronic data processing; explosive detection protocol

EDPM   electronic data processing machine

EDPA   electronic data processing auditor

EDPC   electronic data processing control

EDR   external data representation

EDRAM   enhanced (*or* erasable *or* extended) dynamic random access memory

EDS   external datagram service

EDSAC   electronic delay storage automatic calculator (*or* computer)

EDT   Eastern Daylight Time

edu   education; educational

EDVAC   electrical discrete variable automatic computer

EE   edge enhancement; electrical element; electrical engineering; electron emission; electronic efficiency; equivalence element; extended edition

EEA   Economic Espionage Act

EEC   extended error correction

EECMOS   electrically erasable complimentary metal oxide semiconductor

EEL   epsilon extension language

EEM	enhanced expanded (*or* extended) memory; external event module
EEMAC	Electrical and Electronic Manufacturers of Canada
EEMS	enhanced expanded (*or* extended) memory specification
EENQ	end of enquiry
EEPROM	electrically (*or* electronically) erasable programmable read only memory
EER	effective earth radius
EET	Eastern European Time
EF	electric field; electric force; electrical failure; electrical force; electro-fluor; electronic flash; electronic forms; electronic funds; emitter follower; enable flag; epitaxial film; equipment failure; error free; executive flier; extended file; extended framing
EFA	extended file attribute
EFB	error-free block
EFF	Electronic Frontier Foundation; extended framing format
EFI	electro-mechanical frequency interference
EFP	early failure period
E-FORM	electronic form
EFS	encryption file system; error-free seconds
EFTS	electronic funds transfer system
EG	electron gun; epitaxial growth; exalted gate; except gate; exclusion gate; express graph
e.g.	*exempli gratia* (*Latin:* for example)

EGA	enhanced (*or* extended) graphics adapter
EGAR	extended graphics array resolution
EGNOS	European Geo-stationary Navigation Overlay Service
EGP	exterior gateway protocol
EGREP	extended global regular expression print
EH	electrical heating; embedded hyphen; expert help
EHD	external hard drive
EHF	extremely high frequency
EHLLAPI	emulator high level language application programming interface
EI	effective instruction; electrical impulse; electrical interference; electrode impedance; electrolytic ion; enabled input; enabled interrupt; end instrument; end item; entry instruction; execution instruction; executive instruction; external icon; external interrupt; extract instruction
EIA	Electronic Industries Association
EIDE	enhanced integrated drive electronics
EIRP	effective isotropic radiated power
EIS	executive information system
EISA	enhanced (*or* extended) industry standard architecture
EISCA	enhanced intelligent system cooler architecture
EIT	engineer-in-training; engineering improvement time
EITD	electronic industry telephone directory
EJ	eject; ejection; electron jet
EJT	Eccles-Jordan trigger

EK	electro-kinetics
EL	electrical link; electrical; electricity; electron lens; emotions language; energy level; entry level; envelope learning; erase line; EtherLink; exclusive lock; external label; external link; external lock; extremely low
ELAN	emulated local area network
e-law	E-law; E-LAW; elaw; ELAW; electronic law
ELC	eight level code; embedded linking and control
ELD	electro-luminescent display
ELED	edge-emitting light emitting diode
ELF	executable linking format; extremely low frequency
ELM	EtherNet line monitor; EtherNet local module
ELMER	envelope learning and monitoring via error relaxation
ELS	electro-luminescent screen; emulsion laser storage; entry level system
ELSEC	electronic security
EM	effective memory; electrical motor; electro-metallurgy; electron microscope; electronic mail; electronic multiplier; end of medium; enhanced mode; error message; EtherMail; evoke mode; expanded memory; experimental memory; express modem; extended memory; extensions manager; external modem
EMA	effective memory access; Electronic Mail Association; experimental memory address
EMACS	editing macros
e-mail	E-mail; E-MAIL; email; EMAIL; electronic mail
EMAR	experimental memory address register

EMAT	effective memory access time
EMB	electronic mail box; electronic mail broadcast; extended memory block
EMBARC	electronic mail broadcast to a roaming computer
EMC	electro-magnetic compatibility (*or* compliance); electronic mail connection; e-mail connection; enhanced memory chip; extended mathematics co-processor
EMCC	Eckert-Mauchly Computer Company *(world's first computer company)*
EMD	electro-magnetic delay
EMDL	electro-magnetic delay line
EME	end of medium character
EMF	electro-magnetic field; electro-magnetic flowmeter; electro-motive force; enhanced meta-file
EMI	electro-magnetic induction (*or* inertia *or* interference); electronic numerical integrator
EMIC	electronic numerical integrator and calculator
EML	electronic mail
EMM	enhanced (*or* expanded *or* extended) memory management
EMR	electro-magnetic radiation; electro-magnetic relay; enhanced meta-file record
EMRAB	electro-mechanical relay accessory board
EMS	electron microscope; electronic mail system; electronic message service; enhanced memory specification (*or* system); expanded memory specification (*or* system)

EMSAPI	extended messaging services application programming interface
EMT	Eastern Mediterranean Time; electrical metallic tubing; empty; express modem tool
EMTY	empty
EMW	electro-magnetic wave
EMWAC	European Microsoft Windows Academic Centre (*or* Center)
EN	equivalent network; EtherNet; excess noise
ENC	encoded; encoder; EtherNet card (*or* controller)
ENDEC	encoder-decoder
ENI	electronic numerical integrator
ENIAC	electronic numerical integrator analyzer and calculator (*or* computer) (*first digital computer*)
ENIC	voltage negative-impedance converter
ENQ	enquiry
ENSC	EtherNet spine cable
ENSS	exterior nodal switching sub-system
ENW	equivalent network
EO	electric oscillation; electrical outlet; electron octet; electronic oscillation; emergency operation; even-odd
EOA	end-of-address
EOB	end-of-block
EOC	emergency operating condition; end of conversion
EOD	end-of-data; end-of-day; erasable optical drive

EOEM   electronic original equipment manufacturer

EOF   end-of-file

EOI   end-of-interrupt

EOJ   end-of-job

EOL   end-of-line; end-of-list

EOM   end-of-message

EOR   end-of-run

EOS   earth observing system; emergency operating system; end-of-string

EOSDIS   earth observing system data and information system

EOT   end-of-table; end-of-tape; end-of-text; end-of-track end-of-transmission

EOTC   end-of-transmission character

EP   ear-phone; echo-plexer; echo-print; electric polarization; electric potential; electric power; electrical pole; electrical pulse; electro-photo; electro-plating; electro-polar; electrode position; electrolytic polarization; electron pair; electronic packaging; electronic pen; elliptic polarization; emergency procedure; enlarger printer; entry point; equalizing pulse; EtherPort; EtherPrint; eye pattern

EPA   entry point address; Environmental Protection Agency

EPAD   electrically programmable analog device

EPBX   electronic private branch exchange

EPC   etched printed circuit; even parity check; exploded pie chart

EPDD	electrically programmable digital device
EPE	Epsilon Programmer's Editor
e-pen	**E-pen; E-PEN; epen; EPEN;** electronic **pen**
EPIC	explicitly parallel instruction computing
EPICA	explicitly parallel instruction computing architecture
EPL	effective privilege level
EPLD	electrically programmable logic device
EPP	enhanced parallel port
EPR	equivalent parallel resistance (*or* resistor)
EPROM	electrically-erasable programmable read only memory
EPS	emergency power system; encrypting file system; encapsulated PostScript
EPSF	encapsulated PostScript file
EPT	epitaxial planar transistor; error proof text
EQ	electrical quantity; equal; equalizer; equation
EQD	equalizer delay
EQS	equalizer solver; equalizer statement
EQU	equal; equate; equation
ER	effective resistor; effective rights; electric response; electrical reset; equivalent resistance; equivalent resistor; error; error range; error rate; error ratio; error receiving; exception reporting; executive routine; explicit rate; extension register; external register; effective radiation; exterior route; exterior router; external reference; electronic reading
Er	Erbium

ERA   electronic reading automation; erasable; extended registry attribute(s)

ERAS   electronic routing and approval system; erasure

ERC   error receiving count

ERD   emergency repair disk; estimated round-trip delay

ERIC   Educational Resources Information Center

ERL   enhanced run-length

ERLL   enhanced run-length limited

ERM   electronic recording method

EROM   erasable read only memory

EROS   earth resources observation system

ERP   effective radiated power; enterprise resource planning; error recovery procedure; exterior router protocol

ERR   error

ERS   electrical reset; external reference synchronization

ERTD   estimated round-trip delay

ERU   emergency recovery utility

ERX   electronic remote exchange

ES   earth station; echo suppressor; edit statement; electric susceptibility; electrical schematic; electrical shock; electrical station; electrical switch; electro-sensor; electro-striction; electrolyte strength; electrolytic sensor; electron scanning; electron stream; electronic spreadsheet; electronic storage; electronic switch; elevator seeking; energy saver; engineering sample; error signal; error status; escape sequence; EtherShare; evaluation system; expansion slot; expert system;

extended service; external storage; external symbol; extra segment; extrinsic semiconductor

Es	Einsteinium
ESA	electro-static adhesion; European Space Agency
ESB	electro-static bond(ing)
ESC	EISA system component; Epson standard code; escape; escape character; escape set character; EtherNet spine cable; extended system configuration
ESCD	extended system configuration data
ESCSC	Electronic Still Camera Standardization Committee
ESCM	extended services communications manager
ESCON	enterprise systems connection
ESC/P	Epson standard code for printers
ESD	electro-static discharge; enhanced small device
ESDI	enhanced small device interface; enhanced system device interface
ESDRAM	enhanced synchronous dynamic random access memory
ESE	energy saver extension
ESI	enhanced serial interface; expert system interference; externally specified indexing
ESIE	expert system interference engine
ESM	error service message
ESMP	electro-sensitive matrix printer
ESMR	enhanced specialized mobile radio
ESMX	enhanced statistical multiplexer

ESN   electronic security number

ESO   European Southern Observatory

ESP   electro-static printer; emulation sensing processor; encapsulating security payload; energy star program; enhanced serial port; enhanced service provider; exposed station problem

ESPL   encapsulating security pay-load

ESR   equivalent series resistance (*or* resistor); event service routine

ESRA   event service routine address

ESS   electro-static shield (*or* storage); electronic spread-sheet; electronic switching system; embedded servo system; extended service set

EST   Eastern Standard Time

ESU   editor set-up; electro-static unit

ESW   electro-static watt-meter; equivalent sine wave

ESWM   electro-static watt-meter

ET   echo-talk; electric transducer; electron trap; electronic timing; electronic tuning; enhancement technology; EtherNet type; EtherTalk; exchange termination; excitation table; excitation trigger; execute statement; expander transducer

ETACS   extended total access communication system

ETB   end of transmission block

ETBC   end of transmission block character

ETC   electronic toll collection; enhanced throughput cell EtherNet transmission cable

etc.	*et cetera* (*Latin:* and so on)
ETCG	elapsed time code generator
ETE	extra thermal energy
ETF	enriched text format
ETOM	electron trapping optical memory
e-trade	**E-trade**; **E-TRADE**; **etrade**; **ETRADE**; electronic trade
ETSI	European Telecommunication Standards Institute
ETV	education television
ETX	end of text
EU	end use; Europe; execution unit; external unit
Eu	Europium
EUC	end-user computing; extended UNIX code
EUI	end-user interface
EULA	end user licence (*or* license) agreement
EUV	extreme ultra-violet
EV	electro-valence; envelope
eV	electro-volt; electron volt
EVA	effective virtual address
EVAL	evaluation
EVC	enhanced video connector; external virtual circuit
EVCS	external virtual circuit service
EVE	extensible VAX editor
EVF	extended volume format

EVGA	extended video graphics adapter (*or* array); extended visual graphics adapter (*or* array)
EVM	electronic volt-meter
EW	executive writer
EX	exam; examination; example; exception; exclude; exclusion; exempt; exemption
EXC	except; exception; execution cycle; exchange
ExCA	exchangeable card architecture
EXCH	exchange
EXD	executive diagnostics
EXE	executable; execute; execution; exempt; exemption
EXE2BIN	executable *to* binary
EXEC	executive
EXI	executive image
EXM	exam; examination
EXP	expand; expansion; experiment; exponential; export
EXS	execute statement
EXT	extension; exterior; external; extract; extraction
EXTN	extension; external
EXT/REF	external reference
EXT/RF	external reference
EZ	E/Z; ea*sy*; equals zero
e-zine	E-zine; E-ZINE; ezine; EZINE; electronic magazine

~F~

F	face; factor; Fahrenheit; fail; fall; false; fan; faraday; fast; fat; feed; feet; female; fetch; fibre (or fiber); field; file; final; Finder; fire; fix; flat; float; floating; flow; fluorine; focal; font; foot; force; foreign; form; format; formation; formula; forward; frame; free; frequency; Friday; front; full; function
f	femto; focal; frequency
FA	failure analysis; failure analyzer; false add; file access; file attribute; filing assistant; final address; fixed area; floating address; foreign attachment; four-address; Fourier analysis; frame acquisition; frame alignment; frequency accuracy; frequency agility; full adder; fully automatic; functional address
fA	femto-ampere
FAA	Federal Aviation Administration
FAB	fabrication
FABP	computer chip fabrication plant
FAC	factor; file access code
FACE	field alterable control element
FACT	factor; fully automatic computer translator
FAE	failure analysis engineer
FAHR	Fahrenheit
FAM	frame acquisition mode
FAMA	fixed assigned multiple access

FAMOS   floating-gate avalanche-injection metal oxide semiconductor

FAMOST   floating-gate avalanche-injection metal oxide semiconductor transistor

FAP   file access protocol

FAQ   frequency asked question

FAR   failure analysis report

FARNET   Federation of American Research Networks

FAS   fast address space

FASIC   function and algorithm specific integrated circuit

FAT   failure analysis technician; fat allocation table; file access table; frame acquisition time

FATRE   fat allocation (or access) table read error

FATS   fat allocation (or access) table sector

FATSE   fat allocation (or access) table scan error

FATWE   fat allocation (or access) table write error

FAX   facsimile (facsimile →Latin: make similar) (where X→ cs)

FB   fall-back; fast-back; fat-bit; FAX board; feed-back; feed-box; fill-bucket; flag bit; flat-bed; forward bias; fox box; frame buffer; full byte

FBA   feed-back amplifier

FBB   firmware building block

FBC   feed-back circuit (or control); fully buffered channel

FBCL   feed-back control loop

FBD   feed-back device

FBE	free buffer enquiry
FBF	fixed block format
FBI	feed-back impedance
FBIOS	flash basic input-output system
FBL	feed-back loop
FBP	fall-back procedure; flat-bed plotter
FBR	feed-back resolution; flow based routing
FBS	fall-back switch; feed-back signal; flat-bed scanner;
FBSH	feed-back sample-hold
FBSHI	feed-back sample-hold integrator
FBSR	feed-back shift register
FBT	feed-back transducer
FC	Fairchild; Faraday cage; female connector; fetch cycle; fiber channel; fibre channel; field count; file cache; file capture; final copy; first class; fixed cache; fixed capacitor; fixed cycle; flat card; flex circuit; floppy controller; flow-chart; flow control; flow current; flush capture; flying capacitor; font cartridge; font characteristic; forbidden combination; format capacity; format classification; formatted capacity; forward current; fragment count; frame connector; frame control; front cover; full capacity; full card; function code; fused connection
fc	frequency cut-off (cut-off frequency)
FCAL	FC/AL; fiber (or fibre) channel arbitrated loop
FCB	file compression board; file control block

FCC   Federal Communications Commission; file carbon copy

fcc   flux changes per centimeter

FCCSET   Federal Coordinating Council for Science, Engineering and Technology

FCDC   flush capture on device close

FCEL   FC/EL; fiber (or fibre) channel enhanced loop

FCFS   first-come first-served

fci   flux changes per inch

FCIS   first class intranet server

FCL   fault current limiter; fibre channel loop

FCM   flow control mode; flying capacitor multiplexer; fully connected mesh

fcm   flux changes per meter (or metre)

FCMPX   flying capacitor multiplexer

FCMUX   flying capacitor multiplexer

FCP   fibre channel protocol; full character printer

FCPA   fibre channel protocol architecture

FC-PGA   flip chip — pin grid array

FCR   FIFO control register

FCRP   flat-card resolving potentiometer

FCS   fibre channel standard; frame check sequence

FCSF   frame check sequence field

FCT   flow control transfer; flow-chart template; flush capture time-out; forward collator tray

FCTC	flush capture time-out count
FCTO	flush capture time-out
FD	factory default; fibre dispersion; field density; field discharge; fixed data; fixed disk; floating defect; floppy diskette; flux density; form document; format designator; format detail; forward direction; fragment descriptor; frequency deviation; frequency distortion; frequency diversity; frequency divider; frequency domain; full duplex; function digit; functional diagram
FDA	floppy disk access (or assembly)
FDAC	floppy disk access control
FDC	floppy disk controller; frequency domain concept; full duplex communication
FDCB	floppy disk controller board
FDD	floppy disk drive
FDDI	fibre digital device interface; fibre distributed data interchange (or interface)
FDFA	first-declared first-allocated
FDI	floppy disk interface
FDIS	final draft international standard
FDISK	fixed disk
FDIV	floating-point divide
FDL	file down-load
FDM	frequency division multiplexer (or multiplexing)
FDMA	frequency division multiple access
FDMACU	first direct memory access channels used

FDMUX   frequency division multiplexer (or multiplexing)

FDO   fixed disk organizer

FDR   forged detach request

FDT   fix disk test(ing); floppy disk test(ing); full duplex transmission

FDX   full duplex

FE   ferro-electric; field engineer; field enhancement; field enhanced; file express; file extraction; finite element; fixed expense; font editor; format effector; forward error; frictional error; front end; function element

Fe   Ferrum (Latin: iron)

FEA   finite element analysis

FEB   February; functional electronic block

FEC   fast electonic counter; forward error correction; forward explicit congestion

FECN   forward explicit congestion notification

FED   field emission (or emitter) display

FEFO   first-ended first-out

FEM   finite element modelling

FEP   file extraction program; front end processor

FEPI   front end programming interface

FEPROM   flash electrically-erasable programmable read only memory

FeRAM   ferro-electric random access memory

FERC   Federal Energy Regulatory Commission

FESDK   Far East software development kit

FET	field effect transistor
FEXT	far-end cross-talk (where X→ cross)
FF	fan-fold; FaxFacts; feed form; feed forward; field free; file find; find file; flag field; flat fading; flat file; flip-flop; force flag; form factor; form feed; format factor
FFA	fatal fat allocation; foreign file access
FFAT	fatal fat allocation table
FFATWE	fatal fat allocation table write error
FFC	feed forward control; form-feed character
FFD	flat file data-base; fractional frequency difference
FFDB	flat file data-base
FFDC	first failure data capture
FFE	fast finite element; flip-flop equipment
FFG	free floating grid
FFLE	flip-flop level enable
FFP	fan-fold paper
FFR	Ford-Fulkerson routing
FFS	fast file system; flip-flop string
FFSK	fast frequency shift key(ing)
FFST	first failure support technology
FFT	fast Fourier transform
FG	fast graph; fifth generation; file gap; first generation; flash graphics; floating gate; flux guidance; fourth generation; FoxGraph; frame grabber; function generator

FGC fifth (or first or fourth) generation computer; frame grounding circuit

FGL fifth (or first or fourth) generation language

FGP fore-ground processing; fore-ground program(ming)

FGREP fixed global regular expression print

FGSV forward gate-source voltage

FH file handling; first hand; fixed head; fragmentation header; frequency hopping

FHD fixed hard disk; fixed hard drive; fixed head disk

FH/PFDM FH-PFDM; frequency-hopped and partitioned frequency division multiplex

FHS fan heat-sink

FHSS frequency hopping spread spectrum

FI fan-in; fetch instruction; field inspection; field intensity; finder information; first-in; fork indicator; formatting instruction; functional interleave

FIC fan in circuit

FIE front image enhancer

FIF fractal image format

FIFO first-in first-out

FIFOM first-in first-out memory

FIFOQ first-in first-out queue

FIFOS first-in first-out storage

FIFOSR first-in first-out stack register

FiG first generation

FILESPEC	file specification (or specifier)
FILO	first-in last-out
FILOM	first-in last-out memory
FILOQ	first-in last-out queue
FILOS	first-in last-out storage
FILOSR	first-in last-out stack register
FIP	fetch instruction pointer; file processor buffering
FIPS	Federal Information Processing Standard
FIR	fast infra-red; finite impulse response
FIRST	forum of incident response and security teams
FIT	failure in time
FIU	finger-print identification unit
FIX	Federal Internet Exchange
FK	function key
FKEY	function key
FL	failure log; fault location; feeder loss; fetch load; Fick's law; file locking; Firmi level; first level; fixed length; flex life; float(ing); flow; flow line; fluid; forbidden list; format length; function library; fusible link; fuzzy logic
F/L	fetch-load
FLA	first level address; four letter acronym
FLBIN	floating-point binary
FLC	ferro-electric liquid crystal; form lock clutch
FLD	field; fusible link device

FLG	Freelance Graphics
FLOE	Faraday's law of electrolysis
FLOI	Faraday's law of induction
FLOPS	floating-point operations per second
FLP	fault location program; FORTRAN list processing; full load power
FLR	fixed-length record; folder
FLV	full load voltage
FLW	full load wattage
FM	fade margin; failure mode; fat memory; ferro-magnetic; file maintenance; file management; flat memory; flight memory; flow-meter; flux-meter; fox message; frame maintenance; frame mode; freeze mode; frequency modulation; function multiplier
Fm	fermium
FMB	fast multi-bit
FMBS	fast multi-bit shifter
FMC	frame mode control
FMCS	frame mode control signalling
FMD	frequency modulation detector
FMI	failure mode indicator; frequency modulation index
FMM	fat memory manager; fat memory model; frame maintenance mode
FMN	file maintenance need
FMP	file maintenance protocol
FMR	former; frequency modulation receiver

FMR/F	frequency modulation receiver with feedback
FMS	fast multi-bit shifter; file (or forms) management system
FMT	flight memory tracker; format
FMV	full motion video
FMW	frequency modulated wave
FN	field name; file name; foot-note; form name; free network
FNT	font; Fowler-Noreim tunnelling
FO	fan-out; fast operation; ferric oxide; ferrous oxide; field office; flag object; free oscillation; front office
FOB	fan-out box
FOC	fibre optic cable (or communication or component)
FOCN	fibre optic communication network
FOCUS	forum of control-data users
FOD	facsimile (or FAX) on demand; fold-over distortion
FOF	field of force
FoG	fourth generation
FOH	fibre optic hub
FOIL	file oriented interpretive language
FOIP	fax over Internet protocol
FOIRL	fibre optic internal repeater link
FOLDOC	free on-line dictionary of computing
FOLM	fibre optic local module

FOM	fibre optic modem
FON	Font; phone; fiber (or fibre) optic network
FOR	FORTRAN
FORTRAN	formula translator
FOT	Fibre (fiber) optic test; fibre (fiber) optic transceiver
FOTB	fibre (fiber) optic test procedure
FOTS	fibre(fiber) optic transmission system
FOV	field of vision
FOXI	fibre (fiber) optic transmitter-receiver interface (where X→ transmitter-receiver)
FP	face-plate; facsimile (or FAX) press; failure prediction; fast packet; fast path; fast poll; field-protected; file path; file protection; fixed program; fixed-point; flat package; floating point; focal point; Fontastic Plus; foot-print; FoxPro; fractional programming; functional partitioning
FPA	floating point arithmetic
FPAL	fuse programmable array logic
FPB	floating point binary
FPC	fixed point constant; floating point calculation
FPCE	floating point calculation extension
FPD	flat panel display; floating point divide (or division); flow process diagram; front panel data; full page display
FPDP	front panel data port
FPGA	field programmable gate array

FPI	floating point interface
FPL	Fabry-Perot laser
FPLA	field programming logic array
FPLA/CP	field programming logic array—core patch
FPLA/FMS	field programming logic array—fast multibit shifter
FPLA/PRL	field programming logic array—priority resolver and latch
FPM	fast page mode; four phase modulation
fpm	feet per minute
FPM-RAM	FPMRAM; fast page mode random access memory
FPN	floating point number
FPO	floating point operation; four-plus-one
FPOA	four-plus-one address
FPP	fixed path protocol; floating point pipeline (or processor)
FPR	floating point register (or routine); fixed point representation
FPROM	FP-ROM; field programmable read only memory
FPRS	fixed-point representation system
FPS	floating point standard; frames per second; full proportional servo
fps	feet per second
FPU	floating point unit
FPX	floating point extension
FQDN	fully qualified domain name

FQFP   flat-quad flat-package

FR   facilities request; failure rate; FaxRight; feature register; feed rate; field rate; film resistor; film ribbon; fixed rate; fixed resistor; force reduction; frame reject; frame relay; France; frequency response; from; full range; full read; fuser roller

Fr   francium

FRA   frame relay access; frequency response analysis

FRAD   frame relay access device; frame relay assembler-disassembler

FRAG   fragment; fragmentation

FRAM   F-RAM; ferro-electric random access memory; frame relay access mode

FRBP   feed rate by-pass

FRC   frame relay call (or congestion); frequency response characteristic; functional redundancy check(ing)

FRCC   frame relay call (or congestion) control

FRED   frame editor

FRFZ   full range floating zero

FRI   Friday

F/RJ   FRJ; frame reject

FRM   form; frame; from

FRMR   former

FRN   feed rate number; frame relay network

FROM   ferro-electric (or flash or fusible) read only memory; full range of motion

FROR	feed rate over-ride
FRP	frame relay protocol; full read pulse
FRPA	frame relay protocol architecture
FRPC	flux reversals per centimeter
FRPI	flux reversals per inch
FRS	fixed-point representation system; frame relay sub-layer
FRSL	frame relay sub-layer
FRT	frame re-acquisition time
FS	fail-soft; fatigue sign; feasibility study; Fibonacci search; field strength; file search; file separator; file server; file sharing; file size; file specifier; file statistic; file system; FileShare; fixed storage; fluorescent screen; font size; frame search; frame status; frame synchronization; free standing; full scale; full shift
FSA	floating symbolic address
FSD	file system driver
FSE	file server environment; file sharing extension; full screen editor
FSES	file server environment services
FSF	fixed sequence format; free software foundation; frequency selective fading
FSK	frequency shift key(ing)
FSL	file sharing library
FSM	file sharing monitor; finite state machine; first-shared memory; frequency shift modulation
FSMA	first-shared memory address

FSMAL   first-shared memory address length

FSN   frame sequence number; full service network

FSP   facsimile (or FAX) service program; file service packets; file service protocol

FSPB   file service packets buffered

FSR   feedback shift register; free system resources

FSS   fixed satellite system; flying spot scanner

FST   flat square tube; full stroke time

FT   fast track; fault tolerance; feed-through; feet; file transfer; font tools; foot; form tool; form type; Fourier transform; fractional telecommunication; free time; function table

F/T   FT; full-time

ft   feet; foot

ft-lb   foot-libra (libra →Latin: pound)

FTA   file transfer application

FTAM   file transfer access management (or method)

FTC   fast threshold comparator; fault tolerant computer; foil thermo-couple

FTD   file to download

FTKB   full travel keyboard

FTL   flash transition layer; Fourier transform lens

FTN   fault tolerant node

FTP   ftp; file transfer protocol

FTS   fault tolerant system; Federal Telecommunication System; Fourier transform spectrometer

FTSM	Fourier transform spectro-meter
FTT	function transfer table
FTTC	Fibre (fiber) to the curb
FTTH	Fibre (fiber) to the home
FTX	fault tolerant UNIX
FU	fixed unit; formatting unit; formatting utility
FUI	file update information
FUL	file up-load
FUN	function
FUNC	function
FUT	fibre under test
FV	fixed value; FORTRAN variable
FVC	formant vocoder
FVT	full video transfer; full video translation
FW	firm-ware; font window; forward; four wave; four wire; frame work; free-ware; full write; full wave
FWB	frame-work block
FWBB	firmware building block
FWD	forward
FWHM	full width, half maximum
FWM	four wave mixing
FWO	fragmented write occurred
FWP	full write pulse
FWPS	full wave power supply

FYI   for your information

FZ   Fresnel zone

~G~

G	gain; gamma; gas; gate; gauge; gauss; general; generic; giga; glass; globe; global; glue; grade; gram; graph(ic); gravity; green; grid; gross; ground; group; guess
g	*conductance*; gram; gravitation-constant
GA	generic array; general availability; generated address; genetic algorithm; go ahead; graphing assistant; ground absorption; group address
Ga	Gallium
GaAs	gallium arsenide
gal	Gal; gallon
GAL	gallon; generic array logic
GAM	granularity adjustment module
GAPI	gateway application programming interface
GART	graphics address relocation table
GATT	graphics address translation table
GB	giga-byte; grid ban; grid bias; Great Britain; guard band; guard bit
Gb	giga-bit; gilbert
GBM	grid-bias modulation
GBNAR	go-back-and automatic request
GBNC	go-back-and continuous
GBP	grid by-pass

GBR　　　geographic based routing; Great Britain

GC　　　gamma correction; Gantt chart; gate circuit; gender changer; general control; giga-cycle; global change; graphics card; Gray code; gun control; gun current

Gc　　　giga-cycle

GCC　　　GNU C-compiler; graphics control chip

GCCD　　glass-passivated ceramic chip diode

GCI　　　ground-controlled interception

GCP　　　gate capture playback

GCR　　　generic cell rate; group code recording

GD　　　gap digit; gas discharge; gate driver; general description; general diagnostics; generic decryption; germanium diode; gold doping; graphic device; graphic display; guard digit

Gd　　　gadolinium

GDA　　　global data area

GDAD　　gas discharge alphanumeric display

GDDM　　graphics data display manager

GDE　　　generic decryption engine

GDG　　　generation data group

GDI　　　graphic device interface

GDLC　　generic data link control

GDP　　　graphic draw primitive

GDT　　　generic decryption technique; global descriptor table; gradient descent technique; graphics development tool-kit; ground diffused transistor

GDTR	global descriptor table register
GE	General Electric; generated emission; gross error; Gunn effect
Ge	Germanium
GEC	Gunn effect circuit
GECOS	General Electric comprehensive operating system
GEIS	General Electric information service
GEM	graphics environment manager
GEnie	**GENIE**; General Electric network for information exchange
GEO	geo-stationary earth orbit; geo-stationary; geo-synchronous earth orbit; geography; geometry
GEOS	graphic environment operating system
GER	Germany
GES	graphics editing software
GeV	giga-electron volt
GFC	general flow control; grand-father clock (*or* cycle)
GFCI	ground-fault circuit interceptor (*or* interrupter)
GFI	general format identifier; ground-fault interceptor (*or* interrupter)
GFLOPS	giga floating-point operations per second
GFO	gamma ferric oxide
GFS	global file specification
GG	glare guard
GGP	gateway-gateway protocol

GHz	giga-hertz
GI	General Instruments; graded index
GID	group identification (*or* identifier)
GIF	graded index fibre; graphics interchange format; graphics interface format
GIGO	garbage-in garbage-out
GII	global information infra-structure
GIIS	global information infra-structure
GILS	government information locator service
GINA	graphical identification and authentication
GIRLS	generalized information retrieval and listing system
GIS	geographic information system; global information solution
GIX	global Internet exchange
GJ	grown junction
GJD	germanium junction diode
GKF	global kill file
GKS	graphical kernel system
GL	gap length; gap-less; general ledger; generation language; glass; glue; graphics language; gray level; grid leak; grid lock
4GL	fourth generation language
Gl	Glucinium
g/l	g/L; gl; gL; grams per liter (litre)
GLB	generic logic block; greatest lower bound

GLIS	global land information system
GLM	general linear model
GLOBE	global learning by observations to benefit the environment
GLOCOM	global communication
GLR	graphite-line resistor
GLY	glossary
GM	galvano-meter; Gauss meter; general mechanic; general mode; General Motors; global memory; graphics mode; group mark
gm	gram
GML	generalized markup language
GMP	global mobile professional
GMR	giant magnetic (*or* magneto-) resistance
GMS	global management (*or* memory) system; global messaging service
GMSA	global memory system architecture
GMT	Greenwich Mean Time
GN	Gaussian noise; global navigation
GNCL	general numerical control language
GNCLP	general numerical control language processor
GND	ground
GNN	global network navigator
GNOME	GNU network object model environment
GNSS	global navigation satellite system

GNT   grant

GNU   Gnu's not UNIX

GO   general order

GOSIP   government open systems interconnection profile

gov   GOV; government(al)

GP   galley proof; gang printer; Gantt package; gas plasma; gate pulse; general protection; general purpose; generator polynomial; GeoPort; grade point; graphic panel; graphic plotter; graphics package; ground plane;

GPA   grade point average

GPC   general purpose computer

GPD   gas-plasma display; gated peak detector; general purpose data

GPDC   general purpose data concentrator

GPF   general protection fault; GUI programming facility

GPI   general purpose interface; graphics programming interface; ground position indicator

GPIB   general purpose information (*or* interface) bus

GPPM   graphics pages per minute

GPR   general purpose register

GPRC   glass passivated rectifier chip

GPRF   general purpose register file

GPS   general purpose system; global positioning satellite (*or* system)

GPSD   GeoPort serial driver

GPSS	general purpose system simulation (*or* simulator); global positioning satellite system
GPTA	GeoPort telecommunication adapter
GPTT	GeoPort telephone tool
GR	gamma release; Gaussian response; general register; generalized routine; global replace; global resource; gravity; green; gross; grouped record; guard ring
GRAD	graduate; graduation
GRADD	graphics adapter device driver
GRAFLIB	graphics library *(where F→ ph)*
GRC	guard ring capacitor
GRE	global regular expression; Graduate Record Examinations; graphics engine
GREP	global regular expression print
GRF	general retail format; graph *(where F→ ph)*
GRIF	general retail instructional format
GRIM	global real-time interactive map
GRM	grant rights mask
GRP	Gaussian random process; global routing pool; group
GRTIM	global real-time interactive map
GS	goof sheet; graphics server; gray scale; ground start; group separator; guard signal
Gs	gauss; gravity specific *(specific gravity)*
GSA	group service access
GSAP	group service access point

GSC	grid spaced contact
GSE	ground support equipment
GSI	general server interface
GSM	global shared memory; global system for mobile-communication; ground static monitor; *Groupe Spéciale Mobile* (*French:* Mobile-communication Special Group)
GSNW	gateway service for NetWare
GSP	generic server passer; global service provider
GSS	graphics software system
GSTN	general switched telephone network
GSV	gate-source voltage
GSVP	gas surge voltage protector
GSYIG	gallium substituted yttrium iron garnet
GT	game theory; gate; gate terminal
GTE	General Telephone Electronics
GTF	generalized timing format
GTLD	gTLD; generic top level domain; global top level domain
GTO	gate turn-off; go to; guide to operation
GUI	graphic user interface
GUID	globally unique identifier; global universal identifier
GURU	guide to RAM upgrades
GUT	global universal time
GV	giga-volt; global variable; global voltage

GVM	generating volt-meter
GVS	global variable symbol
GVT	Global Virtual Time
GW	gate-way; giga-watt; gone west
GW-BASIC	Gee Whiz beginners all purpose symbolic instruction code
GWL	gull wing leg
GX	graphics extension
GY	Gy; gray
GYIG	gallium-substituted yttrium iron garnet
gz	GNU zip *(extension)*
GZIP	GNU zip

~H~

H	hair; half; halt; hand; harmonic; hartley; hash(ing); head; header; heap; hear(ing); heart; heat(ing); heater; height; help; helper; henry; heterodyne; heterogeneous; heuristic; hexadecimal; hierarchy; high; hint; histogram; history; hit; hold; hole; hologram; home; homeostasis; hook; hop; horizontal; host; hot; hub; hue; hum; hunting; hydrogen; hysteresis
h	hecto
HA	head actuator; half-adder; half adjust
Ha	Hahnium
HACMP	high availability cluster multi-processing
HAL	hard array logic; hardware abstraction layer; heuristically-programmed algorithmic; house-programmed array logic
HAP	host access protocol
Hart	hartley
HB	hard break; hold button; holding beam; horizontal beam; horizontal blanking; hot buy; hybrid modelling
HBA	host bus adapter
HBI	horizontal blanking interval
HC	half card; half cell; half cycle; Hall constant; Hamming code; handling capacity; hard card; hard case; hard copy; hard core; head cleaning; head crashing; heat capacity; hermaphroditic connector; hexadecimal conversion; hierarchy chart; high concentration;

hole current; Hollerith card; horizontal chart; host computer; house cleaning; Huffman code; Huffman coding; hybrid circuit; hybrid coil; hybrid computer; hyper-card

HCC	Hercules color card; high capacity communication
HCCS	high capacity communication system
HCD	head cleaning diskette
HCE	header control error
HCI	hard copy input; human computer interaction
HCL	hardware compatibility list; hybrid computer link
HCM	half card modem
HCS	hard core section; hybrid computer system
HCSS	high capacity storage system
HCT	hybrid computer translator
HCU	home computer user
HD	half duplex; Hamming distance; hard disk; hard drive; hard drop; harmonic detector; harmonic distortion; head disk; hearing device; high definition; high density; high DOS; histogram data; hole density; home directory; host data; hyphen drop; hysteresis distortion
HDA	hard disk assembly; head disk assembly
HDAC	hybrid digital-to-analog computer
HDB	hierarchical data base; high density bipolar; host data bus
HDB3	high density bipolar 3-zeros
HDBP	high density bi-polar

HDC	half duplex channel (*or* circuit *or* communication); hard disk controller; hexadecimal-to-decimal conversion; high density connector
HDCD	high definition compatible digital
HDD	hard disk drive
HDDM	hard disk drive motor
HDE	horizontal delta encoding
HDF	hierarchical data format
HDI	hard disk interleave; head-to-disk interference
HDL	hardware description language (*or* level); hierarchical data link; high level data
HDLC	hierarchical data link control; high-level data link control
HDM	hard disk menu; hardware device module
HDML	handheld device markup language
HDMS	hard disk menu system
HDO	half duplex operation
HDR	header
HDSC	high density signal carrier
HDSL	high-data-rate digital subscriber line; high-speed digital subscriber line
HDSS	holographic data storage system
HDT	half duplex transmission; hard disk test; host digital terminal
HDTV	high definition television
HDTV-c	high definition television capable

HDVD   high definition volumetric display

HDW   hardware

HDX   half duplex

HE   Hall effect; hyper-editor; hysteresis error

He   Helium

HEC   hybrid electrical car

HEM   high electron mobility

HEMT   high electron mobility transistor

HEX   *Greek:* six; **hex**adecimal

HF   Hall field; hard font; header file; heat flow; high flow; high frequency

Hf   Hafnium

HFA   hot fix area

HFB   hot fix block(s)

HFBA   hot fix block(s) available

HFC   hybrid fibre (fiber) coaxial

HFD   high firm density; hot fix disabled

HFDF   high frequency direction finder

HFE   human factors engineering

HFH   high frequency heating

HFS   hierarchical file system

HFT   high frequency transformer; high function terminal; hot fix table

HFTSt   hot fix table start

HFTSz	hot fix table size
HG	Harvard Graphics; head gap; hologram; hunt group; hyper-game
Hg	*hydrar-gyrum* (*Latin:* mercury)
hg	hecto-gram
HGA	Hercules graphics adapter; high gain amplifier
HGC	Hercules graphics card
HGCP	Hercules graphics card plus
HgDL	*hydrar-gyrum* delay line (*hydrar-gyrum* →*Latin:* mercury) *(mercury delay line)*
HH	half height; header hub; hyphenation help
HHL	host to host layer
HHPC	hand-held personal computer
HHUB	header hub
HI	halt indicator; hanging indent; heterodyne interference; high intensity; hold instruction; hole injection; hybrid interface
HIC	highest incoming channel
HICAPCOM	high capacity communication
HIDM	high information delta modulation
HIFD	high-density floppy diskette
HiFi	HIFI; high fidelity
HIL	human interface link
HIMEM	high memory

HiNIL	HINIL; high noise immunity logic
HIPO	hierarchy input-processing-output
HIPOT	high potential
HIPPI	high performance parallel interface
HIR	host interrupt request
HiRes	HIRES; HI-RES; high resolution
HITS	highway in the sky
HK	hot key; house keeping
HKR	house keeping routine
HKS	hyper-kaleidoscope
HL	hard limit; hard limiting; head-line; header label; high level; high-light; high-low; hyper-link; hysteresis loop
hl	hL; hecto-liter (litre)
HLB	head-line blocking
HLC	high level competition (*or* compiler)
HLD	high level data (*or* debugger *or* design); hold
HLDA	high level design automation
HLDL	high level data link
HLDLC	high level data link control
HLI	hard limited integrator
HLL	high level language
HLLAP	high level language application program
HLLAPI	high level language application program interface
HLM	high level memory (*or* modulation *or* multiplexer)

HLMUX	high level **m**ultiplexer
HLMX	high level multiplexer
HLN	head-line news
HLP	**help**
HLQ	high level **q**ualifier (*or* quality)
HLT	**halt**
HM	Hall mobility; head-meter; help mark; high memory; hole mobility; human machine; humidity measurement; hybrid modelling; hyper-media
hm	hecto-meter (metre)
HMA	high memory access (*or* area)
HMD	head-mounted display
HMI	human-machine interface; humidity measurement instrument
HMMP	hyper-media management protocol
HMOS	high-density (*or* high-speed) metal oxide semiconductor
HMP	host monitoring protocol
HMT	hybrid modelling technology
HN	hexadecimal notation; high noise; host node; host number; Hungarian notation
HNI	high noise immunity
HNIL	high noise immunity logic
HNL	host to network layer
HNW	heterogeneous network

HO	hands-on; harmonic oscillator; Hartley oscillator; high output; higher order; highest order
Ho	Holmium
HOC	highest outgoing channel
HOE	hands on experience; heat of emission
HOS	harmonic oscillator sampling
HOS-SDC	harmonic oscillator sampling signal/distortion converter
HOST	higher order software technique
HOTT	hot off the tree
HP	Hartley principle; heating pump; Hewlett-Packard; high pass; high performance; high position; high potential; high-power; horse-power; hydraulic pump
hp	horse-power
HPA	high-power amplifier
HPC	handheld personal computer; high performance computer (*or* computing *or* connection)
HPCC	high performance computing and communication
HPDJ	Hewlett-Packard Desk Jet
HPF	high performance file; high-pass filter; highest possible frequency
HPFS	high performance file system
HPG	Hewlett-Packard graphics
HPGL	Hewlett-Packard graphics language
HPIB	Hewlett-Packard interface bus
HPLJ	Hewlett-Packard Laser Jet

HPM	Harvard project manager
HPPA	Hewlett-Packard precision architecture
HPPI	high performance parallel interface
HPR	high performance routing
HPSB	high performance serial bus
HPUX	Hewlett-Packard UNIX
HPW	high performance work-station
HQX	*hex*adecimal; high quality extension
HR	hard return; hashing routine; header record; heat rays; heat recovery; heuristic routine; hierarchical routing; high record; high request; high resolution; hit ratio; horizontal resolution; horizontal retrace; hour; human resource(s)
HRG	high resolution graphics
HRO	high record offset
HRP	horizontal retrace period
HRR	high request rate
HRS	hours
HRT	head related transfer
HRTF	head related transfer function
HRTP	horizontal re-trace period
HS	half sinusoid; half subtractor; halt switch; hand-set; hand-shaking; hard sector; hardware system; heat sink; heat spreader; help screen; hierarchical simulation; hierarchical system; high school; high speed; high split; horizontal scroll; hybrid system; hyper-space

HSA	hardware system architecture
HSB	high speed bus; hue, saturation, brightness
HSC	hierarchical storage controller; high speed channel (*or* scanner)
HSDI	high speed digital input
HSDI/OIB	high speed digital input-output interface board
HSDO	high speed digital output
HSF	horizontal scanning frequency
HSI	hue, saturation, intensity
HSL	high speed lens (*or* logic)
HSM	hierarchical storage management
HSN	hyper-stream network
HSP	hand-shaking protocol; hidden station problem; high speed printer (*or* processor)
HSR	half shift register; horizontal scanning rate
HSSI	high speed serial interface
HSSL	high speed storage loading
HST	half splitting technique; Hawaii Standard Time; head settling time; heat sink technology; high speed technology; history; host
HSV	hue saturation value
HSYNC	horizontal synchronization
HT	half time; half tone; half toning; hash total; heat; height; hidden text; high tension; hole trap; holding time; horizontal tabulation; hybrid topology; hybrid transmission; hyper-text

HTC	head to tape contact; highest two-way channel; horizontal tabulation character
HTE	half time emitter
HTL	high threshold logic
html	HTML; hyper-text markup language
html+	HTML+; hyper-text markup language *plus*
HTN	high performance twisted nematic; high tension
HTPM	Harvard total project manager
HTS	high temperature super-conductor
HTSC	high temperature super-conductor
http	HTTP; hyper-text transfer (*or* transport) protocol
HTTP-NG	http-ng; hyper-text transfer (*or* transport) protocol next generation
HTTPS	hyper-text transfer (*or* transport) protocol secured
HTWC	highest two-way channel
HU	hosed-up; hung-up
HUT	Hopkins ultra-violet telescope
H/V	H-V; HV; high voltage; horizontal-Vertical
HVAC	heating, ventilation, and air conditioning; high voltage alternating current
HVD	high voltage differential
HVDC	high voltage direct current
HVP	horizontal-vertical position
HW	half wave; half word; hand wired; hard-ware; hard wire; hertzian wave; home-work; hot wire

H/W	H/W; hand written; hardware; home-work
HWA	hardware assembler; hot wire anemometer
HWAM	hot wire anemo-meter
HWC	hardware check
HWCP	hardware code page
HWD	height, width, depth
HWDL	hardware description language (*or* level)
HWI	hardware interrupt
HWIN	hardware interrupt number
HWL	hard wire logic
HWNC	hand-wired (*or* hard-wired) numerical control
HWR	hardware
HWS	hardware selection (*or* standardization *or* system)
HWSA	hardware system architecture
HYCOL	hybrid computer link
HYCOTRAN	hybrid computer translator
HYDAC	hybrid digital-analog computer
HYP	hyphenation
HZ	hot zone
Hz	hertz
HzW	hertzian wave

~ I ~

I	*current*; identifier; in; increment; index; indexing; input; intensity; Internet; internet; iodine; ion
IA	immediate address; implicit address; in advance; indexed address; indirect address; input area; instruction address; instruction area; instrumentation amplifier; integrated amplifier; internal arithmetic; Internet address; inverting amplifier; isolation amplifier; item advance
IAA	intra-application area
IAB	Internet activities (*or* architecture) board
IAC	integration, assembly, and checkout; inter-application communication; Internet access coalition
IAD	Internet address detector
IAG	instruction address generation
IAGC	instant automatic gain control
IAHC	Internet ad hoc committee
IAK	Internet access kit
IAL	integral action limiter; international algebraic language (*first name of ALGOL*)
IAM	index address mark
IAN	Internet assigned number
IANA	Internet assigned numbers authority
IAP	Internet access provider

IAR	index (*or* instruction) address register
IAS	immediate access store; Institute for Advanced Studies; Internet access server
IAT	import address table; interactive television
IB	impedance bridge; incremental backup; inductance bridge; input block; input buffer; instruction buffer; integral boundary; inter-base; interface bus; interlock bypass; ion beam
IBC	immediate (*or* international) block character; instrument bus computer; interbase current
iBCS	Intel binary compatibility specification
IBF	input buffer full
IBG	inter-block gap
IBI	intelligent bus interface
IBIS	input-output buffer information specification
IBM	International Business Machines *(Company)*
IBM-GL	International Business Machines graphics language
IBP	in-bound packet; interlock by-pass
IBR	input buffer register
IBS	in-band signalling
IBW	incident backward wave
IC	ideal capacitor; ideal component; ideal crystal; illegal character; illegal code; illegal control; immediate cycle; impedance coil; impedance compensator; impedance converter; incremental compaction; image converter; in-circuit; incremental computer; indicator chart; induced charge; induced current; induction coil;

inductive capacitor; inductive circuit; inductive coupling; industrial control; information center; information content; injection current; input channel; input converter; input current; instruction cache; instruction character; instruction code; instruction counter; instruction cycle; instrumentation calibration; instrumentation correction; integrated chopper; integrated circuit; integrated component; integrator capacitor; intelligent cable; interbase current; inter-carrier; inter-change; interface card; interface converter; intermittent control; interprocess communication; internal circuit; interrupt controller; interrupt cycle; intrinsic conduction; ion cluster; ion concentration; ion count; isochronous communication

ICA	integral control action; intelligent console architecture
ICANN	Internet Council on Internet Names and Numbers
ICAP	Internet calendar access protocol
iCAS	ICAS; Intel communicating application specification
ICB	internal circuit board; Internet citizen's band; instruction control bus
ICC	industrial control communication; integrated circuit card; International Color Consortium; International Computer Center; Internet control center
ICCP	Institute for Certification of Computing Professionals
ICD	international code designator; interrupt controlled data
ICDA	interrupt controlled data acquisition
ICDAS	interrupt controlled data acquisition system
ICDIP	integrated circuit dual in-line package

ICE	in-circuit emulator; integrated computing environment; Internet configuration extension
ICES	interference causing equipment standards
ICF	integrated circuit fabrication; Internet connection firewall
ICI	image component information
ICL	inter-connection line
ICLID	incoming-call line identification
ICM	image color matching; in-coming message; initial condition mode; Internet control message; inverted coaxial magnetron
ICMC	Internet control message center
ICMP	Internet control message protocol
ICO	icon
iCOMP	Intel comparative microprocessor performance
ICP	in-coming packet; initial connection protocol; integrated channel processor; interrupt count pulse; invalid connection packet
ICPL	initial control program load
ICQ	I *Seek You* (where CQ→ seek you) (Internet program)
ICR	initial count register; interrupt code (or control) register
ICR	intelligent character recognition; Internet chat relay
ICS	independent clock synchronization; intuitive command structure; inverting current switch
ICSA	International Computer Security Association

ICSAPI	Internet connection services application program interface
ICT	in-circuit test(ing); insulating core transformer; integrated circuit tester
ICU	instruction cache (*or* control *or* counter) unit; Intel configuration utility; ISA configuration utility
ICW	initialization command word
ID	identification; identifier; image dissector; implicit differentiation; impurity diffusion; incremental data; incremental dimension; instruction decoder; instruction diagnostic; interface debugging; internal diameter; interrupt device; intruder detection; isolating diode; isotropic dielectric; item design
I2D	imitation 2 dimension
IDA	incoming data alert; integrated digital access; intelligent data acquisition; intelligent disk (*or* drive) array
IDAI	intelligent data acquisition interface
IDAM	identification address mark
IDAPI	independent data-base application programming interface
IDC	integrated data-base (*or* desk-top) connector; Internet data-base connector
IDDE	integrated development and debugging environment
IDE	imbedded (*or* integrated *or* intelligent) drive electronics; integrated development environment; interactive design engineering; interface design enhancement
IDEA	international data encryption algorithm
IDEAL	interface data environment for an application's life

IDF	integrated data file; intermediate distribution frame
IDI	improved data interchange; initial domain identifier
IDL	interactive data language; interface definition language
IDLE	International Date Line East
IDLW	International Date Line West
IDM	integrated data-base management
IDMS	integrated data-base management system
IDN	integrated digital network
IDNX	integrated digital network exchange
IDO	internal datagram operation
IDOM	isolated digital output module
IDOS	icon driven operating system
IDP	integrated data processing; integrated detector pre-amplifier; Internet-work datagram protocol
IDR	indirect; intelligent document recognition
IDS	integrated data storage
IDT	interface design tool; interrupt descriptor table
IDTR	interrupt descriptor table register
IDTV	improved definition television
IDU	interface data unit
IDX	index
IE	identity element; image enhancement; impulse excitation; indexed entry; induced environment; industrial engineering; inference engine; inherited

error; input editing; integrated emulator; inter-exchange; interface exerciser; intermittent error; internal energy; Internet Explorer

IEC	inter-exchange carrier; International Electro-technical Commission
IED	ideal envelope detector; interrupt enable and disable
IEEE	Institute of Electrical and Electronics Engineers
IEL	instruction execution logic
IEM	Internet electronic mail; isolated expansion multiplexer
IEMSI	interactive electronic mail standard identification
IEN	Internet engineering note(s)
IER	instruction execution rate
IES	isolated expansion slot
IET	instruction execution time
IETF	Internet Engineering Task Force
IESG	Internet Engineering Steering Group
IEU	International Electrical Units
IF	ideal filter; ideal flux; ideal frequency; image file; image filter; incipient failure; indexed file; induced failure; information field; instruction format; interaction factor; interface; interference fading; intermediate frequency; internal font; internal force; internal frequency
I/F	IF; interface
IFB	information feed-back
IFBS	information feed-back system

IFC	Internet foundation classes
IFD	image file directory
IFF	interchangeable file format
IFHS	integrated fan heat sink
IFIP	International Federation of Information Processing
IFM	interrupt freeze mode
IFO	immediate frequency oscillator
IFP	instruction fetch pipeline
IFS	information feedback system; installable (*or* integrated) file system; inter-frame scheme
IFSM	information systems management
IFTA	integrated fault tolerant architecture
IFW	incident forward wave
IG	identity gate; ignore gate; impedance generator; impedance ground; implication gate; impulse generator; inclusion gate; inhibit gate; injector grid; insulated gate; interblock gap; internal gap; internal gate; interword gap
IGA	integrated graphics array
IGBT	insulated gate bipolar transistor
IGC	integrated graphics controller
IGES	initial graphics exchange standard
IGFET	insulated-gate field effect transistor
IGMP	Internet group management (*or* multicast) protocol
IGP	interior gateway protocol

IGR	interior gateway routing
IGRP	interior gateway routing protocol
IGS	internet go server
IH	independent heterodyne; information heading; intelligent hub; internal heat; ionization heat
IHD	internal hard drive
IHL	Internet header length
IHUB	intermediate hub
IHV	independent hardware vendor
II	immediate instruction; impulse inertia; incremental induction; incremental integrator; inhibiting input; input impedance; input intensity; ion implantation; iterative impedance
IIA	implied indirect addressing
IIC	intelligent interface card
IID	interrupt identification
IIF	immediate interface
III	interstate identification index
IIL	integrated injection logic (*or* I^2L); interrupt input line
IIOP	Internet inter-operability protocol; Internet inter-orbital protocol
IIR	immediate impulse response
IIS	Internet information server
IITF	information infra-structure task force
IIU	interrupt is used

IJP   ink-jet printer

IKB   intelligent key-board

IKBS   intelligent key-board system

IKS   intelligent keyboard system

IL   impurity level; in-line; infinite loop; injection logic; intensity level; interconnection line; interlock; internal lock; Internet layer

I²L   IIL; integrated injection logic

Il   Illinium

ILA   image light amplifier; in-line assembly

ILB   internal lock bypass

ILBP   inter-lock by-pass; internal lock by-pass

ILD   injection laser diode

ILEC   incumbent local exchange carrier

ILLIAC   Illinois automatic computer

ILP   in-line package (*or* procedure)

ILS   in-line subroutine

ILSB   in-line sub-routine

ILSG   International Language Support Group

IM   idle mode; injection molding; input module; Instant Messenger; instruction modification; insulated material; integral module; integrated manufacturing; interactive mode; interface management; interface module; interlaced memory; interlacing multiprocessing; internal memory; internal modem; interrupt module; interval marker; intrinsic mobility

IMA	International Multimedia Association
IMACS	image management and communication system
iMac	Internet-access Macintosh
IMAP	interactive mail (*or* message) access protocol
IMAS	interactive mail (*or* message) access System
IMAX	image maximum (*maximum image*)
IMB	interrupt mask bit
IMC	image motion compensation; industrial microcomputer; integrated monolithic circuit; internal modem control
IMD	inter-modulation distortion
IMDB	in-memory data-base
IMDS	image data stream
IMG	image
IMHO	in my humble opinion (*news-group*)
IMI	inner macro-instruction
IML	initial microcode load
IMN	inter-modulation noise
IMP	infant mortality period; interactive multi-processor; information (*or* interface) message processor; interlace multi-processing; Internet mail provider
IMPA	intelligent multi-port adapter
IMPACT	implementation planning and control technique
IMPS	interactive multi-processor system
IMR	Internet monthly report; interrupt mask register

IMS	information management system; Institute of Management Sciences; interactive multiprocessor system; Internet mail service; Internet measurement system
IMSP	Internet message support protocol
IMT	improved mobile telephone
IMTC	International Multimedia Teleconferencing Consortium
IMTS	improved mobile telephone system
IMTV	interactive multimedia television
IMU	internal measurement unit
IMUX	inverse multiplexer
IMW	interrupt mask word
IN	impulse noise; inch; induction noise; inductive neutralization; infix notation; input; input noise; internal; internal noise
In	Indium
INC	increase; increment
Inc.	incorporated
INCA	interleaved native compiled code architecture
INCH	integrated chopper
IND	ideal noise diode; index; India; indicator
I-Net+	Internet +
INF	infinite; infinity information
INFO	information
INFS	Internet network file system

INI	initial; initialization; initialize
INIT	initial; initialization; initialize
INM	integrated network management
InP	indium phosphate
INR	internal noise reduction
INRS	internal noise reduction system
INS	instruction; instrument; integrated network server; International Network Service; Internet news search
INT	integer; internal; interrupt; international
InterNIC	Internet Network Information Center
INTL	international
INTR	interrupt; introduction
INTRQ	interrupt request
INW	Internet work
INWG	International Network Working Group
IO	illegal operation; interpreter operation
I/O	IO; input-output
Io	Ionium
IOA	input-output address (*or* architecture)
IOB	input-output bound (*or* bus)
IOC	input-output cable (*or* card *or* channel *or* controller); inter-office channel
IOCC	input-output channel converter; input-output controller chip

IOCS	input-output control system
IOD	input-output device
IODP	input-output device polling
IOE	input-output error (*or* executive)
IOEC	input-output error count
IOI	input-output instruction (*or* interface); iso-planar oxide isolation
IOM	input-output memory (*or* module *or* multiplexer)
IOMA	input-output memory address
IOMS	input-output mapped system
IOP	input-output ports (*or* processor *or* programming); instruction operation
IOPL	input-output privilege level
IOPS	input-output programming system
IOR	index of refraction; input-output register (*or* request)
IORW	input-output request word
IOS	input-output switch
IOSGA	input-output support gate array
IOT	input-output table (*or* test)
IOTP	input-output test program
IOU	immediate operation use
IP	image processing; image program; impact printer; impedance poles; in phase; in post; in-put; incoming packet; indium phosphate; inductive potentiometer; information processing; initial point; initial packet; initialization packet; input program; inquiry

	processing; instantaneous power; instruction pointer; integrated programming; interactive processing; Internet protocol; Internet provider; interpret program; interprocess; irreversible process; iterative process
IPA	intelligent programming algorithm; Internet protocol address
IPC	industrial personal computer; industrial process control; information processing center; instructions per clock; inter-process communication
IPCP	Internet protocol control protocol
IPD	incoming packet discarded; input device; intelligent peripheral device
IPDC	Internet protocol device control
IPDS	intelligent printer data stream
IPE	interpret parity error
IPFC	information presentation facility compiler
IPI	intelligent peripheral interface
IPL	independent program loader; information programming language; initial program load(er); interrupt priority logic; ion projection lithography
IPM	images per minute; inductive potentiometer; integrated photo masking; intelligent power mode (*or* module)
ipm	inches per minute
IPMI	intelligent platform management interface
IPN	Internet protocol number
IPng	IPNG; Internet protocol next generation
IPOI	iso-planar oxide isolation

IPOS	input-processing-output-storage
IPOT	inductive potentiometer
IPP	Internet printing protocol
IPQP	in-phase and quadrature-phase
IPR	instruction pointer register
IPRA	Internet Policy Registration Authority
IPS	intelligent power system; interpretive programming system; interrupt processing structure
IPSE	integrated project support environment
IPsec	IPSEC; Internet protocol (*or* provider) security
IPT	inductive pressure transducer; interval polling timer
IPTC	International Press Telecommunications Council
IPX	Internet packet exchange
IQ	in-phase and quadrature-phase; intelligence quotient
IQL	Interactive query language
IR	image response; impedance ratio; implicit reference; implicit rights; incremental representation; index register; indirect address; inductive resistor; information retrieval; infra-red; initial review; input reference; input resolution; instruction register; instruction repertoire; internal radius; internal record; internal resistor; ionic radius
Ir	iridium
IRAN	inspect, repair as necessary
IRC	information reduced carrier; Internet relay chat
IRCC	International Radio Consultative Committee

IRCS	information reduced carrier synchronization
IRD	integrated receiver-descrambler
IrDA	IRDA; Infra-red Data Association
IRE	Institute of Radio Engineers
IRET	interrupt return
IRF	inheritance rights filter; intermediate routing function
IRG	inter-record gap
IRH	invalid reply header
IRHC	invalid reply header count
IRL	interactive reader language; inter-repeater link
IrLAP	IRLAP; infra-red link access protocol
IrLED	IRLED; infra-red light emitting diode
IRM	information resource management; inherent rights mask; interface (*or* Internet) reference manual
IRN	Iran
IRP	initial receiving point; interior router protocol
IRQ	interrupt request; Iraq
IRQL	interrupt request level
IRR	input request register
IRS	internal reference synchronization
IRT	interrupt response time
IRTF	Internet Research Task Force
IrTP	IRTP; infra-red transfer protocol
IRV	Intel raw video

IRW	indirect reference word
IRX	information retrieval experiment
IS	ideal signal; ideal system; identification system; image sensor; image setter; imperative statement; impulse speed; in string; incremental system; independent software; index sensing; inductosyn scale; information separator; information society; information system; initial state; input signal; input stream; input symbol; inquiry station; inserted subroutine; instruction set; integrated software; integrated system; interacting simulator; interactive software; interface standard; intermediate system; internal signal; internal storage; international standard; intrinsic semiconductor; item size
ISA	indexed sequential access; Industry Standard Architecture; information system access; instruction set architecture
ISAL	information system access line
ISAM	indexed sequential access management (*or* method)
ISAPI	Internet server application program interface
ISB	independent side-band
ISBN	international standard book number
ISC	instruction set computer; interlaced status checking; inter-system communication; intrinsic semiconductor; invalid slot count
ISDN	integrated services digital network
ISE	International Standard Electric
ISF	indexed sequential file; interrupt signal feedback
ISFB	interrupt signal feed-back

ISH	information super highway; ideal sample-hold
ISI	inter-symbol interference
ISIS	integrated system and information service
ISL	interactive system language
ISM	industrial-scientific-medical; Internet service manager
ISMM	International Symposium on Memory Management
ISN	information systems network; invalid sequence number
ISNC	invalid sequence number count
ISO	International Standardisation Organisation (*International Organization for Standardization*)
ISOC	Internet Society
ISP	in-system programming; internally stored program; Internet service provider; interrupt stack pointer; interrupt status port
ISR	information storage and retrieval; inserted sub-routine; interrupt service routine; interrupt status register
ISSN	international standard serial number
IST	in-service testing; internal self-test
ISV	independent software vendor
IT	icon tools; idea tree; ideal terminal; idle time; information technology; information theory; input transformer; input translator; installation time; instruction time; interactive television; interference trap; internal timer
ITB	intermediate text block; Internet traffic block
ITC	Internet traffic control

ITDM	isochronous time division multiplexing
ITG	internal track gap
ITI	interactive terminal interface
ITM	individual test menu
ITN	identification tasking and networking
ITO	indium tin oxide
ITP	interpretive translation program
ITR	Internet talk radio
ITT	International Telephone and Telegraph; invitation to transmit
ITU	International Telecommunication Union
ITU-DS	International Telecommunication Union—Development Sector
ITU-RS	International Telecommunication Union—Radio-communications Sector
ITU-TSS	International Telecommunication Union—Telecommunication Standardization Sector
ITU-TIES	International Telecommunication Union—Telecommunication Information Exchange Service
ITUG	International Telecommunications User Group
ITV	interactive television; interrupt table vector
IU	information user; information utility; instruction unit
IUAP	Internet user account provider
IUF	in-use flag
IUP	instruction unit pipeline

IUPL	instruction unit pipe-line
IUS	interchange unit separator
IV	ideal value; index value; induced voltage; interrupt vector
IVC	internal virtual circuit
IVDS	integrated voice and data system; interactive video-disc system
IVDT	integrated voice-data terminal
IVI	involuntary interrupt
IVIF	interchangeable virtual instrument foundation
IVIS	interactive video information system
IVP	integrity verification procedure
IVR	interactive voice response
IVS	interactive video set (*or* system)
IVV	IV&V; independent verification and validation
IW	identifier word; ImageWriter; input wave; input waveform; instruction word
IWA	Internet-work address
I-WAY	IWAY; information high-way
IWF	input wave-form
IWG	inter-word gap
IWMM	International Workshop on Memory Management
IWQ	input work queue
IWR	index word register

IXC   inter-exchange carrier

IXL   induction and extremely large

~J~

J	jabber; jack; jam; jet; jitter; job; jog; join; joint; joule; journal; joystick; jump; jumper; junction; junk; junior; justify; justification
JA	jump address
JAD	joint application design
JAN	January
JANET	joint academic network
JAR	Java archive
JB	jitter budget; junction box
JBOD	just a bunch of disks
JC	job count; joint commission; junction circuit; junior college
JCAF	Java control and automation frame-work
JCF	job control flag
JCL	job control language
JCP	job control program
JCS	job control statement
JD	joint denial; junction diode
JDBC	Java data base connectivity
JDG	joint denial gate
JDK	Java development kit

JDZ	joystick dead zone
JE	job entry; job exit; joule effect
JEDEC	Joint Electronic Devices Engineering Council
JFET	junction field effect transistor
JEIDA	Japanese Electronics Industry Development Association
JES	job entry system
JET	job entry time; job exit time; Joint European Torus
JETAG	Joint European Test Action Group
JEVA	Japan Electric Vehicle Association
JF	jabber field; job file; junction field
JFC	Java foundation classes; job flow control
JFET	junction field effect transistor
JFIF	JPEG file interchange format
JFH	job file handle
JFN	job file name
JFS	journal file system
JG	job group; jumbo group
JHG	joule heat gradient
JI	joint industry
JIC	joint industry conference
JIPS	JANET Internet protocol service
JIS	joint input stream
JIT	just-in-time

JITC	just-in-time computer
JJ	Josephson junction
JJM	Josephson junction memory
JLIP	joint level interface protocol
JLS	junction light source
JM	Jackson method; joule magneto-striction
JMAPI	Java management application program interface
JMF	Java media frame-work
JMP	jump
JMS	Java message service; joule magnetic (*or* magneto-) striction
JN	job number; Johnson noise
JNI	Java native interface
JNK	junk
JNZ	jump not zero (*jump if not zero*)
JOE	Java objects everywhere
JOHNNIAC	John Neumann integrator and automatic computer
JOSS	JOHNNIAC open shop system
JOT	job oriented terminal
JP	jack panel; jack part; jet propulsion; job position; job processor
JPC	job processing control
JPEG	Joint Photographic Experts Group
JPG	Joint Photographic (Experts) Group

JPL	Jet Propulsion Laboratory
JPN	Japan
JPW	job processing word
JQ	job queue
JR	job route; Josephson rate; jump routine
JRE	Java run-time environment
JS	job schedule; job step; job stream; joy-stick; junction summing
JSDZ	joy-stick dead zone
JSE	job scheduling executive
JSS	Java style sheet
JST	Japanese Standard Time
JT	job type; junction transistor
JTA	job turn-around
JTAG	Joint Test Action Group
JTAPI	Java telephony application programming interface
JTC	Joint Technical Committee
JUL	July
JUN	June
JVC	Japan Victor Company (Victor Company of Japan)
JVM	Java virtual machine
JX	junction box
JZ	jump zero (jump if zero)

~K~

K	*kalium* (*Latin:* potassium); *Kathode* (*Greek:* cathode); Kelvin; kinetic; kilo *(thousand)*; kit
k	kilo
Ka	*Kathode* (*Greek:* cathode)
KAB	Kelvin ampere balance
KAM	keep alive memory (*or* message)
KB	key-board; kilo-bauds; kilo-byte
Kb	kilo-bit
KBC	key-board circuit
KBCK	key-board control key
KBD	key-board; key-board display
KBE	key-board encoder; knowledge based engineering
KBF	key-board function
KBFK	key-board function key
KBL	key-board lock
KBP	key-board processing (*or* processor)
KBps	kilo-bytes-per-second
Kbps	kilo-bits per second
KBPWR	key-board power
KBS	knowledge based system
KBSR	key-board send-receive

KBWK	key-board wake up
KBT	key-board template
KC	key code
kc	kilo-cycle
kCi	kilo-curie
KCK	keyboard control key
KCPS	kilo-characters per second
kcps	kilo-cycles per second
KCS	kilo-characters per second
KDT	key definition table
KE	Kelvin effect
KEYB-BE	KEYBBE; KB-BE; keyboard—Belgium
KEYB-BR	KEYBBR; KB-BR; keyboard—Brazil
KEYB-CF	KEYBCF; KB-CF; keyboard—Canadian French
KEYB-CZ	KEYBCZ; KB-CZ; keyboard—Czechoslovakia)
KEYB-DK	KEYBDK; KB-DK; keyboard—Denmark
KEYB-FR	KEYBFR; KB-FR; keyboard—France
KEYB-GR	KEYBGR; KB-GR; keyboard—Germany
KEYB-HU	KEYBHU; KB-HU; keyboard—Hungary
KEYB-IT	KEYBIT; KB-IT; keyboard—Italy
KEYB-LA	KEYBLA; KB-LA; keyboard—Latin America
KEYB-NL	KEYBNL; KB-NL; keyboard—Netherlands
KEYB-NO	KEYBNO; KB-NO; keyboard—Norway

KEYB-PL	**KEYBPL; KB-PL; keyb**oard—Poland
KEYB-PO	**KEYBPO; KB-PO; keyb**oard—Portugal
KEYB-SF	**KEYBSF; KB-SF; keyb**oard—Swiss French
KEYB-SG	**KEYBSG; KB-SG; keyb**oard—Swiss German
KEYB-SL	**KEYBSL; KB-SL; keyb**oard—Slovak
KEYB-SP	**KEYBSP; KB-SP; keyb**oard—Spain
KEYB-SU	**KEYBSU; KB-SU; keyb**oard—Suomi *(Finland)*
KEYB-SV	**KEYBSV; KB-SV; keyb**oard—Svenska *(Sweden)*
KEYB-UK	**KEYBUK; KB-UK; keyb**oard—United Kingdom
KEYB-US	**KEYBUS; KB-US; keyb**oard—United States
KEYB-YU	**KEYBYU; KB-YU; keyb**oard—Yugoslavia
K_{eq}	*konstante* **eq**uilibrium *(konstante →Greek:* constant) *(constant equilibrium)*
KF	key field
KFK	keyboard function key
kg	kilo-gram
kg-cal	kilo-gram calorie
kgf	kilo-gram force
kgps	kilo-grams per second
kHz	kilo-hertz
K_i	ionization *konstante (konstante →Greek:* constant) *(constant ionization)*
KIF	knowledge interchange format
kJ	kilo-joule

KKN	Kid's Korner Network
kl	kL; kilo-liter; kilo-litre
KL	Kirchoff's laws
kM	kilo-mega
KM	kilo-meter; kilo-metre
K-map	Karnaugh map
kMC	kilo-mega-cycle
kms	kilometers per second
KOS	knock-out switch
KP	key-pad
kPa	kilo-Pascal
KPI	kernel programming interface
kpsi	kilo-pounds per square inch
KQML	knowledge query and manipulation language
KR	Kipp relay
Kr	Krypton
KRS	knowledge retrieval system
KSD	key-switch debouncing
KSPH	key-strokes per hour
KSR	keyboard send-receive
KT	Kelvin temperature
kVA	KVA; kilo-volt-ampere
K_w	specific *konstane* of water (*konstante* → *Greek:* constant) (*water specific constant*)

KW	key word
kW	**KW**; **k**ilo-**w**att
KWH	**kW-H**; **KW-h**; **k**ilo-**w**att-hour
KW-HR	**KW-hr**; **k**ilo-**w**att-hour
KWIC	**k**ey **w**ord **i**n **c**ontext

~L~

L   label; language; lasso; last; latch; late; latency; law; layer; layout; lead; leader; leak; legend; level; lid; light; limit(er); line; linear; link; list; liter (*or* litre); load(er); lobe; local; location; lock; log; logarithm; logic; logo; long; longevity; loop(ing); loose; loss; low(er); lug; luminance; lump; lurk(ing)

LA   language assembler; large area; line art; line assembly; linear amplifier; linear art; link address; logarithmic amplifier; logical analyzer; look ahead; loss angle

La   Lanthanum

LAA   local administered (*or* area) address

LAC   load accumulator; look ahead carry

LACG   look ahead carry generator

LAD   local area data

LADDR   layered device driver architecture

LADT   local area data transport

LAF   logical addressing format

LAG   load and go

LAID   local area identification (*or* identifier)

LALL   longest allowed lobe length

LAN   language; local allocation number; local area network (*or* number)

LANAC   local area network adapter card

LANACS   local area network asynchronous connection server

LANAD   local area network administrator

LANDP   local area network distributed platform

LANE   local area network emulation

LANEC   local area network emulation client

LANES   local area network emulation server

LANG   language

LANIU   local area network interface unit

LANMU   local area network management utilities; local area network manager for UNIX

LAP   link access procedure

LAPB   link access procedure balanced

LAPD   link access procedure on digital-channels

LAPF   link access procedure for frames

LAPM   link access procedure for modems

LAR   load access rights

LARAM   LA-RAM; line addressable random access memory

LARC   Livermore Atomic Research Computer

LAS   logical address space; local area storage

LASER   light amplification by stimulated emission of radiation

LAST   local area storage transport

LAT   local access terminal; local area transport

LATA   local access and transport area

LAVC	local area VAX cluster
LAWN	local area wireless network
LB	latency buffer; learning block; learning bridge; line buffer; link bit; load balancing; logical block; logical bomb; loop-back
lb	*libra* (*Latin:* pound)
LBA	leaky bucket algorithm; logical block address(ing)
LBL	label
LBM	logical blocking map
LBP	loop-back plug
LBR	library
LBT	listen-before-talk
LBX	local box; local bus extension
LC	leakage current; life characteristic; life cycle; line circuit; line clipping; line code; linear control; link control; liquid crystal; load capacitor; load(ing) coil; load curve; logarithmic compression; logic circuit; logic comparator; logical card; logical connective; longitudinal current; loop code; loop command; loop configuration; loop counter
L/C	luminance-color
LCB	line control block
LCC	leadless chip carrier
LCCN	library of congress control number
LCD	liquid crystal display; lowest common denominator
LCE	logic coincidence element

LCF	link control field; low cost fibre
LCL	local
LCN	logical channel (*or* connection) number; loop control number
LCO	local central office
LCP	limited contention protocol; link control protocol; logical construction of program
LCR	laser cartridge replacement; least cost routing; line control register
LCS	line conditioner and stabilizer
LCU	last cluster used
LD	laser disc; lattice dynamics; liar's dice; line driver; linear distortion; liquid drop; load; locking directive; logic design; logic diagram; logical decision; logical difference; logical drive; long directory; longitudinal delay
LDA	logical device address
LDAP	light-weight directory access protocol
LDC	logical drive count; longitudinal delay line
LD/F	LDF; long directory file-name
LD/FN	LDFN; long directory file-name
LDIP	long distance Internet provider
LDM	liquid drop model; long distance modem
LDO	low drop-out
LDS	load delay slot; local distribution system
LDT	linear displacement transducer; local descriptor table

LDTD	long distance television distribution
LDTR	local descriptor table register
LDUA	local dial up access
LE	Lindemann electrometer; linear energy; link(age) editor; little endian; load effective; local echo; local exchange; logic element; logic error; loop error; low earth
LEA	load effective address
LEC	LAN emulation client; lecture; local exchange carrier
LECS	LAN emulation configuration server
LED	light emitting diode; link encryption device
LEF	log-in enabled flag
LEM	language extension module; Lindemann elecrtrometer
LEO	low earth orbit; Lyons electronic office
LEP	lowest effective power
LES	LAN emulation server; laser emulsion storage; level enable signal
LET	letter; linear energy transfer
LF	Larmor frequency; lattice filter; line feed(er); loading factor; lock flag; logic file; logic flowchart; loss factor; lost frame; low format; low frequency
L2F	layer 2 forwarding
LFAP	light-weight flow admission protocol
LFB	loop feed-back
LFC	line feed character; logic flow-chart

LFF	Laplacian edge enhancement
LFI	last (*or* long) file indicator
LFMP	linearly frequency modulated pulse
LFN	long file name
LFT	leap frog test; low function terminal
LFU	least frequently used
LG	line generator; line graph; logic gate; loop gain
LGA	leadless grid array
LGDT	load global descriptor table
LGN	logical group number
LH	logic high
LHM	long haul modem
LHS	low-high selector
LHT	light; long haul trunk
LI	language interpreter; limited integrator; line impedance; linear interpolation; link indicator; loaded impedance; log-in; logical instruction; loop initialization; loop input
Li	lithium
LIA	lock-in amplifier
LIAS	library information access system
LIB	liberal; library
LIC	licence; line integrated circuit; line interface coupler; loop iteration count; lowest incoming channel
LICS	Lotus international character set

LID	logic interface device
LIDE	LED indirect exposure
LIDT	load interrupt descriptor table
LIEP	large Internet exchange packet
LIF	long instruction format; low insertion force
LIFMOP	linearly frequency modulated pulse
LIFMP	linearly frequency modulated pulse
LIFO	last-in first-out
LILO	last-in last-out
LIM	Lotus-Intel-Microsoft
LIM-EMS	Lotus-Intel-Microsoft expanded memory specification
LIM-M	Lotus-Intel-Microsoft memory
LIMA	Lotus-Intel-Microsoft-AST
LIMDO	light intensity modulation direct overwrite
LIMM	light intensity modulation method
LIMS	library information management system
LIP	large Internet packet; linear integer programming
LIPS	light-weight Internet person schema; logical inferences per second
LISP	list processing
LIT	literal; log-in time
LIU	LAN interface unit
LIW	long instruction word
LJ	laser jet; left justify; loop jump

LK   locking key

LL   leased line; Lenz's law; linking loader; load(ed) line; local line; local load; local loop; logic level; logic low; logical link; logical lock; long link; low level; low light; low loss; lumped leading

LLC   logical link control; long link communication; low level controller

LLCL   logical link control layer

LLCS   long link communication set

LLD   load local descriptor

LLDT   load local descriptor table

LLF   low level format

LLL   low level language; low level logic

LLM   leased line modem; low level modulation (*or* multiplexer)

LLR   load limiting resistor

LM   linear modulation; link management; loading match; location manager; lock manager; logical multiplication; logical multiply; longitudinal magnetization

lm   lumen

LMBCS   Lotus multi-byte character set

LMD   last modification date

LMDS   local multipoint distribution service

LME   location manager extension

LMG   location manager guide

LMI   link (*or* local) management interface

LMM	location manager module
LMO	load modulated oscillator
LMPDS	local multi-point distribution service
LMR	land mobile radio
LMS	linear magnetic striction; linear magneto-striction
LMSW	load machine status word
LMT	limit; limitation; linear matrix transformation
LMU	LAN management utilities; LAN manager for UNIX
LN	lattice network; line number; load number; logical name; Lukaseiwicz notation
ln	logarithm natural *(natural logarithm)*
LNA	line number access; low noise amplifier
LNG	long
LNK	link
LNW	lattice network; linear network
LO	lay-out; linear optimization; literal operand; local oscillator; logic operation; logic(al) operator; low; low-order
LOC	local; location; lowest outgoing channel
LOCIS	Library of Congress Information System
LOD	lack of data
LOF	line of flux; line of force
log	LOG; logarithm
LOL	laughing out loud *(news-group)*

LON   local operating network

LOP   line of pulse; linear operation; logical operation

LORE   line oriented editor

LOS   line of sight; loop output signal; loss of signal

LOT   laws of thoughts

LP   Larmor precession; light pen; line pairs; line printer; linear program; lingering period; list processing; logic probe; logic product; logic pulser; long packet; long play; longitudinal parity; loop program; loss packet; low pass; low power; low pressure; low pulse; lumped parameter

LPA   light pen attention; linear power amplifier

LPAR   logic programming and automated reasoning

LPC   linear predictive coding; local procedure call

lpc   LPC; lines per centimeter

LPE   low performance equipment

LPF   light pen function; low pass filter; low power field

LPI   low probability of intercept

lpi   LPI; lines per inch

LPL   list processing (or programming) language

LPM   laser printer memory; linear potentio-meter

lpm   LPM; lines per minute

LPMU   laser printer memory upgrade

LPN   logical page number

LPR   line printer remote; liquid photo resist; listen packet request

LPRINT	line **print**(er)
LPRNT	line **print**(er)
LPS	linear **p**ower **s**upply; list processing structure; low power **S**chottky
LPSM	low **p**ower **s**leep **m**ode
LPT	line printer terminal
LPX	low **p**rofile e**x**tended (*or* extension)
LQ	letter **q**uality; low **q**uality
LQM	letter **q**uality **m**ode; link **q**uality **m**onitoring
LQP	letter **q**uality **p**rinter
LR	Larmor radius; leakage radiation; leakage reactance; linear rectifier; linear resistor; link register; loader routine; loading routine; local repeater; logical relation
Lr	Lawrencium
LRAD	Lossev **rad**iation
LRC	local register cache; longitudinal redundancy check(ing)
LRG	low **r**esolution **g**raphics
LRL	least **r**ecently **l**oaded; logical record lock
LRLT	logical record lock threshold
LRM	language **r**eference **m**anual; logical **r**ing **m**aintenance
LRO	low **r**ecord **o**ffset
LRS	last record **s**een
LRU	least **r**ecently **u**sed; line replaceable **u**nit

LRUB   least recently used block

LRUBD   least recently used block dirty

LS   large scale; laser spooler; lattice spacing; least significant; library software; light sensitive; line segment; line spectrum; line support; linear selection; link state; list structure; load select(ion); load sequence; local signal; local socket; local station; lock status; log sheet; logic shift; logic swing; logic; symbol; logical shift; low(er) side; low(er) signal; low(er) speed; low(er) state; luminance signal

LSA   LAN-SCSI adapter; line sharing adapter

LSAPI   licence services application program interface

LSB   laser spooler board; least significant byte; lower side band

LSb   lsb; least significant bit

LSC   least significant character

LSD   least significant digit

LSDN   log-in sub-directory name

LSE   line segment enhancement

LSI   large scale integration

LSIB   large scale integration board

LSIBT   large scale integration board tester

LSL   line support layer

LSM   local scope model

LSP   link state packet

LSR   link state routing

LSS	low speed storage
LST	last; list
LSTTL	low-power Schottky transistor-transistor logic
LSW	library software
LT	language translator; laser trimming; late; latent time; letter; light; limiter tube; line terminator; line test; linear time; local terminal; LocalTalk; lock type; log-in time; logic tester; long term; loop test; low tension
LTA	line (*or* low) turn-around
LTC	lowest two-way channel
LTE	line termination equipment
LTF	loop transfer function
LTI	linear time invariant
LTM	link tool manager; long term memory
L2TP	layer 2 tunnelling protocol
LTR	left to right; letter; lighter; load task register
LTWC	lowest two-way channel
LU	large unit; logical unit
Lu	lutetium
LUA	logical unit application
LUD	loop up-date
LUI	local user input
LUIS	library user information service
LUN	large (*or* logical) unit

LUT	look-up table
LV	large view; linear variable; logical volume; low voltage; lumped voltage
LVD	low voltage differential
LVDS	low voltage differential signalling
LVDT	linear variable differential transformer; low voltage differential transceiver
LVM	logical volume management
LVS	large view screen
LYR	lyrics
LW	large word; LaserWriter; light-weight; long wait; long word; low wattage
LWD	larger word; low wattage display
LWDAP	light-weight directory access protocol
lx	lux
LXC	local exchange carrier
LZ	lazy; leading zero
LZC	Lempel-Ziv coding
LZW	Lempel-Ziv-welch

~M~

M	machine; made; magazine; magenta; magnet; magnetic; magnetron; magnification; magnify; magnitude; mail; main; maintenance; major; majority; make; male; malfunction; man; manager; manganite; mantissa; manual; manuscript; map; margin; mark; mask(ing); mass; master; mat; match; matrix; maximal; maximum; Maxwell; mean; meaning; measurand; measure; measurement; mechanic; media; median; medium; meeting; mega; member; memory; menu; merge; mesh; message; metal; meter (*or* metre); microphone; middle; migration; million; minimal; minimum; minute; mirror; mistake; mix; mixture; mock; mode; model; modification; modifier; modify; modular; modulate; modulation; module; moire; moisture; mold(ing); mole; molecule; monitor; monolithic; month; more; morning; morph; mosaic; motor; mount; mouse; move; multiple; multiplication; multiply; music; mute; muting
m²	meter meter; meter *square*; metre metre; metre *square*
MA	machine address; magnetic analysis; memory address
M.A.	MA; Master of Arts (*Latin original: Artium Magister*)
mA	ma; milli-ampere
M.A.A.	MAA; Master of Applied Arts
MAB	memory address bus
M.A.B.E.	MABE; Master of Agricultural Business and Economics

MAC   Macintosh; macro; media (*or* medium) access control; memory address counter; message authentication code; minimum (*or* mnemonic) access code; multiple access computers; multiple address code; multiply and accumulation

Mac   MAC; Macintosh

Mac OS   Mac O/S; Macintosh Operating System

MACA   multiple access with collision avoidance

MACH   multilayer actuator head

MAD   magnetic anomaly detection; memory address driver; Michigan algorithm decoder

MADBT   micro-alloy diffused base transistor

MADE   manufacturing and automated design engineering

MADYMO   mathematical dynamic modelling

MAE   Macintosh application environment; metropolitan area EtherNet

M.A.E.   MAE; Master of Aeronautical Engineering

M.A.Ed   MA ED; MA Ed; Master of Arts in Education

MAGMA   minimal architecture for generalized markup applications

mAH   mAh; milli-ampere hour

MAI   mail; multiple applications interface

MAJC   microprocessor architecture for Java computing

MAN   manager; manual; metropolitan area network

MANIAC   mathematical analyzer numerical integrator and computer

MAP	manufacturing automation protocol; memory allocation map; minimum access programming; modular arithmetic processor; multiple access protocol
MAPI	mail (*or* messaging) applications programming interface
MAPICS	manufacturing, accounting and production information control system
MAR	March; mars; memory address register; minimum access routine; multi-alternate routing
MARC	multi-technology automated reader card
MARS	manufacturing analysis reporting system
MARVEL	machine assisted realization virtual electronic library
MAS	master; medium access sublayer; microprocessor alarm system
MASER	microwave amplification by stimulated emission of radiation
MASM	macro assembler
MASS	maximum availability and support subsystem
MAT	memory access time; memory address table
MAU	media access unit; media adapter unit; multiple access unit; multi-station access unit
MAVDM	multiple application virtual DOS machine
MAVICA	magnetic (*or* magneto-) video camera
MAX	maximum
MB	magnetic bias; mail bridge; mail-box; main block; mask bit; mega-byte; memory bank; memory bus; message

blocking; metallic bond; module board; molecular beam; molecular bond; monitor bit; mother-board; multi-bus; multiple bits; multiple bytes

Mb	mega-bits
M.B.A.	MBA; Master of Business Administration
MBA	magnetic bubble annihilator
MBB	multicast back-bone
MBC	mini-bundle cable
mbCCD	million-bit charge coupled device
MBCS	multi-byte character set
MBE	molecular beam epitaxy
MBGA	micro ball grid array
Mbit	mega-bits
MBM	magnetic bubble memory
MBN	mixed base notation; multiple bus network
MBO	monadic Boolean operator
MBone	multicast back-bone
MBP	multiple base pages
MB/s	mega-bytes *per* second
MBps	mega-bytes per second
Mbps	mega-bits per second; million bits per second
MBR	master boot record; memory buffer address
MBS	microprocessor bus system; multiple bus structure
Mbyte	mega-bytes

MBX	mail-box
MC	machine code; machine cycle; machining center; magnetic circuit; magnetic coating; magnetic code; magnetic core; magnetic cycle; major cycle; majority carrier; male connector; Manchester coding; marginal check; Markhov chain; master clock; material control; mathematical check; mathematics co-processor; maximum characters; Meissner circuit; memory cache; memory cycle; meta-ceramic; meta-compiler; micro-channel; micro-circuit; micro-code; micro-command; micro-computer; micro-controller; micro-cycle; mini-cartridge; mini-computer; minor cycle; minority carriers; modular connection; modular converter; modulated carrier; modulation code; modulo-check; monochrome connector; monostable circuit; motion control; motor control; multi-cast; multi-channel; multi-chip; multiplexing channel
Mc	mega-cycle
MCA	micro-channel adapter (*or* architecture); micro-computer application; microprocessor code assembler; motor control application
MCAD	mechanical computer aided design
MCB	memory (*or* message) control block; microwave circuit board
MCC	Macintosh compatible cable; Maxwell's circulating current; micro-channel card; micro-code compaction; mono-chrome connector; Mosaic Communications Corporation
MCCL	multi-channel current loop
MCCRT	mono-chrome cathode ray tube
MCCS	micro-computer control section (*or* signal)

MCD   major control data; master clerical data; memory chip density; Microsoft certified developer; modem control device; mono-chrome display

MCDA   mono-chrome display adapter

MCDDS   micro-computer disk development system

MCDS   micro-computer development system; micro-controller design system; Microsoft COBOL development system

MCE   machine check enable; micro-computer enclosure

MCF   meta content frame-work; micro-channel flag

MCG   Monte Carlo generator

MCGA   multi-color graphics adapter (*or* array)

MCHS   micro-computer hydraulic system

MCI   machine check indicator; machine code instruction; master control interrupt; media control interface; micro-circuit isolation; micro-computer instrument; micro-controller interface; Microwave Communications, Inc.

MCIK   micro-computer interfacing kit

MCK   micro-computer kit

MCKA   micro-computer kit assembler

MCL   multi-channel current loop

MCLK   master clock

MCM   magnetic core memory; main command menu; mathematical control mode; micro-control memory; microprocessor cache memory; Monte Carlo method; multi-chip module

MCMC	micro-computer machine control
M.C.N.E.	MCNE; Master Certified Novell Engineer
MCOSPF	multi-cast open shortest path first
MCP	maintenance control panel; master (*or* message) control program; mathematics co-processor
M.C.P.	MCP; Microsoft Certified Professional
MCPGA	MC-PGA; metallized ceramic pin grid array
MCPOS	micro-computer point-of-sale
MCPS	micro-computer prototyping system
M.C.P.S.	MCPS; Microsoft Certified Product Specialist
Mcps	mega-cycles per second
MCPU	micro-programmed central processing unit
MCQFP	MC-QFP; metallized ceramic quad flat pack
MCR	master control routine; minimum cell rate; modem control register; multi-cast routing
MCRT	monochrome cathode ray tube
MCS	master (*or* motion) control station; microcomputer control section; microprocessor control signal; multiple channel system
MCSA	motor control system application
MCSD	micro-computer support device
M.C.S.D.	MCSD; Microsoft Certified Systems Developer
M.C.S.E.	MCSE; Microsoft Certified Systems Engineer
MCT	memory cycle time; micro-computer terminal; modular cable tester; multiple console terminal

M.C.T.   MCT; Microsoft Certified Trainer

MCTC   micro-computer traffic control

MCTE   multiple console terminal eliminator

MCTM   micro-computer timing module

MCTS   multi-channel television sound

MCU   micro-controller unit; microprocessor (*or* microprogram) control unit; multi-chip unit

MD   magnetic damping; magnetic disk; magnetic drum; main document; make directory; marking distortion; material dispersion; mechanical dictionary; mechanical differential; media developer; medical doctor; memory diagnostic; memory dump; micro-diskette; mini-disc; mini-disk; mirrored device; modular design; module dissipation; monochrome display; mosaic detector; multi-drop

Md   Mendelevium

MDA   monochrome display adapter

MDB   master directory block; Microsoft data base

MDCU   memory-device control unit

MDDBMS   multi-dimensional data base management system

MDDS   microcomputer disk development system; microprogram disk development system

MDE   machine diagnostic expert

MDF   main distribution frame; menu definition file

MDG   majority decision gate

MDI   manual data input; memory display interface; multiple document interface; multiply divide instruction

MDIC	Manchester decoder and interface chip
MDK	multimedia developers kit
MDL	magnetic (*or* mercury) delay line; microprocessor data logging
MDLP	mobile data link protocol
MDLS	modulated down-link signal
MDM	magnetic disk memory; medium distance modem; moving domain memory
MDMAC	Motorola direct memory access controller
MDP	microprocessor debugging program; multiply-divide package
MDPE	medium density poly-ethylene
MDR	memory data register; minimum design requirement; modal damping ratio; multi-destination routing
M-DRAM	**MDRAM**; multibank dynamic random access memory
MDS	maximum data size; micro-data switch; micro-device sequencer; microcomputer development system; microcontroller design system; modulated down-link signal
MDT	Mountain Daylight Time; multiple data terminal
MDU	multiple dwelling unit
MDY	month-day-year
ME	machine equation; magnetic energy; magneto-electric; majority element; measurement error; mechanical engineer(ing); Meissner effect; memory extender; message exchange; micro-electronics; micro-enhancer;

microprocessor evaluation; modulating electrode; mole electronics

MEALS   micro-electronic advanced laser scanner

MEB   memory expansion board; module extended board

MEC   mix error count

MEF   microprocessor economic feasibility

MEG   mega-byte

Meg   mega-ohm (*or* **meg**ohm)

MEGAR   maximum enhanced graphics adapter resolution

MEM   memory

MemMaker   Memory Maker

MEMS   micro-electro-mechanical system

MEN   menu

MEO   medium earth orbit

M.E.R.C.I.   Multimedia European Research Conferencing Integration (*or* MERCI)

MEP   microprogram emulation process

MES   microprocessor educator system

MESA   Macintosh entertainment software alliance

MESFET   metal semiconductor field effect transistor

MESI   modified-exclusive-shared-invalid

MET   memory enhancement technology; meta-file; Middle European Time

METC   micro-processor equipped traffic control

MeV	mega-electron volt
meV	milli-electron volt
MF	magnetic ferrite; magnetic field; magnetic flux; main frame; Massey formula; medium frequency; mega farad; memory fill; message formatting; meta-file; micro-Farad; micro-fiche; micro-film; miscellaneous flags; miscellaneous function; malfunction
mF	milli-farad
MFB	mixed functional block
MFC	main frame computer; Microsoft Foundation Class; multi-fibre cable
MFCC	mel-frequency cepstral coefficient
MFD	magnetic flux distribution; micro-farad; micro-function decoder; mode field diameter; multi-function drive
MFF	magnetic flip-flop
MFFS	Microsoft flash file system
MFI	magnetic field intensity (*or* interference)
MFJ	modified final judgement
MFL	multi-function lamination
MFLOPS	million (*or* mega-) floating-point operations per second
MFM	mixed functional module; modified frequency modulation
MFO	manual feed-rate over-ride; maximum frequency operation
MFOC	Microsoft FORTRAN optimizing compiler

MFP	multi-function peripheral
MFPI	multi-function peripheral interface
MFR	matched filter reception; metallic film resistor
MFS	magnetic-tape field scan; metropolitan fibre system
MFT	master file table
MG	Macintosh guide; mail gateway; majority gate; master group
Mg	Magnesium
mg	milli-gram
MGA	monochrome graphics adapter
MGE	modular GIS environment
MGML	minimal generalized markup language
MGNT	management
MGP	macro-generating program
MGR	manager
MGT	management
MGW	mail gate-way
MHD	magnetic (*or* magneto-) hydro-dynamics
MHL	magnetic hysteresis loop
MHS	message handling service (*or* system); microcomputer hydraulic system
MHW	machine hardware
MHz	mega-hertz; million hertz

MI	machine infinity; machine instruction; magnetic induction; magnetic ink; magnetic instability; magneto-ionic; management interface; manual input; matching impedance; material implication; mechanical interface; memory interface; memory interleaving; micro-instruction; microprocessor instrument; microprocessor intelligence; modulation index; multiple interrupts; mutual inductance
MIB	management information base; metro image base
MIC	macro interpretive command; media interface connector; microphone; mobile industrial computer; monolithic integrated circuit; microwave integrated circuit
MICR	magnetic ink character reader (*or* recognition)
MicROM	microcode read only memory (*or* micROM)
MICs	macro interpretive commands
MID	machine identification; micro-instruction decoder (*or* display); multi-image driver
MIDI	musical instrument digital interface
MIE	Microsoft Internet Explorer
MIF	management information format (*or* file)
MIG	manual input generator; metal in gap
MII	Microsoft-IBM-Intel
MIIS	metal-insulation-insulation-semiconductor
MIK	microcomputer interfacing kit
MIL	machine interface layer; military
MILSPEC	military specification

MIM	map image metafile; metal-insulator-metal
MIMD	multiple instruction multiple data
MIME	multimedia (*or* multipurpose) Internet mail extension
MIN	minimal; minimum; minute; mobile identification number; multistage interconnection network
MIND	Microsoft Internet developer
M/IO	MIO; memory input-output
MIPS	million instructions per second; microprocessor without interlocked pipeline stage
MIR	memory information register; micro-instruction register
MIS	management information system; micro-instruction sequence; microprocessor instruction set; multimedia information source
MISC	miscellaneous
MISD	multiple instruction single data
MIT	Massachusetts Institute of Technology
MITRE	Massachusetts Institute of Technology Research and Engineering
MIX	member information exchange
mJ	milli-joule
MJP	modular junction panel
MK	micro-kit
MKA	microcomputer kit assembler
MKB	magnetic (*or* membrane) key-board
MKDIR	make directory

mks	meter-kilogram-second
mksa	meter-kilogram-second-ampere
MKSA	meter-kilogram-second-ampere system
ML	machine language; machine learning; machine length; machine logic; magnetic leakage; mailing list; maximum line; Maxwell's law; mega-link; message length; message line; meta-language; micro-logic; milli-liter; millennium; modification loop; monolithic; multi-layer
ml	mL; milli-liter; mili-litre
MLA	microprocessor language assembler; multi-level address
MLAPI	multi-lingual application programming interface
MLB	multi-layer board
MLBR	multiplexed low bit rate
MLC	micro-logic card; minimal latency coding; multiple layer ceramic; multiple level cell
MLD	machine logic design
MLE	microprocessor language editor; multiple line editor
MLFPB	mega-link four port buffer
MLI	multiple link interface
MLID	multiple link interface driver
MLM	mail-list manager
MLML	multi-longitudinal mode laser
MLP	machine language program; multi-link protocol
MLPPP	multiple link point to point protocol

MLS   monolithic storage; multiple level signal

MLSR   maximum locked sweep rate

MLT   memory latency time; modem link tool; multiply

MM   magnetic material; magnetic media; magnetic memory; magnetic mirror; magnetic moment; mail merge; main memory; maintenance manager; manual mode; master menu; mathematical model; memory management; memory manager; memory map; memory module; message mode; micro-module; microprocessor monitor; milli-meter; multi-media; multi-meter

MMA   main memory allocation; Microcomputer Managers Association

MMB   main memory bandwidth (*or* block); memory mail box

MMBW   main memory band-width

MMC   matched memory cycle; metal matrix composite; microcomputer machine control; Microcomputer Marketing Council; microprocessor maintenance console; Microsoft management console; monolithic micro-circuit; multi-media card

MMCD   multi-media compact disc

MMCX   multi-media communication exchange

MMD   modem multiplexer diagnosis; multi-mode device; multi-mode dispersion

MMDT   modem multiplexer diagnostic test

MMF   magneto-motive force; multi-mode fibre; multiple micro-instruction format

mmg   milli micro-gram

MMH   memory management hardware

mmHg	milli-meters (metres) *hydrar-gyrum* (*hydrar-gyrum*→ *Latin:* mercury) *(milli-meters mercury)*
MMHW	memory management hardware
MMI	man-machine interface; memory mapped input; memory module interface
MMIC	monolithic microwave integrated circuit
MMIF	multiple micro-instruction format
MMIME	multi-media Internet mail extension
MMI/O	memory mapped input-output (*or* MMIO)
MMIS	materials manager information system
MML	moderated mailing list; multi-longitudinal mode laser
MMM	modern memory manager
MMN	multi-media network
MMP	multi-media programming
MMPC	multi-media personal computer
MMPM	multi-media presentation manager
mmpm	milli-meters (metres) per minute
MMR	memory management register
MMS	main memory system; memory management software; micro-miniature speaker
MMU	memory management unit
MMV	monostable multi-vibrator
MMVF	multi-media video file
MMX	matrix manipulation extension; multi-media extension

MN	member name; mesh network
Mn	Manganese
M-n-C	modulo-n-check
MNM	Microsoft NetMeeting
MNOS	metal nitride oxide semiconductor
MNP	Microcom networking protocol; Micron networking protocol
MNS	maximum number of servers
MNU	menu
MNW	mesh network
MO	magnetic oxide; magneto-optical; mail order; main office; master oscillator; memory overlay; micro-operation; monadic operation; money order; month; multiplexed operation
Mo	Molybdenum
MOB	memory-order buffer
MOBO	mother-board
MOC	maximum open connections; mnemonic operation code
MOD	magnetic optical disk (*or* drive); manager on duty; modern; module; modulation; modulus; moving domain
MODEM	modulator-demodulator
MOH	mail-order house
MOHLL	machine oriented high level language
MOL	machine oriented language; memory over-lay

mol	mole; molecule
MOLAP	multi-dimensional on-line analytical processing
MOM	manufacturing operations management; Microsoft Office Manager
MON	Monday; monitor
MONET	multi-wavelength optical networking
MONO	monophone; monophonic
MONOS	monitor out of sequence
MOO	MUD object-oriented
MOP	maintenance operation protocol
MOPS	million operations per second
MOS	magnetic optical storage; maximum open sockets; metal-oxide-semiconductor; multi-processing operating system; multi-tasking operating system
MOSCG	metal-oxide-semiconductor character generator
MOSFET	metal-oxide-semiconductor field effect transistor
MOSM	metal-oxide-semiconductor memory
MOSPF	multicast open shortest path first
MOSROM	metal-oxide-semiconductor read only memory
MOST	metal-oxide-semiconductor transistor
MOTD	message of the day
MOV	metal oxide varistor; move; movement; movie
MOVPE	metal organic vapor phase epitaxy
MP	magnetic path; magnetic potential; magnetic potentiometer; main program; maintenance processor;

major part; mathematical programming; matrix printer; media protocol; memory page; memory parity; memory protect; metric prefix; micro-parameter; micro-phone; micro-processor; micro-program; motion picture; multilink protocol; multi-processor; multi-program; multiple precision; multiplexing polling

MP3 MPEG layer 3

MPA micro-processor analyzer

M.P.A. MPA; Master of Public Administration

MPAS micro-processor assembler simulator

MPC maximum possible connections; memory port controller; message passing computer; micro-processor card (*or* chip *or* code); micro-program counter; multimedia personal computer; multiple path channel

MPCA micro-processor code assembler

MPCL2 micro-processor code level 2

MPCL3 micro-processor code level 3

MPCM micro-processor cache memory

MPCPU MP-CPU; micro-programmed central processing unit

MPCS micro-processor control section (*or* signal)

MPCU micro-programmed control unit

MPD multiple platter disk

MPDDS micro-program disk development system

MPDL micro-processor data logging

MPDP micro-processor debugging program

MPE	memory parity error; micro-processor evaluation; mid-point equalization; multi-programming executive
MPEF	micro-processor economic feasibility
MPEG	Motion (*or* Moving) Picture Experts Group
MPEG3	Motion (*or* Moving) Picture Experts Group—layer 3
MPEP	micro-program emulation process
MPES	micro-processor educator system
MPETC	micro-processor equipped traffic control
MPF	multi-path fading
M.P.H.	MPH; Master of Public Health
MPI	message passing interface; micro-processor instrument (*or* intelligence) micro-program index (*or* instruction); multiple protocol interface
MPIME	multi-purpose Internet mail extension
MPIS	micro-processor instruction set
MPL	multi-point line; multi-programming level
MPLA	micro-processor language assembler
MPLE	micro-processor language editor
MPM	magnetic potentio-meter; message passing library; micro-processor monitor; miles per minute; micro-processor monitor; multi-pole moments; multi-port memory
mpm	meters per minute; metres per minute
MPMC	micro-processor maintenance console
MPMD	multiple processor multiple data
MPN	multi-point network

MPO	Miller-Pierce oscillator
MPOA	multi-protocol over ATM
MPOM	multi-processor operating mode
MPOS	multi-processing operating system
MPP	manual part programming; massively parallel processor; message posting protocol; message processing program; micro-programmable processor; micro-programming parameterization; Microsoft PowerPoint; multi-phase program
MPQP	multi-protocol quad port
MPR	micro-processor register; multi-part repeater; multi-port register (*or* repeater); multi-protocol router
MPROM	MP-ROM; mask programmable read only memory
MPS	maximum possible sockets; micro-print spooler; micro-processor slice (*or* system); micro-programmed sequencer (*or* subroutine); microcomputer prototyping system; multi-processor specification (*or* system)
MPSA	micro-processor system analyzer
MPT	micro-processor timing; multi-port transceiver
MPTA	micro-processor training aid
MPTN	multi-protocol transport network
MPTS	multi-protocol transport service
MPU	micro-processor unit
MPX	multiplex(er, ing)
MPY	multiply
MQ	multiplier quotient

MQFP	metric quad flat package
MQI	message-queue interface
MQN	magnetic quantum number
MQR	multiplier quotient register
MQW	multiple quantum well
MR	magnetic recording; magnetic resonance; magnetic rigidity; magneto-resistive; malfunction routine; mark reader; mask register; maximum resolution; memory receive; memory register; memory resident; message routing; microprocessor register; modem ready; modem relay; moderating ratio; modulation rate
M-RAM	MRAM; magnetic random access memory
M-RAMS	MRAMS; minimum random access memory speed
MRB	mother-board
MRC	memory read cycle; motor run capacitor
MRCF	Microsoft real-time compression format
MRCI	Microsoft real-time compression interface
MRF	multiple register file
MRI	magnetic resonance imaging
MRJ	Macintosh run-time for Java
MRLW	magnetic resonance line width
MRM	maximum rights mask
M-ROM	MROM; microprocessor read only memory
M-ROMP	MROMP; microprocessor read only memory programmer
MRN	multiple reflection noise

MRP   material requirement planning

MRPL   main ring path length

MRS   maximum rated speed; media recognition system minimum RAM speed

MRT   mean repair time

MRU   maximum receive unit

MS   magnetic saturation; magnetic shield; magnetostriction; mail server; mail slot; major state; mass spectrometer; mass storage; master scheduler; master-slave; master slice; master station; master synchronizer; matrix storage; matrix switch; measured signal; mechanical splice; memory scan; memory storage; memory system; menu standard; mercury storage; message store; message switching; metric system; microprocessor slice; Microsoft; mid-splitter; modem scripts; modem splitter; modular system; modulating signal; monitoring station; monolithic storage; more segments; multiple scan; multi- segment; multi-stage; multi-state; multi-statement; multiple system; multiplexed sampling; multiplication shift; mutual synchronization

M.S.   MS; M.Sc.; MSc; *Scientiae Magister* (*Latin:* Master of Science)

ms   micro-second

MSA   microprocessor system analyzer

MSACM   Microsoft audio compression manager

MSAU   multi-station access unit

MSAV   Microsoft anti-virus

MSB   most significant byte

msb	MSb; most significant bit
MSBF	mean swaps between failures
MSC	midi show control; mobile switching center; mono-stable circuit
M.Sc.	MSc.; M.S.; MS; *Scientiae Magister* (*Latin:* Master of Science)
M.Sc.(E.E.)	MSEE; Master of Science in Electrical Engineering
MSCDEX	Microsoft compact disc extensions
MSCHAP	Microsoft challenge handshake authentication protocol
MSCW	mark stack control word
MSD	mass storage device (*or* dump); microcomputer support device; Microsoft system diagnostics; most significant digit
MSDL	magneto-strictive delay line
MSDN	microsoft developer network
MS-DOS	MSDOS; Microsoft Disk Operating System
MSDR	multiplexed streaming data request
MSDS	Microsoft developer support
MSE	multi-segment EtherNet
msec	milli-second
M.S.E.E.	MSEE; Master of Science in Electrical (*and/or Electronic*) Engineering
MSEL	memory select
MSFR	mark sense form reader; minimum security function requirement

MSG	message
MSI	medium scale integration
MSIE	Microsoft Internet Explorer
MSIIS	Microsoft Internet information server
MSIN	multi-stage interconnection network
MSK	minimum shift keying
MSL	mirrored server link
MSLG	major state logic control
MSM	magnetic surface memory; magnetic (*or* mass) spectrometer; multi-scanning monitor
MSMP	master-slave multi-programming
MSMQ	Microsoft message queue-server
MSMV	mono-stable multi-vibrator
MSN	master-slave network; Microsoft Network; multistage switching network; multi-state noise
MS-NET	MSNET; Microsoft Network
MSNW	master-slave network
MSO	multi-system operator
MSOS	Microsoft operating system
MSP	memory scratch pad; Microsoft paint; modem surge protector
MSR	machine state register; magnetic shift register; meta stepwise refinement
MSRP	manufacturer suggested retail price

MSS	managed security service; mass storage system; multi-protocol switched services
MST	magneto-striction transducer; memory space time; Mountain Standard Time; multi-statement transaction; multiplexer settling time
MSTF	memory space time function; Microsoft terminal server
MSTS	Microsoft terminal (*or* transaction) server
MSW	machine status word; Microsoft Word
MT	MacinTalk; magnetic tape; maintenance time; marginal test; mercury tank; median time; metropolitan trunk; microprocessor timing; modular tap; multi-task; multi-thread; multi-trace; multiplication time
Mt	metric ton
MTA	Macintosh telephony architecture; message transfer agent; microprocessor training aid; multiple terminal access
MTBB	mean time between breakdowns
MTBF	mean time between failures
MTBJ	mean time between jams
MTBO	mean time between outages
MTC	memory traffic controller; microcomputer traffic control
MTD	magnetic tape diagnostics; memory technology driver; Moscow Time Daylight
MTDR	multi-function time delay relay
MTF	magnetic tape format; magnetic thin film; Microsoft tape format; modulation transfer function

MTFS	magnetic tape field scanning
MTG	meeting; memory timing generator
MTL	memory technology layer; merged transistor logic
MTM	microcomputer timing module; multi-tracker module
MTO	maximum time-out; multi-trace oscilloscope
MTP	MacinTalk Pro
MTR	magnetic tape reader
MTRP	maximum transfer rate performance
MTS	message transfer service (*or* system); Moscow Time Standard; multichannel television sound
MTSAT	multi-functional transport satellite
MTSO	mobile telephone switching office
MTSR	mean time to service restoral
MTT	microwave theory techniques; multi-transaction timer
MTTD	mean time to diagnose
MTTF	mean time to failure
MTTR	mean time to repair
MTU	maximum transfer (*or* transmission) unit
MTV	music television
MU	machine unit; magnetic unit; master unit; memory unit; multi-user
mU	milli-unit
MUA	mail user agent

MUD	multi-user dialogue; multi-user dimension; multi-user domain; multi-user dungeon
MUDS	maximum used dynamic space
MUG	Macintosh User Group
MUL	multiplexer; multiplication; multiplier; multiply
MULTICS	multiplexed information and computer system; multiplexed information and computing service
MUMPS	Massachusetts utility multi-programming system
MUP	multi-unit processor
MUSE	multi-user shared (*or* simulated) environment
MUT	make-up time; monitor under test
MUX	multiplex(er, ing)
MV	machine variable; major version; manipulated variable; measured variable; mega-volt; molecular volume; move; multi-variable; multi-vibrator
Mv	mendelevium
mV	mv; milli-volt
MVB	multimedia viewer book
MVC	magnetic video camera; marginal voltage check; multi-variable control; multimedia viewer compiler
MVDM	multiple virtual DOS machines
MVGA	monochrome video graphics array
MVGAR	maximum video graphics array resolution; maximum visual graphics adapter resolution
MVIP	multi-vendor integration protocol
MVP	multimedia video processor

MVS	multiple virtual storage
MVT	mercury vapor tube
MW	machine word; MacWrite; mega-watt; magnetic wire; memory window; Microsoft Word; micro-wave; mirror writing; multi-wave; multi-wire
mW	milli-watt
m.w.	**mw;** molecular weight
MWC	memory write cycle
MWCB	micro-wave circuit board
MWIC	micro-wave integrated circuit
MWIPS	microprocessor without interlocked pipeline stage
MWPR	MacWrite Pro
MWT	mean waiting time
MX	mail exchange(r); mix; mixture
Mx	Maxwell
MXR	mask index register
MXS	Microsoft exchange server
My	May
myg	myria-gram
MZ	minus zone
MZR	multi-zone recording

~N~

N   name; narrow; negation; negative; negatron; nesistor; nest; net; network; neuron; neutral; neutron; new; news; newton; nitogen; node; noise; north; notation; note; number; numeral; numeric; nylon

n   nano

NA   network administrator; network analyzer; network architecture; network assistant; node address; not applicable; not assigned; numerical analysis; numerical aperture; numerical apparatus

N/A   NA; not applicable

Na   *Natrium* (*Latin:* sodium)

NAB   National Association of Broadcasters

NAC   network access control; network adapter card

NACD   National Association of Computer Dealers

NACS   National Advisory Committee on Semiconductors; NetWare asynchronous communication server

NAEP   National Assessment of Educational Progress

NAK   negative acknowledgement

NAL   network access layer

NAM   network access module; numeric assignment module

NAMI   network adaptive multimedia image

NAMPS   narrow-band analog mobile phone service

NAN   non-dedicated advanced NetWare; not a number

NAND   not **AND** *(gate)*

NANP   North American numbering plan

NAP   network access point (*or* protocol)

NAPLPS   North American presentation level protocol syntax

NAS   NetWare access server; network application support; non-arithmetic shift

NASA   National Aeronautics and Space Administration

NASI   NetWare asynchronous services interface

NASIRC   NASA automated systems Internet response capability

NASV   non-automatic self-verification

NAT   natural; network address translation; node address type

NATO   North Atlantic Treaty Organization

NAU   network addressable unit

NAV   navigator; Norton Anti-Virus

NB   narrow band; natural binary; negative bias; network bridge; network buffer

Nb   Niobium

NBAM   narrow band angle modulation

NBC   narrow band coder

NBFM   narrow band frequency modulation

NBFSK   narrow band frequency shift key(ing)

NB-ISDN   narrow band integrated services digital network

NBMA   non-broadcast multi-access

NBP	name binding protocol
NBS	narrow band socket; National Bureau of Standards
NBW	nominal band-width; Nyquist band-width
NC	negative conductance; negative conductor; negative crystal; network calculator; network constant; network courier; neutral conductor; neutralizing capacitor; no carrier; no case; no charge; no connection; no cost; no contact; non-conductor; non-contention; normal contact; normally closed; not closed; not connected; numerical code; numerical constant; numerical control
NCA	network communications adapter; network computing architecture
NCAR	National Center for Atmospheric Research
NCC	network control center; Netscape Communications Corporation
NCCT	non-congestion control traffic
NCD	network computing device; non-coherent detection
NCF	NetWare command file
NCGA	National Computer Graphics Association
ncJFET	negative-channel junction field effect transistor
NCM	numerically controlled machine
ncMOS	negative-channel metal oxide semiconductor
NCMT	numerical control for machine tools
NCOS	network computer operating system

NCP   NetWare core protocol; network configuration plan; network control processor (*or* program *or* protocol); network core protocol; not copy protected

NCPMUX   NetWare core protocols multiplexer

NCR   non-return to change recording

NCS   no carrier sense

NCSA   National Center for Supercomputing Applications; National Computer Security Association

NCSC   National Computer Security Center

NCSI   network communication services interface

NCV   number of custom variables

ND   no detection; node delay; not detected; noise digit; noise diode; numerical data

Nd   Neodymium

NDA   Newton Developers Association

NDD   Norton disk doctor

NDEF   not defined

NDF   normal direction flow

NDI   network device interface

NDIF   new disk image format

NDIS   network device (*or* driver) interface specification

NDL   network data language; nickel delay line

NDN   non-destructive network

NDP   numerical data processor

NDR   network data representation; non-destructive read;

NDRM	non-destructive read memory
NDRO	non-destructive read-out
NDS	NetWare directory service; network development system; node data structure; non-destructive system; Novell directory service
NDX	index
NE	negative electricity; negative electrode
Ne	neon
NEBW	noise equivalent band-width
NEC	National Electrical Code; Nippon Electric Company; non-embedded command
NECC	Naval EHF communications controller
NECT	near-end cross-talk
NEE	non-equivalence element
NEG	negate; negation; negative; negatron
NEMA	National Electrical Manufacturers Association
NEP	network entry point; noise equivalent power
NEO	non-equivalence operation
NERC	North American Electric Reliability Council
NES	non-executable statement
NEST	Novell embedded systems technology
NET	network
NetBIOS	network basic input-output system
NetBEUI	network BIOS extended user interface

Netiquette	ne**t**work **etiquette** (*etiquette on the Internet*)
Netizen	**ne**twork ci**tizen** (*citizen of the Internet*)
NetLib	**NETLIB**; ne**t**work **lib**rary
NETMON	ne**t**work **mon**itor
NETRJE	ne**t**work **r**emote **j**ob **e**ntry
NETRJS	ne**t**work **r**emote **j**ob **s**ervice
Netserial	**NETSERIAL**; ne**t**work **serial**
Network+	**Network+** (*CompTIA computer certificate*)
NEU	**n**umeric **e**xecution **u**nit
NEWS	**N**et**W**are **e**arly **w**arning **s**ystem; **n**etwork **e**xtensible **w**indow **s**ystem; **N**orth-**E**ast-**W**est-**S**outh
NEXT	**n**ear-**e**nd ***cross***-**t**alk (*where X→cross*)
NEXTC	**n**ear-**e**nd ***cross***-**t**alk **c**oupling (*where X→cross*)
NEXTCL	**n**ear-**e**nd ***cross***-**t**alk **c**oupling **l**oss (*where X→cross*)
NF	**n**atural **f**requency; **n**on-**f**ault; **n**ot **f**ixed
NFB	**n**egative **f**eed-**b**ack
NFF	**n**o **f**ault **f**ound
NFG	**n**atural **f**unction **g**enerator
NFI	**n**ear **f**ield **i**maging
NFP	**n**ormal **f**ailure **p**eriod; **n**ormalized **f**loating **p**oint
NFPN	**n**ormalized **f**loating **p**oint **n**umber
NFS	**n**etwork **f**ile **s**ystem; **n**on-**f**ault **s**ystem
NFY	**n**ot **f**ixed **y**et
NG	**n**egation **g**ate; **n**o **g**round; **n**ot **g**rounded

NGC	network gone count
NGI	next generation Internet
NGME	New Grolier Multimedia Encyclopedia
NH	network header
NHA	next higher assembly
NHRP	next hop resolution protocol
NI	negative impedance; negative ion; network information; network interference; nickel; noise immunity; nominal impedance; non-inductive; non-inversion
N/I	non-interlaced; not included
Ni	nickel
NIA	next instruction address
NIC	negative impedance converter; network information center; network interface card; network interface controller; nickel; non-inductive capacitor (*or* circuit); not in contact
NICs	network interface cards
NiCa	nickel-cadmium
NiCad	NICAD; nickel-cadmium
NICOLAS	network information center on-line aid system
NID	new interactive display
NIG	negative ignore gate
NIM	network installation management
NIMH	nickel-metal-hydride
NIO	native input-output

NIP	non-impact printer
NIPS	network input-output per second
NIQ	new input queue; not in queue
NIR	network information retrieval
NIS	network information service; non-isolating error
NISC	nickel-iron secondary cell
N-ISDN	NISDN; narrow-band integrated services digital network
NISO	National Information Standards Organization
NISP	network information services project
NIST	National Institute of Standards and Technology
NITC	National Information Technology Center
NIU	network interface unit
NJCL	network job control language
NJE	network job entry
NKR	number of known routes
NL	native language; natural language; nesting level; nesting loop; network layer; network library; new line; next loop; noise level; no lead; no-load; non-linear; normal logic
NLC	new line character; non-linear capacitor
NLD	non-linear distortion; number of local drives
NLF	non-listening failure
NLI	non-linear interference; normal logic input
NLL	non-loading line

NLM	NetWare loadable module
NLN	non-linear network
NLO	normal logic output
NLP	natural language processing (*or* processor); non-linear programming
NLQ	near letter quality
NLQPB	near letter quality print buffer
NLR	non-linear resistance
NLS	no lead speed; non-linear system
NLSFUNC	National Language Support Function
NM	native mode; network management; network model; network monitor; new message; new model; no mistake; noise margin; noisy mode; non-mistake; normal magnetization; normal mode; null modem; Nusselt number
nm	nano-meter
NMA	null modem adapter
NMB	no mother-board
NMC	null modem cable
NMHS	NetWare message handling service
NMI	non-maskable interrupt
NMM	NetWare management map
NMOS	negative-channel metal oxide semiconductor
NMP	network management protocol
NMR	normal mode rejection; nuclear magnetic resonance

NMRA	new millennium remote agent
NMRB	no mother-board
NMS	named mail slot; network management system
NMT	Nordic Mobile Telephone
NMVT	network management vector transport
NN	natural noise; network name; network node; network number; new number
NND	non-numerical data
NNDP	non-numerical data processor
NNI	network-network interface
NNM	network node manager
NNS	NetWare name service; neuron network simulation
NNT	network news transfer
NNTC	network news transfer center
NNTP	network news transfer (*or* transport) protocol
NO	no operation; non-operative; normal operation; normally opened; not open
No	nobelium
no	NO; No; *numero* (*Latin:* number)
NOC	network operations center; normal operating Condition
NOI	non-operable instruction; non-operative instruction
NOMA	National Office Management Association
NOP	no operation; number of packets

NOPAC	network on-line public access catalogue
NOR	negative **OR** *(gate)*; not **OR** *(gate)*; number of operator retries
NOS	network operating system; number of servers
NOSP	number of servers processed
NP	named pipes; negative point; negative pulse; network protocol; Neumann principle; new program; no power; non-powered; number of pieces; numerical point
Np	Neptunium
nP	nano-processor
np	neper
NPA	network printer alliance
NPB	non-persistent binding
NPC	nano-program control; nano-programmed computer
NPD	network protocol data
NPDU	network protocol data unit
NPF	no problem found
NPI	network printer interface
NPL	National Physical Laboratory; non-procedural language
NPM	non-programmed memory
nPM	NPM; nano-program memory
NPO	negative-positive-*zero*
NPP	non-powered port
NPPS	non-powered port sharing

NPPSD	non-powered port sharing device
NPS	negative pulse stuffing
N.P.S.	NPS; Novell Productivity Specialist
NPSHM	non-powered short haul modem
NPTN	National Public Telecomputing Network
NPU	natural processing unit; numerical point (*or* processing) unit
NPX	numeric processor extension
NQS	network queing system
NR	negative resistance; network relay; no record; no router; noise ratio; non-real; non-removable; non-return; normal response; not rated; not read; not ready; Nyquist rate
N(R)	number-receive(d)
NRBC	no receive buffers count
NRC	National Research Council; non-return to change
NRC-R	non-return to change—recording
NREN	National Research and Educational Network
NRF	no router found; non-recursive filter
NRFC	no router found count
NRM	network resource manager; non-removable memory; normal response mode
NRT	non-real time
NRZ	non-return to zero
NRZ-I	NRZI; non-return to zero—invert

NRZ-L	**NRZL**; non-return to zero—level
NRZ-O	**NRZO**; non-return to zero—one
NRZ-R	**NRZR**; non-return to zero—recording
NS	name-space; national security; native signal; negative signal; NetWare support; network security; network service; network shell; network stabilization; network synthesis; neuron simulation; neutral state; new shape; new system; news signal; no sound; noise signal; noise source; non-stop; non-switched; non-synchronous; normal state; normal system; North-South; notation system; number system; numeric sort; numeric source
N(S)	number-send; number-sent
ns	nano-second
NSAP	Needham-Schroeder authentication protocol; network service access point
NSAPI	Netscape server application program interface
NSC	nano-second circuit; never same color; numeric source count
NSCBBS	National Support Center Bulletin Board System
NSE	NetWare support encyclopedia
NSERC	National Sciences and Engineering Research Council
NSF	National Science Foundation; no symptom found
NSFnet	**NSFNET**; National Science Foundation Network
NSI	NASA Science Internet
NSIA	National Security Industrial Association
NSL	non-switched line

NSP	native signal processing; network service protocol (*or* provider); network shell program
NSR	noise-signal ratio
NSS	Novell storage services
NSSC	NASA Standard Spacecraft Computer; no space for service count
NSSP	next set starting point
NSTC	National Science and Technology Council
NSTL	National Software Testing Laboratories
NT	need troubleshooting; new technology; news time; network; network terminal; network termination; network terminator; network topology; network transfer; neutral temperature; night time; no test; no tone; non-trial; non-transfer
NTAS	new technology advamced server
NTC	negative transconductance
NTF	network transfer function; no trouble found
NTFS	new technology file system
NTIA	National Telecommunications and Information Administration
NTIS	National Technical Information Service
NTLAN	new technology local area network
NTP	native signal processing; network time protocol
NTRAS	new technology remote access services
NTSC	National Television Standards Committee; never twice the same color

NTTC	National Technology Transfer Center
NTU	network termination unit
NTV	non-trial version
NUI	network user identification (*or* interface)
NUL	null
NUMA	non-uniform memory access (*or* architecture)
NUS	non-uniform system
NV	no voltage; non-volatile
NVM	non-volatile memory
NVN	numeric variable name
NVOD	near-video on demand
NVR	NVRAM; non-volatile RAM
NVRAM	NVR; non-volatile random access memory
NVT	network (*or* Novell) virtual terminal
NW	numeric word
NWB	network bridge; network buffer
NWDS	NetWare diagnostic services
NWFS	NetWare file system
NWG	network working group
NWI	network information
NWL	network library
NWM	network management
NWN	network number

NWS   NetWare web server

NWSB   NetWare for small business

NZ   neutral zone

NZT   New Zealand Time

O	output; oxygen
O^2	oxygen
OA	object access; office automation; one address; open architecture; open area; operational amplifier; operational area; output area
OAC	operator aborts count
OAD	open architecture driver
OAG	online air guide
OAI	open applications interface
OAL	object access library; over-all loss
OAM	operation and maintenance
OAS	one-to-all scatter
OAT	operating ambient temperature
OB	object; open book; option board; ordering bias; output buffer; output bus
OBC	offset binary code
OBD	on-board diagnostics; output bus driver
OBEX	object exchange
OBID	object identification (*or* identifier)
OBJ	object
OBR	open book repository

OBS   out-band signal(ling)

OC   object code; ohmic contact; open circuit; open code; open count; open coupler; operating condition; operation code; operational character; optical carrier; optical coupler; optical fibre; optimizing control; optimum code; opto-coupler; origin counter; output capacitance; output channel; over-coupling

OCA   optimizing control action

OCAL   on-line cryptanalytic aid language

OCC   other common carrier

OCE   open collaborative environment

OCF   objects component frame-work

OCI   optical coupled isolation

OCIA   optical coupled isolation amplifier

OCL   online computer library; operation (*or* operator) control language

OCLC   online computer library catalogue

OCP   optional character printing

OCR   one's complement representation; optical character recognition

OCS   one cell switching; operand call syllable

OCT   October

OCWR   optical continuous wave reflectometer

OCX   oven controlled *crystal* (*where X→ crystal*)

OCXO   oven controlled *crystal* oscillator (*where X→ crystal*)

OD	object dancer; ohmic drop; open data; operational decoder; optical disc; original data; original destination; output device; over-damp(ing)
ODA	one digit adder; open document architecture
ODAA	open data acquisition association
ODAPI	open data-base application programming interface
ODBC	object-oriented data base connectivity; open data base connection (*or* connectivity)
ODBMS	object-oriented data base management system
ODC	optical directional coupler
ODI	open data-link interface; open device interconnect
ODIF	open document interchange format
ODL	object definition language
ODLI	open data-link interface
ODM	object data manager; optimized distribution model
ODMA	open document management API
ODP	online data processing; open document processing
ODS	open data service; open document setup
ODSI	open directory service interface
ODT	object data type; open desk-top
OE	odd-even; off emergency; original equipment; outlet expansion; output enhancement
O/E	optical to electrical
Oe	Oerstad
OEC	odd-even check

OEI	odd-even interleaving
OEM	original equipment manufacturer
OEP	operand execution pipe-line
OEPS	outlet expansion power strip
OF	object file; optical fibre; output formatter; over-flow
OFB	optical fibre bus; output feed-back
OFBM	output feed-back mode
OFD	optical fibre device
OFDM	orthogonal frequency division multiplexing
OFHS	oxygen-free high conductivity
OFI	over-flow indicator
OFK	on-off key(ing)
OFM	output feedback mode
OFMT	output format
OFO	one-for-one; over-flow operation
OFP	over-flow position
OFS	object file system; optical fibre star; output field separator
OG	open-ground; OR gate
OGM	out-going message
OH	off hook; over-head
OHB	over-head bit
OHCI	open host controller interface

OI	operator indicator; operator interrupt; optical image; optical isolator; opto-isolator; output impedance; output indicator; output-input; overflow indicator
OIA	operations impact assessor
OIC	optical image chip
OIDB	optically isolated driver board
OIDL	object interface definition language
OIS	office information system; operator intervention section
OL	object language; object link; off-line; off-load; on-line; open-link; open-load; open-loop; operations-logistics; outside loop; overall loss; over-lay; over-load(ing)
OLA	on-line activity
OLAP	on-line activity (*or* analytical) processing
OLC	over-load capacity
OLCP	on-line complex processing
OLCS	open loop control section (*or* system)
OLD	on-line data (*or* debugging *or* diagnostics); over-lapping data
OLDC	over-lapping data channel
OLDP	on-line data processing
OLE	object linking and embedding
OLFSH	open loop follower sample-hold
OLG	open loop gain
OLGA	on-line guitar archive
OLI	optical line interface

OLM	over-lay module; over-load module
OLMC	output logic macro-cell
OLMT	over-load module test
OLN	open loop network
OLO	off line operation
OLP	over-lay path (*or* program)
OLR	on line repair; open loop response; over-lay region; over-load recovery
OLRT	over-load recovery time
OLS	one level storage; on-line replacement; on-line service; on-line storage; over-lay supervisor
OLSP	on-line service provider
OLT	on-line test; over-lay tree
OLTF	on-line test facilities
OLTP	on-line transaction processing
OM	object management; object manager; ohm-meter; on mode; open message; operation(s) manual; optical mark; optical mouse; output meter; output module; over-modulation
OMA	object management architecture
OME	open messaging environment
OMF	object module format; open media frame-work; open message format
OMG	object management group
OMI	open messaging interface; outer micro-instruction
OML	object manipulation language

OMM	optical (*or* opto-) mechanical mouse
OMR	optical mark recognition
OMT	overload module test
OMV	output module valve
ON	object name; open network; order number; output noise
ONA	open network architecture
ONC	open network computing
ONDS	open network distribution services
ONE	open network environment
ONL	object name length
ONMS	open network management system
ONP	open network provision
ONU	optical network unit
OOB	out of band
OOBS	out of band signalling
OODB	object-oriented data-base
OODMS	object-oriented data-base management system
OOG	object-oriented graphic
OOK	on-off key(ing)
OOL	object-oriented language
OOM	object orientation manipulator
OOOS	object-oriented operating system
OOP	object-oriented programming

OOPL   object-oriented programming language

OOS   object-oriented system

OOST   out of service testing

OOT   object-oriented technology

OOUI   object-oriented user interface

OP   object program(ming); odd parity; open poll; operand; operating procedure; operation; operation personnel; optimum program(ming); original post; out-put; over-punch; overflow position

OPAC   online public access catalogue

OPAL   open platform alignment linkage

OPALS   opto-electronic, photonic, advanced laser simulator

OP-AMP   OPAMP; operational amplifier

OPC   odd parity check; organic (*or* optical) photo-conductor

OPCODE   operational code

OPD   original post date; output device

OPI   open pre-press interface

OPM   operations per minute

OPOA   one-plus-one address

OPPI   open pre-press interface

OPS   open profiling standard

OPT   open protocol technology; optimum; option(al)

OPUS   octal program updating system

OQL   object query language

OQP	offset quadrature phase
OQPSK	offset quadrature phase shift key(ing)
OR	object request; ohmic resistor; open raid; open resistor; open route; open routine; operational relay; operation research; optical read; original request; output record; output register; output regulation; over record
ORB	object request broker
ORD	original request date
ORDVAC	ordnance variable automatic computer
ORF	original request form
ORG	organization
ORI	online retrieval interface; original
ORL	optical return loss
O-ROM	OROM; optical read only memory
ORS	output record separator
ORT	overload recovery time; overshoot rise time
OS	object security; off-set; off state; on state; one shot; open shop; open software; open subroutine; open system; operating system; optical scanner; optical sensor; optional stop; ordinary symbol; out-side; output steering; output stream; over-scanning; over-shoot
Os	osmium
OS/2	operating system 2
OSA	open scripting (*or* system) architecture
OSD	open software distribution; orderly shut down

OSDC	on state drain current
OSDPM	operating system directed power management
OSE	office server extension; optical shaft encoder
OS/E	operating system environment
OSF	open socket failures; open software foundation
OSI	open system interconnection
OSO	one step operation
OSP	on-screen programming; optical storage processor; over-sized packet
OSPF	open shortest path first
OSPFP	open shortest path first protocol
OSPM	operating system power management
OSQL	object structured query language
OSR	open sub-routine
OSRT	over-shoot rise time
OSW	open software
OT	object technology; object type; open transport; over-time
OTA	operation-triggered architecture
OTD	optical time-domain
OTDR	optical time-domain reflection (*or* reflectometer)
OTF	on-line test facility; open token foundation
OTL	open transport library
OTO	one-to-one

OTP	one-time programmable
OTS	off-the-shelf
OURS	open users recommended solutions
OUT	outage; outline; output
OV	output voltage; over-view
OVAL	object-based virtual application language
OVD	over-view diagram
OVL	over-lay
OVR	over
OW	over-write
OWL	object (*or* open) Windows library
OZR	one to zero ration

~P~

P   pack; package; packet; page; paint; pair; palette; panel; paragraph; parallel; parameter; parent; parity; part; partial; partition; pass; paste; patch; path; pattern; peak; Pentium; peripheral; peta; phase; picture; pilot; pitch; pixel; plain; planar; plane; plasma; plate; poise; polar; pole; poll; pop; population; port; portable; post; potential; power; phosphorus; print; private; process; program; protocol; pulse; pure

p   pico

PA   packet assembly; page addressing; parallel adder; parametric amplifier; peak amplitude; phase angle; physical address; polar axes; positive addressing; power amplifier; pre-amplifier; program activity; program address; pulse amplifier; pulse amplitude

Pa   Pascal; Protactinium

PAAM   plugable authentication and authorization module

PAB   personal address book

PABS   peek-a-boo-system

PABX   private automatic branch exchange

PAC   program address counter

PACE   priority access control enabled

PACS   picture archiving and communication system

PACSL   public access computer systems list

PAD   packet assembler-disassembler

PADS   pen application development system

PAF	photo animator file; positive addressing format
PAG	power amplifier with gain
PAIH	public access Internet host
PAIS	public access Internet site
PAK	pack; package; packed; positive acknowledgement
PAL	palette; phase alternating line; platform alignment linkage; programmable array logic; programming assembly language
PALASM	programmable array logic assembler
PALC	plasma-addressed liquid crystal
PALCD	plasma-addressed liquid crystal display
PALS	principles of alphabet literacy system
PAM	production automation microcomputer; pulse amplitude modulation
PAN	personal area network; print alpha-numerically
PAP	packet level procedure; password authentication protocol; printer access protocol
PAR	parabola; parallel; partial; particle; personal animation recorder; pixel aspect ratio; positive acknowledgement with re-transmission; precision approach radar; program address register
PARA	paragraph
PARC	Palo Alto Research Center
PARD	periodic and random deviation
PARISC	PA-RISC; precision architecture reduced instruction set computer

PAS	PASCAL; physical address space; point and shoot; production automation system
PASC	production automation system component
PASCAL	Blaise **Pascal** (*one who invented the PASCAL language*)
PAT	patch; pattern; phonograph audio technology; program activity transmission
PATN	pattern; port access telephone number
PAU	position analog unit
PAX	portable archive exchange; private automatic exchange
PB	Packard Bell; packet buffer; page break; paint-brush; panel-board; parity bit; patch-board; peripheral bus; peta-byte; piggy backing; plotting-board; prototyping board
Pb	*Plumbum* (*Latin:* lead)
PBA	Packard Bell Assembly; physical block address; printed board assembly
PBASIC	parallax beginners all-purpose symbolic instruction code
PBBDR	parallel bidirectional bus driver-receiver
PBC	parallel by character; pulling by crystal
PBD	processing of binary data
PBF	Poisson distribution function; poly-silicon blown fuse
PBGA	plastic ball grid array
PBI	processor basic instruction
PBM	peripheral bus mode; piggy-back module
PBN	Packard Bell Navigator; private business network

PBNEC   Packard Bell Nippon Electric Company

PBP   packet burst protocol; phase by phase; portable battery pack

PBR   provider based routing

PBS   Public Broadcasting Service

PBSRAM   pipe-lined burst static random access memory

PBW   pulse band-width

PBX   private branch exchange

PC   packet communication; pad character; paging channel; paired cable; parallel circuit; parallel connection; parallel conversion; parasitic capacitor; parity check; peak clipper; peaking circuit; periodic current; peripheral controller; personal computer; phantom circuit; phasing capacitor; pin connection; pin contact; point contact; polar coordinates; polar crystal(s); polarized capacitor; policy certification; polling characters; position code; positive charge; power check; power computing; power console; power consumption; primary constant; primary current; printer circuit; printer controller; priority control; process control; program code; program conversion; program counter; programmable calculator; programmable clock; programmable controller; propagation constant; proportional control; protocol converter; pulse carrier; pulse code; pulse counter; punched card

PC-DOS   PCDOS; personal computer disk operating system

PCA   parallel contention arbitration; policy certification authority; printed circuit assembly; programmable communication adapter

PCACIAS   personal computer automated calibration interval analysis system

PCAM	process control analog module
PCB	printed circuit board; process control block
PCBA	printed circuit board assembly
PCBB	printed circuit bread-board
PCBC	plain (*or* propagating) cipher block chaining
PCBCP	printed circuit board control point
PCBP	printed circuit board package
PCBPS	printed circuit board power shut-off
PCBPT	printed circuit board portable tester
PCBTL	printed circuit board test language
PCBTP	printed circuit board test point
PCC	peripheral controller chip; pin connect crystal; power control center; printed circuit card; process control compiler (*or* computer)
PCCK	personal computer cleaning kit
PCD	photo compact disc; point contact diode; programmer's console diagnostic
PCDM	process control digital module
PC-DOS	personal computer - disk operating system
PCDP	photo compact disc player
PCE	paper checking exercise; personal computer emulation
PCEB	PCI to EISA bridge
PCEC	printed circuit epoxy coating
PCF	personal computer fortress; point coordination function

PCI	peripheral command (*or* component) interconnect; peripheral component interconnect (*or* interface); personal component interconnect (*or* interface); program check interruption; program control instruction; programmable communication interface
PCIA	personal computer industrial application
PCIB	peripheral component interconnect bus
PCIC	personal computer interface (*or* interrupt) controller
PC-I/O	program controlled input-output
PCKBS	personal computer key-board switch
PCL	printer command language; path control layer; printer control language; process control language (*or* loop)
PCLK	processor clock
PCM	personal computer manufacturer; photo cell matrix; printer cartridge metric; pulse code modulation; pulse counting module
PCMA	paired carrier multiple access
PCMC	PCI, cache, memory controller
PCMCIA	Personal Computer Memory Card International Association
PCMIA	Personal Computer Memory-Card Industry Association
PCMIM	personal computer media interface module
PCN	personal communication (*or* computer) network
PCNFS	personal computer network file system
PCO	point of control and observation; programmable calculating oscilloscope

PCP	photo compact-disc player; primary control program
PCPS	personal computer printer switch
PCR	peak cell rate; point contact rectifier
PCROM	programmed control read only memory
PCS	parallel conversion system; personal communication service (*or* system); personal computer service; personal conferencing specification; physical coordinate system; plastic clad silica; positioning contouring system; printed circuit switch; process control system
PCSK	personal computer service kit
PCSM	personal computer serial modem
PCSMC	personal computer serial modem cable
PCT	picture; private channel (*or* communication) technology; percentage; pneumatic crimp tool; point contact transistor; processor cycle time
PCTC	personal computer token card
PCTV	personal computer television
PCU	program control unit
PD	packet density; parallel data; parametric diode; passive device; peak distortion; periodic damping; peripheral device; phase delay; phase detection; phase dictionary; phase difference; phase discriminator; physical device; physical disk; pin diode; pixel depth; pixel doubling; plasma display; polar diagram; portable document; post doctorate; potential difference; power dissipation; power dump; program documentation; propagation delay; protocol discriminator; public domain; pulse derivation; pulse detector; pulse digit; pulse discriminator; pulse drive(er); pulse droop; pure density

Pd   Palladium

PDA   personal digital assistant; plant-wide data acquisition

PDAC   plant-wide data acquisition configuration

PDB   punch down block

PDC   parallel data connector; peripheral device control; physical disk channel; personal digital cellular; physical drive count; primary domain controller

PDD   physical device driver; portable digital document

PDE   processor detected exception

PDF   portable document file (*or* format); printer description file; probability distribution function

PDI   parallel digital interface

PDIAL   public dial-up Internet access list

PDIB   parallel digital interface board

PDIO   parallel digital input-output

PDIOC   parallel digital input-output card

PDIP   plastic dual in-line package

PDL   packet (*or* physical) data link; page (*or* program) description language; parameter definition list; physical data link; program design language; programmable digital logic

PDLI   packet data link interface

PDLP   packet data link processor

PDM   product data management; programmable data mover; programmed defined macro; pull down menu; pulse duration modulation

PDN	private domain name; public data network
PDO	portable distributed object
PDP	parallel data processing; peripheral data packet; plasma display panel; programmed data processor
PDPT	peripheral data packet transfer
PDS	packet driver specification; permanent dynamic storage; portable document software; premises distribution system; processor direct slot; program development system; public domain software; push down stack
PDSS	post development and software support
PDT	Pacific Daylight Time; performance diagnostic tool; physical drive tape; portable diagnostic terminal; programmable drive table; programmed data transfer; pulse decay (*or* delay) time
PDTE	packet-mode data terminating equipment
PDTR	peak data transfer rate
PDU	position dependent unfairness; power distribution unit; protocol data unit
PDUN	packets discarded unknown net
PDX	printer description extension
PE	parity error; parity even; pass element; peripheral equipment; permanent error; phase encoding; photo-electric; physical element; piezo-electric; point effect; poly-ethylene; port expander; positive electricity; positive electrode; post edit; post equalization; primary electrons; primary emission; processing element; Professional Engineer; program editor; program error; proximity effect; pulse equalizer
PEA	pocket EtherNet adapter

PEC	piezo-electric crystal
PECL	positive-supply emitter coupled logic
PED	piezo-electric device
PEE	photo-electric effect; piezo-electric effect
PEM	privacy enhanced mail; processing element memory; processor evaluation module
PEMDAS	parenthesis, exponentiation, multiplication, division, addition, subtraction
PEP	packet exchange protocol; peak envelope power
PER	program event recording
PERC	power edged RAID controller
PERL	practical extraction and report language
PERT	program evaluation and review technique
PES	packetized elementary stream; photo-electric scanning; positioning error signal; processor enhancement socket
PET	photo-electric threshold; piezo-electric transducer; print enhancement technology
PEY	photo-electric yield
PF	page fault; page frame; parts family; peak follower; permanent fault; pin-feed; power factor; power fading; power failure; power frequency; primary flow; program form
P-F	PF; power-fail
pF	pico-farad
PFB	positive feed-back; printer font binary

PFC	personal filing cabinet; power factor correction
PFD	peak flux density; phase frequency distortion; power failure detection; pulse flatness deviation
PFDM	partitioned frequency division multiplex; power failure detection module
PFE	programmer's file editor
PFET	programmable field effect transistor
PFG	paper feed guide; potentiometer function generator
PFL	power-fail logic; power failure logic
PFM	power factor meter; printer font metrics; pulse frequency modulation
PFR	power-fail restart; power failure rate (*or* recovery)
PFS	packet field strength; processor, file-manager, spread-sheet
PFV	peak forward voltage
PG	parity generator; penta-grid; pixel graphic; potential gradient; power gain; program generator; proportional gain; pulse generator
PGA	pin grid array; professional graphics adapter
PGC	parity generator checker; program group control
PGDN	page down
PGL	printing graphic library
PGML	precision graphics markup language
PGP	Pretty Good Privacy
PGR	pager
PGS	photographic storage; program generation system

PGUP   page up

PH   packet handling; passive hub; phase; phone; photo; photograph; picture height

ph   phot

PHEMT   pseudo-morphic high electron mobility transistor

PHF   packet handling function

PHIG   programmer's hierarchical interface to graphic

PHIGS   programmer's hierarchial interactive graphics standard

PHO   phone; phonograph

PHPS   personal handy-phone system

PHS   personal handy-phone system

PHV   property has value

PI   parabolic interpolation; parallel interface; parity interrupt; performance index; peripheral interface; phase inverter; polling interval; program instruction; program interruption; programmable interrupt; programmed instruction; pulse interleaving

PIA   peripheral interface adapter

PIABI   peripheral interface adapter bus interface

PIARW   peripheral interface adapter read-write

PIC   peripheral interface channel; personal information carrier; personal intelligent communicator; picture; planar (*or* plasma) integrated circuit; powdered iron core; priority (*or* programmable) interrupt controller

PICMG   PCI Industrial Computer Manufacturers Group

PICS   platform for Internet content selection

PICT	picture
PICU	priority interrupt control unit
PID	potentiometric input device; process (*or* product) identification; proportional integral derivative
PIE	plug-in electronics; post installation evaluation
PIER	procedure for Internet re-numbering
PIF	picture interchange format; program information file
PIFB	point information feed-back
PIFS	point information feedback system
PIHS	plug-in heat sink
PII	program integrated information
PIII	plasma immersion ion implantation
PILOT	program inquiry, learning or teaching
PilotACE	pilot automatic computing engine
PIM	peripheral (*or* processor) interface module; personal information manager; priority interrupt module; protocol independent multicast
PIN	personal (*or* process) identification number; positive-intrinsic-negative
PINE	program for Internet news and electronic-mail
PING	packet Internet Gopher
PINO	positive-input negative-output
P-in-P	picture-in-picture
PIO	parallel (*or* processor *or* programmable) input-output
PIOC	programmable input-output channel

PIOD	programmable input-output device
PIP	pattern and information processing; picture in picture; problem isolation procedure; programmable interconnect point
PiP	picture in picture
PIPO	parallel-in parallel-out
PIR	protocol independent routing
PIS	positive ion sheath
PISO	parallel-in serial-out
PISP	plug-in surge protector
PIT	priority interrupt table; programmable interval timer
PIX	*Latin:* pitch
PIXEL	picture—voxel
PJ	paper jam; point junction; pulse jitter
PJT	point junction transistor
PK	pack; primary key; private key; public key
PKC	private (*or* public) key cryptography
PKE	private (*or* public) key encryption
PKR	public key ring
PL	paper-less; peak limiter; peak load; pen-light; phase library; phase logic; physical layer; physical lock; pipe- line; place; polling list; polling loop; positive logic; power level; power line; power lock; power loss; private line; private link; program library; program listing; programmable logic; programming language; proof listing

PL/1	programming language one
PL/M	programming language for micros
PLA	programmable logic array
PLAIF	programmable logic array instruction fetch
PLAOL	programmable logic array output latch
PLC	programmable logic controller
PLCC	plastic leaded (*or* leadless) chip carrier; programmable logic control case
PLD	processor level design; programmable logic design
PLDS	pilot land data system
PLL	phase locked loop
PLLML	phase locked loop motor control
PLM	power line monitor; pulse length modulation
PL/M	programming language for micros
PLMN	public land mobile network
PLO	paper-less office; phase locked oscillator
PLP	packet level procedure; phone line protector
PLS	primary link station
PLT	pilot; plate; platter; plot; plotter; process loop test; protocol level timer
PLV	production level video
PLY	play
PM	page mode; paragraph mark; permanent magnet; permanent memory; phase modulation; physical media; physical medium; polar mode; polar molecule; post

	mortem; power management; PrintMonitor; program module; programmable memory; programming module; protected mode; protocol machine; pulse mode; pulse modulation
Pm	promethium
p.m.	pm; P.M.; PM; *post meridiem* (*Latin:* afternoon)
PMA	physical memory address
PMAC	programmable multi-axis controller
p-mail	P-mail; P-MAIL; PMAIL; pmail; paper mail
PMB	phased microwave beam
PMC	PCI mezzanine connector; potentio-meter circuit
PMD	packet mode data; physical media (*or* medium) dependent; post mortem dump; presentation manager debugger
PMFG	potentio-meter function generator
PMI	phase modulation index; processor memory interface; protected mode interface
PMM	Pentium memory management; portable multi-media; power management
PMMU	paged memory management unit
PMOS	positive-channel metal oxide semiconductor
PMP	physical memory page; program maintenance procedure; pump(ing)
PMR	phase modulation recording
PMT	photo multiplier; potentio-meter transducer
PMVI	protected mode virtual interrupt

PMW	pulse modulation width
PN	page number; physical node; Polish notation; port number; processing node; program name; public network
P/N	part number
PNA	physical node address; programmable network access
PNG	portable network graphics
PNET	private network; public network
PNL	panel
PNM	Petri net model
PNNI	private network to network interface
PNP	pnp; positive-negative-positive
PnP	plug and play
pnp	PNP; positive-negative-positive
PNTG	painting
PNTR	pointer
PNW	peaking network; peer network; public network
PO	page orientation; parallel operation; parametric oscillator; parasitic oscillation; parcel order; parity odd; part operation; pilot operation; pin out; pixel operation; portrait orientation; post operation; power on; push operation
Po	polonium
POC	point of contact
POH	power-on-hours
POI	point of information; priority ordered interrupt

POL	Physician On-Line; Poland; problem (*or* procedure) oriented language
POM	photo-optic memory
POP	package for on-line programming; Pentium overdrive processor; point of presence (*or* purchase); post office protocol
POR	Portugal; power-on reset; power-on rest
POS	point of sale; position; positive; product of sums; programmable option select
POSIX	portable operating system interface for UNIX
POSS	point of sale system
POST	point of sale terminal; power-on self-test
POSTNET	postal numeric encoding technique
POT	potential; process object table; pulse origin time
POTS	plain old telephone service
POWER	performance optimization with enhanced RISC
PowerPC	performance optimization with enhanced RISC performance computing
PP	page printer; page protection; paint program; paper pack; parallel port; parallel processing; parent population; part programmer; partial program; path profile; planar process; plastic package; polarized plug; post processing; power pack; program parameter; program patch; programmable peripheral; proprietary program; push- pull
P-P	peak to peak
P3P	PPPP; platform for privacy preferences project

PPA	pixel processing accelerator; push-pull amplifier
PPAL	physical platform alignment linkage
PPC	parallel printer connection (*or* connector); phenolic printed circuit; power performance computing; push-pull circuit
ppc	points per cycle
PPD	peak phase deviation; PostScript printer description
PPDC	proportional plus derivative controller
PPDS	personal printer data stream
PPGA	plastic pin grid array
PPI	precise pixel interpolation; programmable parallel (*or* peripheral) interface
PPIC	proportional plus integral controller
PPM	parameter potentio-meter; parts per million; pulse position modulation
ppm	pages per minute
PPOST	programmable point of sale terminal
PPP	parallel plate package; point-to-point protocol
PPPB	program patching plug-board
PPPL	Princeton Plasma Physics Laboratory
PPPP	P3P; platform for privacy preferences project
PPQ	post-print queue, pre-print queue
PPROM	plug programmable read only memory
PPRP	PowerPC reference platform

PPS	packets per second; parallel processing system; personal productivity software; positive pulse stuffing
pps	pulses per second
PPSEB	parallel processing system evaluation board
PPSI	packets per send interval
PPT	periodic pulse train; potentiometric pressure transducer
PPTP	point-to-point tunnelling protocol
PPU	peripheral processing unit
PQFP	plastic quad flat package
PR	packet radio; packet(s) received; parallel resonance; partial response; pattern recognition; photo resist; physical record; poll response; power relay; power response; primary register; product; program register; program run; proposed response; pulse ratio
Pr	praseodymium
PRA	print alpha-numerically; print address
PRACSA	Public Remote Access Computer Standards Association
PRAM	parallel random access machine; parameter random access memory
PRB	paper refold basket; prime read block
PRC	parallel resonant circuit; pseudo-random code
PRD	printer driver (*or* dump); product; production
PRDP	packets received during processing
PRE	packet receiver error; physical read error

Pref	preference
PREP	preparation
PReP	PowerPC reference platform
PRF	preference; pulse repetition frequency
PRG	program
PRGM	program
PRI	primary; primary rate interface
PRISM	photo-refractive information storage material
PRJ	project; projection; projector
PRL	physical record lock
PRLC	physical record lock count
PRLT	physical record lock threshold
PRMD	private mangement domain
PRMEC	packet receiver miscellaneous error count
PRN	print numerically; printer; pseudo-random number
PRNG	pseudo-random number generator
PRNS	pseudo-random number sequence
PRO	packet receiver overflow; professional; profile
PROC	packet receiver overflow count; procedure; process; processor
PROD	producer; product; production
PROG	program; programmer
PROJ	project; projection; projector
PROLOG	programming in logic

PROM   programmable read only memory

PROT   protocol

PRP   page replacement policy; photo resist process; printer ready protocol

PRR   physical read request; pulse repetition rate

PRT   platinum resistance thermometer; print; printer; program reference table

PRTBC   packet receiver too big count

PRTSC   packet receiver too small count; print screen

PS   packet size; packet switching; page size; parallel search; parallel storage; parallel system; parallel-series; parametric subroutine; parasitic stopper; parasitic suppressor; particle size; passive star; periodic signal; permanent storage; phase shift; phase splitter; pilot system; polarizing slot; poly-silicon; position sensor; position storage; PostScript; power sag; power search; power semiconductor; power spike; power strip; power supply; power switch; primary storage; program scheduler; program segment; program specification; program stack; program statement; program step; program storage; proprietary slot; protocol stack; pulse stuffing

ps   pico-second

PS/2   programming system 2

PSAPI   presentation space application programming interface

PSBF   poly-silicon blown fuse

PSC   parallel-series circuit; peripheral support computer; permuted cycle code; personal super computer; poly-styrene capacitor; Public Service Commission

PSD	peripheral software driver; positive sensitive detector; power spectral density; programmable sharing device
PSDN	packet-switched data network
PSDS	packet-switched data service
PSE	portable stream environment; program sensitive error; power system engineering
PSF	pattern sensitive fault; permanent swap file; PostScript font
p.s.f.	pound-force per square foot (*or* psf)
PSFCC	production support flight control computer
PSG	polyphase synchronous generator
PSI	performance systems international; program stop instruction
p.s.i.	pound-force per square inch
PSID	PostScript image data
PSJ	pulse stuffing jitter
PSK	phase shift key(ing)
PSL	pipe status list
PSM	power switch module
PSN	packet sequence number; packet switching network (*or* node)
PSP	PostScript printer; program segment prefix; public service provider
PSPDN	packet-switched public data network
PSR	parametric sub-routine; processor state register
P-SRAM	pseudo-static random access memory (*or* PSRAM)

PSRT   PostScript round table

PSS   personal signalling system; physical simulation system; print spooler software

PST   Pacific Standard Time

PSTN   public-switched telephony network

PSU   page set-up; power supply unit; program storage unit

PSW   processor (*or* program) status word

PT   packet transmission; packet type; page table; paper tape; parallel transfer; parallel transmission; part-time (*or* P/T); partition table; pentode transistor; phase transition; picture tube; pig-tail; planar transistor; plasma torch; power transformer; power transistor; PowerTalk; primary task; proving time

Pt   Platinum

P/T   PT; part-time

PTB   Physikalisch-Technische-Bundesanstalt *(German)*

PTC   positive temperature coefficient

PTE   packet transmitter error

PTEC   packet transmitter error count

PTG   pulse train generator

PTM   pulse time modulation

PTMEC   packet transmitter miscellaneous error count

PTN   public telephone network

PTNW   public telephone network

p.t.o.   please turn over

PTP   peak-to-peak; peer-to-peer; point-to-point

PTPA	peak-to-peak amplitude
PTPC	point-to-point configuration
PTPE	peer-to-peer exchange
PTR	peak transfer rate
PTS	phone test set; program test system; push-to-talk switch
PTSA	product term sharing array
PTT	picture tube type; post, telegraph and telephone; processor transfer time; program testing time; push-to-talk
PTTBC	packet transmitter too big count
PTTS	push-to-talk switch
PTTSC	packet transmitter too small count
PU	physical unit; pick-up
Pu	plutonium
PUB	public; publication; publicity; publish
PUL	push-up-list
PUM	pop-up-menu
PUN	physical unit number
PUP	PARC universal packet; peripheral unit processor
PUPS	portable un-interruptible power supply
PUR	poly-urethane
PUS	processor upgrade socket; Public Utility Commission; push-up-storage
PUV	pick-up-value

PV	peak value; peak voltage; phantom voltage; phase velocity; pixel value; poly-valence; propagation velocity
PVA	protected virtual address
PVAM	protected virtual address mode
PVC	permanent virtual circuit; poly-vinyl-chloride
PVI	protected-mode virtual interrupt
PVM	parallel virtual machine; pass-through virtual machine
PVN	poly-valent notation
PVP	parallel vector processing; permanent virtual path
PVR	precision voltage reference
PVS	parallel visualization server
PW	password; picture width; pulse width
pW	pico-watt
PWB	printed wire board; programmer's work-bench
PWBRT	packets with bad request type
PWD	print working directory
PWE	physical write error; pulse width encoder;
PWM	pulse width modulation
PWR	physical write request; power; pulse width recording
PWSCS	programmable work-station communication service
PXP	pocket exchange protocol
PZ	plus zone; private zone; public zone; pulse zone
PZN	positive-zero-negative
PZNPS	positive-zero-negative pulse stuffing

Q   quad; quadrant; quadrature; quality; quantity; quantum; quarter; quartz; question; queue; quiz; quote; quotient

q   *charge*; quintal

Q&A   question & answer

QA   quadrature amplitude; quality assurance; question-answer

QAM   quadrature amplitude modulation; quick access memory

QB   quick basic; quick break

QBC   qui-binary code

QBE   query by example

QBF   query by form

QBIC   query by image content

QC   quality control; quantum clock; quartz clock; quartz crystal; quenching circuit; queue control; quick chart; quick code; quiescent current; quiet cable

QCAM   queued content addressed memory

QCB   queue control block

QCD   quad clock driver; quick configuration device

QCIF   quarter common intermediate format

QD   quad density; qualified diagnostic; quantizing distortion; quick disconnect; QuickDraw

QD3D   QuickDraw 3 dimension

QDI   Quicken dictionary

QDOS   quick and dirty operating system

QDT   Quicken data

QE   quality engineering; quantum efficiency; quantum electronics

QEMM   Quarterdeck expanded memory manager

QF   quality factor; quick format

QFA   quick file access

QFE   quick fix engineering

QFP   quad flap package

QIC   quarter inch cartridge

QICD   quarter inch cartridge drive

QIF   Quicken import file

QIL   quad in line

QISAM   queued indexed sequential access method

QL   query language; quick link

QLT   quality

QLTY   quality

QMS   quality management service

QN   qualified name; quantity number; quantization noise; quantum number; queue name

QNT   quantity

QNTM   quantum

QNTY	quantity
QOS	quality of service
QP	qualified personnel; qualified product; quartz plate; quick power
QPE	quoted printable encoding
QPG	quantum phase gate
QPL	qualified products list
QPOST	Q-POST; quick power on self-test
QPPA	quiescent push-pull amplifier
QPR	quadrature partial response
QPSK	quadrature phase shift key(ing)
QPT	quartz pressure transducer
QR	quick reaction
QRT	quart; quarter; quartz
QS	query station; queue status; quick start; quick stop; quoted string
QSA	queued sequential access
QSG	quenched spark gap
QT	qualified tester; quality test; quart; quarter; query type; queue type; queued telecommunications; queuing theory; queuing time; quick test; QuickTime
QTAM	queued telecommunications access method
QTC	QuickTime conferencing
QTP	queuing theory problem
QTR	quarter

QTS	QuickTime setting
QTZ	quartz
QUAM	quadrature amplitude modulation
QW	quantum well; quarter wave
QWIP	quantum well infra-red photo-detector
QWP	quarter wave plane

~R~

R	race; rack; radio; radius; radix; range; Rankine; rapid; rate; rating; ratio; ray; read; ready; real; reboot; receive; record; redundant; reference; register; relation; relative; relay; remote; repeat; reserve; residue; resistance; resistor; resource; return; right; ring; ripple; rise(r); robot; roentgen; root; row
RA	random access; RealAudio; reference address; register address; relative address; remote access; reserve amount; return address; return authorization
Ra	Radium
RAB	random access buffer
RAC	random access channel
RACF	resource access control facility
RAD	radian; radiation; radium; random access device; rapid access disk; rapid application development
rad	radian; radiation
RADA	random access discrete address
RADAR	radio detection and ranging
RADB	routing arbiter data base
RADIUS	remote architecture dial-in user service
RADSL	rate adaptive digital subscriber line
RAF	register address field
RAG	resource allocation graph; row address generator

RAID	redundant array of independent disks (*or* drives); redundant array of inexpensive drives
RAIS	redundant array of inexpensive systems
RAL	rapid access loop; relative address label
RALU	register and arithmetic logic unit
RAM	random access memory; Real Audio meta-file; real address mode; relative addressing mode; repeated addition multiplication; resource allocation mapping
RAMA	random access memory address
RAMAR	random access memory address register
RAMDAC	random access memory digital-to-analog converter
RAMP	remote access maintenance protocol
RAMPS	resources allocation and multi-projects scheduling
RAN	read around number; remote acknowledge number
RAP	random access program(ming); rapid application prototyping
RAR	RAM address register; read-around ratio
RAROM	reprogrammable associative read only memory
RARP	reverse address resolution protocol
RAS	remote access service (*or* setup); risk analysis software; row address select (*or* strobe)
RASAPI	remote access service application programming interface
RAT	random access time
RAVE	rendering acceleration virtual engine

RB	radio button; rain-bow; read block; read buffer; reboot; recycle bin; reference block; reference book; remote bridge; return to bias; reverse bias; right button; roll back
Rb	rubidium
RBBS	remote bulletin board system
RBC	read-back check
RBCS	remote bar code system
RBL	reference black level
RBM	request bit-map
RBOC	Regional Bell Operating Company
RBP	remote batch processing
RB-ROM	remote boot read only memory (*or* RBROM)
RBS	read block size; reliable byte stream
RBSS	roll back snap-shot
RBU	reference binary unit
RBUDC	reference binary unit distance code
RBW	read beyond write; reflected backward wave
RC	radio circuit; radio connection; radix complement; range conversion; reactance chart; receiver card; rectifier crystal; redundancy check(ing); redundant code; relative code; relative coordinates; relay contact(s); reliability control; remote connection; remote console; remote control; repeat counter; resident compiler; residual current; residue check(ing); resistance-capacitance; resistor-capacitor; reversible capacitance; revision cycle; ring counter; ripple counter; riser connector

RCA   Radio Corporation of America; resistance capacitance amplifier; ripple carry adder

RCC   redundancy check character; resistance capacitance coupling; resistors, capacitors circuit

RCD   recordable compact disc

RCF   raised cosine filter

RCID   remote connection identification (*or* identifier)

RCL   rotate carry left

RCN   residential communication network; resistors, capacitors network

RCO   representative calculating operation; resistors, capacitors oscillator

RCP   reception; remote control panel; remote copy; restore cursor position

RCR   rotate carry right

RCS   remote control signal; removable cartridge system; revision control system

RCSS   records communications switching system

RCT   resistance continuity tester

RCTL   resistor capacitor transistor logic

RCW   return control word

RD   raw data; read; read data; receive data; recording density; rectifier diode; relay driver; removable disk; remove directory; request disconnect; rescue dump; research and development; research data; resistance drop; resolver differential; reverse direction; root directory

RD/CHK	read/check
R&D	research *and* development
RDA	remote data access
RDB	receive data buffer; relational data base
RDBMS	relational data base management system
RDC	remote data connection
RDCLK	received clock
RDD	read deleted data
RDF	recursive digital filter; resource description framework
RDL	resource description language
RDP	reliable datagram protocol; remote desktop protocol
RDR	reader; receive data register; recover data register; remote data recover
RDRAM	Rambus dynamic random access memory (R-DRAM)
RDSR	receiver data service request
RDT	rebuilding desk-top; remote data transmitter
RDTO	receive data transfer offset
RDX	realistic display mixer
RE	real; regarding; remote enable; reverse engine; rounding error
Re	rhenium
REC	receive(r); record(er); recreation; rectifier; re-transmit error checking
RECT	rectifier

REF	reference
REG	register; registration; registry; regular
REGAL	rigid epoxy glass acrylic laminate
REJ	reject
REL	relating; relation; relative; relay
REM	remark; remission; remote; remote electronic mail; reminder; ring error monitor
REN	rename
REP	repeat(er); repetition; reply; report; represent; representation; representative
REQ	request; requirement
RES	remote execution service; rescue; reserve; reset; residue; resolution; resolver; resonance; resonant; resonator; resource; respond; response; restore
RESISTORS	Radically Emphatic Students Interested in Science, Technology, and Other Research Studies
RESOL	resolution; resolver
RET	resolution enhancement technology; retire; retrieve; retry; return; rural exchange trunk
REV	review; revise; revision; revolution
REX	remote execution
REXX	restructured extended executor
RF	radio frequency; radius ferrule; random failure; record format; recovery factor; relative file; relative frequency; reservation field; resident font; resource fork; ripple factor; ripple filter; runt frame
Rf	Rutherfordium

RFA	radio frequency amplifier
RFC	request for comment(s)
RFD	relative frequency drift; request for discussion
RFFB	recovery from fall-back
RFI	radio frequency interface; request for information
RFIC	radio frequency integrated circuit
RFID	radio frequency identification
RFM	radio frequency modem
RFP	register file pointer; request for proposal
RFQ	request for quotation
RFS	radio frequency switch; remote file sharing (*or* system); resource fork size
RFT	rich text format
RFU	reserved for future use
RFW	reflected forward wave
RFZT	return from zero time
RG	receiver gate; receiver gating; record gap; reflection gain; report generator; restorer generator; reverse gate
RGB	red-green-blue
RGC	reverse gate current
RGM	re-generative memory
RGS	release guard signal
RGSV	reverse gate source voltage
RGT	rate grown transistor; resonance gate transistor

RH	recording head; relative humidity; route hop
Rh	rhodium
RHR	receiver holding register
RHT	right
RI	raster image; reduced instruction; reference input; reflected impedance; refractive index; relay input; reliability index; request initialization; reverse image; reverse interrupt; ring indicator; ring interface; roll-in; routing information
RIAA	Recording Industry Association of America
RIB	ring indicator box
RID	refractive index difference
RIFF	resource interchange file format
RIM	relay input module; remote installation and maintenance; request initialization mode
RIME	relay-net international message exchange
RIP	raster image processing (*or* processor); ripple; remote imaging protocol; routing information protocol
RIPS	raster image processing system
RIS	reference input signal
RISC	reduced instruction set computer
RIT	raw input thread
RIU	ring interface unit
RJ	random jitter; right justify; remote job
RJE	remote job entry
RJEP	remote job entry protocol

RK	resistance of *kathodos* (*kathodos* →*Greek:* cathode) (*cathode resistance*)
RL	RAID level; random logic; record length; record locking; reference listing; reflection loss; register lower; relay; relay logic; re-load; resistance ladder; resistance lamp; resistance, load-inductance; result list; rotational latency
RLD	random logic device; received line detect; relocation dictionary
RLE	run length encoding (*or* encoded)
RLF	resistance of low frequency
RLL	run length limited
RLLC	run length limited code
RLM	re-circulating loop memory
RLN	remote LAN node
RLSD	received line signal detected
RLSI	ridiculously large scale integration
RLY	relay
RM	random memory; reactance modulator; reactive mode; real mode; receive mode; reference mirror; reference model; regenerative memory; register manipulation; relative magnitude; remote; reserved memory; reset mode; resident module; resistance material
R_m	resistance meter
RMA	reserve memory access; resident macro-assembler; return material (*or* merchandise) authorization
RMC	read multiple command

RMDIR   remove directory

RMF   rich music format

RMI   remote messaging interface; remote method invocation

RMM   read mostly memory

RMON   remote monitor(ing)

RMP   remote maintenance processor

RMS   reliable message stream; remote multiplexing system

rms   root mean square

RMW   read-modify-write

RN   radix notation; random noise; random number; read news; real number; reference noise; registered number; remote network; remote node; routing node

Rn   radon

R_n resistance negative (*negative resistance*)

RND   round

RNG   random noise (*or* number) generator

RNP   regional network provider

RNR   receive(r) not ready

RNW   remote network

RO   read only; read-out; relational operator; ring oscillator; roll out

R/O   receive only

R_o resistance of output (*output resistance*)

ROB   re-order buffer; robot(ics)

ROD	read-out device
ROI	return on investment
ROL	roller; rotate left
ROLAP	relational on-line analytical processing
ROLC	rotate left with carry
ROM	read only memory; relay output module
ROMON	receive only monitor
ROOM	real-time object-oriented modelling
ROP	raster operation; RISC operation
ROR	rotate right
RORC	rotate right with carry
ROS	read only storage
ROSCOE	remote operating system conversational online environment
ROT	rear output tray; rotate; rotation; rotator; rotor; running object table
R$_{out}$	resistance of output *(output resistance)*
RP	radix point; random pick; random pulse; recovery program; reference pilot; reference point; relative path; reset pulse; reversible process; ring purge
RPC	remote procedure call
RPG	report program generator; restorer pulse generator
RPL	relocatable program loader; requested privilege level; resident programming language
RPN	real page number; reverse Polish notation

RP-PROM	**RPPROM**; re-programmable programmable read only memory
RPQ	request for price quotation
RPR	relative performance rating
RPS	request reply service
RPT	reference program table; round-trip propagation time
RQBE	relational query by example
RQSCS	read queue server current status
RR	receive ready; receiver register; reference record; refresh rate; residual resistance
RRA	removable random access
RRM	revoke rights mask
RRP	random replacement policy; resource reservation protocol
RR-ROM	**RRROM**; remote reset read only memory
RRT	random read test; reverse recovery time
RRTC	remote real time control
RS	raster scan; rating system; read sector; received signal; recommended standard; record separator; recording signal; reference search; reference station; reference surface; regeneration signal; relay switch; remote socket; remote station; request to send; reset; reset-set; resource set; reverse scan(ning); right shift; root segment; run switch
RSA	Ronald Rivest, Adi Shamir, Leonard Adleman
RSAA	Rivest-Shamir-Adleman algorithm
RSAC	Recreational Software Advisory Council

RSB	read sector buffer
RSC	relay switching circuit
RSCS	remote spooling communications system
RSD	reference surface diameter; remote serial driver; repeated subtraction division
RSDB	remote serial driver board
RSET	Reset
RSH	remote shell
R_{sh}	resistance of shunt (*shunt resistance*)
RSI	repetitive strain (*or* stress) injury
RSIB	resistance sensor input board
RSL	request-status link
RSN	requested socket number
RSPX	remote sequenced packet exchange
RST	reset; restart; restart time
RSTS	resource sharing time sharing
RSV	reserve
RSVD	reserved
RSVN	reservation
RSVP	reserved protocol
R.S.V.P.	RSVP; *répondez s'il vous plaît* (*French:* please reply)
RSW	ready status word
RSX	realistic sound experience

RT   real time; record type; recovery time; reel tape; reference time; relay tree; reliability test(ing); reluctive transducer; remote terminal; research and technology; reservation table; reserved time; response time; response type; restart time; return; ring topology; RISC technology; rise-time; route-time; run-time

R/T   receive-transmit

RTAM   remote telecommunication (*or* terminal) access method

RTB   return to bias

RTC   real (*or* relative) time clock; received timing clock

RTCC   receiver-transmitter communication controller

RTCD   real time clock diagnostic

RTD   rebuilding the desktop; resistance temperature detector

RTDM   real time data migration

RTE   real time execution; run time error

RTF   radio-telephone (*where F→ ph*); rich text file (*or* format)

RTFM   read the friendly manual

RTG   real time guard

RTI   real time interface (*or* interrupt)

RTIS   real time information system

RTL   register transfer language (*or* level); resistor-transistor logic; right to left; run-time library

RTM   real time mode; real (*or* response) time monitor; register transfer module; run time manager

RTMP	routing table maintenance protocol
RTO	real time operation; receive time out; red tape operation
RTOS	real time operating system
RTP	rapid transport protocol; real time protocol
RTPT	round-trip propagation time
RTR	real time routine
RTRI	real time remote inquiry
RTS	real time sampling; request to send; run time state
RTSP	real time streaming protocol
RTT	real time trace; real time trigonometry
RTTF	real time trigonometric function
RTTFG	real time trigonometric function generation
RTTI	run time type information
RTTY	radio tele-typewriter
RTU	remote terminal unit
RTV	real time video
RTX	run time extension
RU	register upper
Ru	ruthenium
RV	random variable; reference voltage; reverse video
RVA	relative virtual address
RVI	reverse interrupt
RVS	read verify sector

RW	random walk; re-writable; read wire; read-write; receiving window; response window
R/W	read-write; red/white; rewind; re-writable
RWC	read-write counter
RWH	read-write head
RWI	read-write initialization (*or* initialize)
RWITM	read with intent to modify
RWL	reference white level
RWM	read-write memory
RWMM	read-write memory module
RX	receive-*transmission* (*where X→ transmision*)
RXD	receive-*transmission* data (*where X→ transmision*
RY	relay
R/Y	red/yellow
RZ	reset to zero; return to Zero

~S~

S sale; sample; save; scalar; scale; second; secure; search; send; sensor; series; session; set; shape; shunt; siemens; sign; signal; single; sink; slave; slim; slow; snail; sort(er); source; space; spacing; spare; spark; spike; spool; square; stack; star; stock; storage; store; sulfur; sum; system

SA search algorithm; search attribute; selective availability; sequential access; sequential alarm; serial adder; server address; signature analysis; simultaneous access; slice architecture; smart actuator; source address; spark absorber; special address; spectrum analysis; stack architecture; storage allocation; storage area; sub-address; subroutine address; subtracter-adder; surface area; symbolic addressing; symbolic assembler; synchronous allocation; system analysis; system analyst; system area; system attribute

SAA systems application architecture

SABM set asynchronous balanced mode

SABME set asynchronous balanced mode extended

SAC single attachment concentrator; store and clear

SACI successive approximation conversion interface

SAD sequential access device

SADL synchronous data link control

SAF store and forward

SAIDI system average interruption duration index

SAINT symbolic automatic integrator

SAL   secured access line; shift arithmetic left; system access limitation

SAM   sample; sampling; sequential (*or* serial) access memory; single application mode; status activity monitor; surface to air missile

SAME   specific area message encoding; studio appearance management environment

SAMI   synchronized accessible media interchange

SAN   system area network

SAP   sapphire; second audio program; security and privacy; service access (*or* address) point; service address (*or* advertising) protocol; stand alone program; symbolic assembly program

SAPI   service access point identifier; speech application program interface

SAR   search and replace; segmentation and re-assembly; set asynchronous response; shift arithmetic right; successive approximation register; synthetic aperture radar; system address register

SARM   set asynchronous response mode

SARME   set asynchronous response mode extended

SAS   sequential (*or* serial) access storage; single attached station; single audio system; stand alone system; statistical analysis system; successive approximation system; symbolic assembly system

SASI   Shugert Associates system interface

SAT   saturate(d); saturation; Saturday; security administrator tool

SATAN   security administrator tool for analyzing network

SATD	saturated
SAW	surface acoustic wave
SAWFC	stop and wait flow control
SAWS	surface acoustic wave sensor
SAV	save(d)
SAVDM	single application virtual DOS machine
SB	sample block; save buffer; Schottky barrier; shunt box; side band; sign bit; simple buffering; skip bus; soft boot; soft break; sound blaster; sound board; stand-by; start bit; starting block; status bit; stop bit; super band; surface barrier; switch box; switching blank; system board; system bus
Sb	Stibium *(antimony)*
sb	stilb *((candela per square meter (metre)))*
SBA	scene balance algorithm; Small Business Administration; stand-by application
SBC	sensor based computer; single board computer; single byte character; small business computer; stacked bar chart
SBCS	single byte character set
SBD	Schottky bipolar decoder
SBE	symmetry breaking effect
SBI	sound blaster instrument
SBL	Schottky bipolar latch
SBLAC	Schottky bipolar look ahead carry
SBLAN	server based local area network

S John S. DeSousa, B.S.E.E., M.S.E.E.

SBLP	switch-board loop panel
SBM	Schottky bipolar memory (*or* microcomputer); search bit map; stand-by mode
SBMP	stand-by monitor present
SBO	single bus orientation
SBP	Schottky bi-polar; set break point
SBPD	Schottky bi-polar decoder
SBPL	Schottky bi-polar latch
SBPS	stand-by power system
SBR	stand-by register; switch bounce routine
SB-RAM	SBRAM; Schottky bipolar random access memory
SBS	side-band signal; smart battery specification (*or* system); step by step; synchronous bus system
SBS-RAM	SBSRAM; synchronous burst static random access memory
SBT	stand-by time; system board test
SBUV	sun-burning ultra-violet
SC	satellite computer; saturated color; saturated current; scan converter; scanner; script; secondary channel; select command; selected configuration; selection check; selector channel; selector circuit; semiconductor; semiconductor contact; sensor scan(ning); sequence checking; sequential circuit; sequential computer; sequential control; shift control; short circuit; show-case; side carrier; side circuit; signal conditioning; signal constellation; signal converter; simplex circuit; simultaneous computer; skeletal coding; smart card; smooth contact; soft copy; solid conductor; sort command; sound card; source code;

space character; special character; special code; specific conductivity; spelling check(er); splice closure; stack control; standard code; standard component; standard converter; star configuration; static charge; statistical concentrator; step counter; storage capacity; storage cell; storage cycle; sub-command; sub-schema; sub-script; subsequent counter; substitute character; sum check(ing); super computer; super conductivity; sweep circuit; Swiss cheese; switching circuit; symbolic code; symbolic concordance; synchronous capacitor; synchronous communication; synchronous computer; syntax checker; system check(ing)

Sc	scandium
SCA	single connector attachment; software cross assembler; solar cell array; supervisory control action
SCADA	supervisory control and data acquisition
SCAM	SCSI configuration automatically
SCB	sub-system control block; system configuration block
SCBD	system controller and bus driver
SCC	self-correcting code; serial communication channel (*or* controller); serial controller chip; shielded control cable; signal conditioning component; single card connector; snoopy cache controller; super computer center; synchronous channel check(ing)
SCCS	source code control system
SCD	standard color display
S-CDMA	SCDMA; synchronous code division multiple access
SCE	single cycle execution; system command executive
SCEMP	simple (*or* small) cost effective micro-processor

SCF	system control facility
SCFF	sign control flip-flop
SCH	schedule; schematic; scheme; school
SCI	scalable coherent interface; science; scientific; serial (*or* synchronous) communication interface; short circuit impedance; source code instruction; subroutine call instruction
SCID	source connection identification (*or* identifier)
SCJD	Sun Certified Java Developer
SCK	serial cable kit
SCL	stroke center line
SCLM	software configuration and library management
SCM	server client model; single chip microcomputer; software configuration management; static column mode; system check module
S-CMOS	**SCMOS**; static complementary metal oxide semiconductor
SCOPE	simple communication programming environment
SCP	server control procedure; session control protocol; shaped card potentiometer; short circuit parameter; system control program
SCPC	single channel per carrier
SCR	screen; script; sector count register; sequence control register; silicon-controlled rectifier; sustainable cell rate
SCRC	side circuit repeating coil
SCRN	screen

SCRS	scalable cluster of RISC system
SCRT	symbol cross reference table
SCS	single channel system; subtractive color system; synchronous channel splitter
SCSA	signal computing system architecture
SCSI	small computer system interface
SCT	Schottky clamped transistor; semi-conductor trap; storage cycle time; subroutine call table; system configuration test
SCW	solder covered wire
SD	sample delay; sampled data; Schottky diode; select data; selective dump; semiconductor diode; semiconductor doping; send data; serial data; sign digit; signal distance; silicon diode; single data; single document; slow death; sorted directory; source data; space distortion; space diversity; standard definition; standard deviation; standard dictionary; startup disk; starting delimiter; static dissipation; static dump; station doubler; step down; storage device; straight decision; streaming data; structured design; sub-directory; sudden death; super density; switching device; switching diode; symbolic debugging; synchronous data; synchronous detection; synchronous dynamic; system design; system diagnostics; system disk; system drive; systematic drift
S/D	signal-distortion; synchronization to digital
SDA	software disk array; source data automation; step down amplifier; storage data acceleration; system design aid; system display architecture
SDAM	single DOS application mode
SDB	symbolic debugger; system data bus

SDC   serial data controller; signal-distortion converter; step-down counter

SDCR   segment descriptor cache register

SDCT   star daisy chain topology

SDCU   secondary DMA channels used

SDCUIF   secondary DMA channels used in flag

SDD   software description data-base

SDDS   Sony dynamic digital sound

SDF   space delimited file (*or* format); standard data format

SDG   synchronous differential generator

SDH   synchronous digital hierarchy

SDI   single document interface; software development interface

SDK   software development kit

SDL   serial (*or* synchronous) data link; sonic delay line; specification and description language

SDLC   serial (*or* synchronous) data link control

SDM   standard dialogue manager; system development multi-tasking

SDMS   SCSI device management system

SDN   software defined network; sub-directory name

SDNS   secured data network service

SDO   source data operation

SDP   streaming data procedure; system development project

SDR	streaming data request
SDRAM	**SD-RAM;** synchronous dynamic random access memory
SDROM	**SD-ROM;** super density read only memory
SDS	space division switching; specific dielectric strength
SDSL	single-line digital subscriber line; symmetric digital subscriber line
SDT	segment descriptor table; serial data transfer; standard display tube; synchronous data transmission
SDTV	satellite distributed television; standard definition television
SDU	serial data unit; service data unit; simulator debug utility; static dissipating unit
SDV	switched digital video
SDX	storage data *acceleration (where X→ accleration)*
SE	search engine; semantic error; sensing element; serial extension; single element; skin effect; soft error; software engineering; software evaluation; source editor; static eliminator; static error; statistical error; storage element; stroke edge; syntactic error; system engineering
Se	selenium
SEA	standard extended attribute
sea	self extracting archive *(extension)*
SEAC	standards eastern automatic calculator *(or* computer)
SEAL	screening external access link

SEC	second; secondary; section; secure; single error correcting; single error correction
SECAM	*sequential couleur avec mémoire* (*French:* Sequential Color With Memory)
SECBR	severely errored cell block rate
SECC	single edge contact cartridge
SECDED	single-error correcting, double-error detecting
SECT	section; sector
SED	stream-oriented editor
SEDM	software evaluation and development module
SEF	single error flag; source explicit forwarding
SEG	segment
SEH	structured exception handling
SEINT	spot effective input noise temperature
SEL	select(ion); syntax error list
SEM	scanning electron microscope; standard electronic module
SEN	spontaneous emission noise
SEP	September
SEPP	secured encryption payment protocol; single-edge processor package
SEPT	September
SER	serial; series; server; service; system error rate
SERCOS	serial communication system
SERV	server; service

SES	spooler enhancement switch
SET	secured electronic transaction; system elapsed time
SETC	set carry
SETEXT	structure enhanced text
SF	scale factor; scanning frequency; selective fading; send failure; sequential file; shift forward; sign flag; signal frequency; sinusoidal field; skip flag; snow flake; soft font; sporadic fault; standard form; step function; storage fragmentation; swap file; system file; system folder
SFA	spring finger action
SFB	semiconductor functional block
SFC	system file checker
SFCMA	still frame compression multimedia adapter
SFCTR	static forward current transfer ratio
SFD	start frame delimiter
SFDR	spurious-free dynamic range
SFE	source file editor
SFF	storage flip-flop
SFK	special function key
SFN	signal frequency noise
SFQL	structured full-text query language
SFS	system file server
SFT	system fault tolerance
SFTE	system fault tolerance error

SFTET system fault tolerance error table

SFTL system fault tolerance level

SFW system firmware

SG sampling gate; second generation; signal gain; signal generator; silica gel; sixth generation; specific gravity; speech generator; static gain; stationary gap; strain gauge; symbol generator; system gain; system gamma

SGA shared global area

SGC second (*or* sixth) generation computer

SG-CMOS SGCMOS; silicon gate complementary metal oxide semiconductor

SGDT stored global descriptor table

SGE secondary grid emission

SGEN signal (*or* system) generator

SGM shaded graphics modelling

SGML standardized general markup language

SGPT strain gauge pressure transducer

SGR set graphics rendition

SG-RAM SGRAM; synchronous graphics random access memory

SGT safe-guard timer

SH sample-hold; sector header; semaphore handle; stream head

S/H sample-hold; shipping and handling

SHA sample-hold amplifier (*or* application); secure hash algorithm

SHAT	sample-hold acquisition (*or* aperture) time
SHAUT	sample-hold aperture uncertainty time
SHB	system hand-book
SHC	sample-hold characteristics (*or* counting)
SHD	sample-hold device
SHDR	sample-hold decay rate
SHED	segmented hyper-graphic editor
SHF	super high frequency
SHFT	sample-hold feed through
SHL	shift left
SHLA	shift left with arithmetic
SHM	short haul modem
SHMH	short haul modem hub
SHR	shift right; split horizon routing
SHRA	shift right with arithmetic
SHS	self-propagating high-temperature synthesis
SHST	sample-hold settling time
SHTML	static hyper-text markup language
S-HTTP	SHTTP; secured hyper-text transfer (*or* transport) protocol
SI	search index; send interval; serial input; serial interface; shift-in; shift instruction; short instruction; short interval; single injector; single instruction; single inter-phasing; software integrity; software interrupt; source impedance; source index; speech interpolation; standard interface; static interface; status information;

step index; synchronous information; synchronous input; system inaccuracy; system information; system input; system integration; system interface; *système international* (*French:* International system)

Si   Silicon

SIA   segmented instruction addressing; Semiconductor Industry Association; subtracter instrumentation amplifier

SIAU   second input-output address used

SIAUL   second input-output address used length

SIB   series interface board

SIC   semiconductor integrated circuit; shift-in character; standard industrial code; synchronous idle character

SICR   synchronous idle character register

SID   security identifier; serial input data; server (*or* system) identification; symbolic interactive debugger

SIDF   system independent data format

SIDL   server identification list

SIDN   server identification number

SIDT   store interrupt descriptor table

SIE   single instruction execute

SIF   step index fibre

SIFS   short information feedback system; short inter-frame scheme

SIFT   Stanford information filtering tool

SIG   sign(al); signature; special interest group

SiGe	silicon germanium
SIL	speech interface level; statistical interpretive language
SILP	single in-line package
SIM	simple(x); simulate; simulated; simulation; simulator
SIMD	single instruction multiple data
SIMM	single inline memory module
SIMTEL	simulation and tele-processing
SIMULA	simulation language
SIN	sine; single; sinus
SINT	sintering
SINU	second interrupt numbers used
SINUIUF	second interrupt numbers used in use flag
S/IO	SIO; serial (*or* simultaneous *or* strobed) input-output
SIOAU	second input-output address used
SIOAUL	second input-output address used length
SIOBI	simultaneous input-output bus interface
SIOM	stored input-output method
SIP	single inline package; single inter-phasing
SIPC	simply interactive personal computer
SIPO	serial-in parallel-out
SIPP	simple Internet protocol plus; single inline pin package
SIR	serial infra-red; static input resistance
SIRDS	single image random dot stereogram

SISD	single instruction single data
SISO	serial-in, serial-out; shift-in, shift-out
sit	StuffIt *(extension)*
SIU	slot in use; system interface unit
SJ	semiconductor junction; shorted junction; stacked job; summing junction
SJD	shorted junction device
SJP	stacked job processing
SK	side kick; soft key; sort key; storage key
SKP	**skip**
SKT	socket
SKU	stock keeping unit number
SL	scanning line; scatter load; scattering loss; second level; sequential logic; servo-link; session layer; shared logic; shunt lead; signal level; silicon link; simulation language; sine law; single line; slave; sleeve; slim; slip; slope; slope line; slot; slug; software library; sound level; source language; source level; source library; square loop; status line; straight line; string length; subscriber loop; surface leakage; symbolic language; symbolic logic; synthetic language; system loader; system log
SLA	second level addressing; slice look ahead
SLAC	Standard Linear Accelerator Center
SLAM	single layer metalization
SLBB	solder-less bread-board

SLC	solder-less connector; straight line coding; subscriber line concentrator
SLD	source level debugging
SLDO	super low drop out
SL-DRAM	SLDRAM; synchronous link dynamic random access memory
SLDT	store local descriptor table
SLED	single large expensive disk; surface-emitting light emitting diode
SLF	single loop fibre; socket longevity flag
SLI	subroutine linkage instruction
SLIC	system level integrated circuit
SLIP	serial (*or* service) line Internet protocol; serial (*or* service) line Internet provider; spatial light modulator
SLL	single-line laser
SLM	semiconductor LSI memory; shared library manager; single-longitudinal mode; single loop memory; slice latch mask; Starlan local module; straight line microprogram
SLMR	silly little mail reader
SLP	second level protocol; single (*or* station) line protector; sleep; slip; slop
SL-PROM	SLPROM; silicon link programmable read only memory
SLR	storage limit register
SLSI	super large scale integration
SLSS	system library subscription service

SLT   slate; solid logic technology; source language translation; surface life time

SLW   slow; solder-less wrap

SM   scattering matrix; scheduled maintenance; search mode; secondary memory; security mailer; semiconducting material; serial mouse; servo-mechanism; servo-motor; servo-multiplier; shared memory; sign magnitude; single mode; slave mode; sleep mode; slice memory; small; source module; special mask; speech manager; stack manipulation; standard mode; standby mode; static memory; status message; stepper motor; storage medium, storage module; string manipulation; sub-miniaturization; sub-modular; sub-module; supervisor mode; surface mount; switch matrix; switching module; system management; synchronous machine

Sm   samarium

SMA   shape-memory allow

s-mail   S-mail; S-MAIL; S-Mail; s-Mail; snail mail

SMART   self-monitoring, analysis and reporting technology

SMB   server message block; speed matching buffer; system management bus

SMBP   sign magnitude bi-polar

SMC   serial modem cable; servo-motor controller; set multiple command; silver mica capacitor; static magnetic cell; static memory card; surface mount connector; synchronous mode computer

SMCS   simultaneous multi-channel system

SMD   storage module device (*or* drive); surface mount design (*or* device)

SMDS   switched **m**egabit **d**ata (*or* **d**igital) **s**ervice; switched multi-megabit data (*or* digital) service

SMDR   station message detail recording

SME   synchronous modem eliminator

SMF   single mode fibre (fiber)

SMI   static memory interface; structure of management information; system management information (*or* interrupt)

smi   self-mounting image *(extension)*

SMIF   standard mechanical interface

SMIL   synchronized multimedia integration language

S/MIME   **S-MIME**; **SMIME**; secured multimedia (*or* multipurpose) Internet mail extension

SMIT   system management interface tool

SML   single mode laser; **small**; standard meta language; surface mount leg

SMLD   single-mode laser diode

SMM   special mask mode; specific magnetic moment; system management mode

SMM-RAM   **SMMRAM**; system management mode random access memory

SMO   surface mount oscillator

SMOLTS   single-mode optical loss test set

SMOS   static metal oxide semiconductor

SMOS-RAM   **SMOSRAM**; static metal oxide semiconductor random access memory

SMP   sample; sampler; simple management protocol; single and multiple passes; standby monitor present; surface mount package; symbolic manipulation program; symmetric multi-processing; symmetric multi-processor

SMPC   shared memory parallel computer

SMPS   switching mode power supply

SMPX   statistical multiplexing; system mutiplexer

SMR   sign magnitude representation; smear; specialized mobile radio

SM-RAM   SMRAM; system management random access memory

SMS   serial memory system; small messaging system; standard micro-system; static magnetic storage; storage management service (*or* system); system management server

SMT   specialized mobile radio; surface mount transistor (*or* technology *or* transformer)

SMTP   simple (*or* small) mail transfer protocol

SMU   system management utility

SMUX   statistical multiplexer

SN   saturated noise; saturation noise; segment number; sequence number; server name; short noise; sky noise; socket number; source node; static noise; stochastic noise; stock number; sub-net; swish noise; switching node; symbolic name; system noise; systematic noise

S/N   SN; serial number; signal to noise

Sn   Stannum

SNA   snuffer network analyzer; system network architecture

SNAP	sub-network access protocol
SND	serial number display; sound
SNET	source network
SNEWS	secured news server
SNMP	simple network management protocol
SNOBOL	string oriented symbolic language
SNP	silicon nitride passivation
SNR	signal to noise ratio
SNRM	set normal response mode
SNRME	set normal response mode extended
SNW	stub network
SO	sampling oscilloscope; service organization; shift out; spin out; spurious oscillation; stable oscillation; storage oscilloscope; stream oriented; sweep oscillator; synchronous operation; synchronous output
S/O	SO; send only; shop order
SOA	spatial operator algebra; start of authority; state of art
SOB	synchronization on blue
SOC	shift out character; social; society; system on a chip
SOD	slope overhead distortion
SODA	Shift-key, Option-key, Delete-key, Apple-command-key
SO-DIMM	SODIMM; small outline dual in-line memory module
SOE	standard operating environment

SOF	stack over-flow
SOG	synchronization on green
SOH	start of header (*or* heading)
SOHD	slope over-head distortion
SOHO	small office, home office
SOI	silicon on insulator
SOIC	small outline integrated circuit
SOIT	silicon on insulator technology
SOL	simulation oriented language; solenoid; solution; solvant; supervisor over-lay
SOJ	small outline J-lead
SOM	self-organizing machine; start of machine (*or* message); system object model (*or* module)
SON	server order number
SONC	standing on nines carry
SONET	synchronous optical network
SOP	small outline package; standard operating procedure; sum-of-products
SOR	synchronization on red
SOS	silicon on sapphire; sophisticated (*or* supervisor) operating system; standards open system
SOS-RAM	SOSRAM; silicon on sapphire random access memory
SOST	silicon on sapphire transistor
SOTA	state of the art

SOX   sound exchange

SP   sampling period; Schottky process; search path; search procedure; self-powered; send packet; serial port; serial printer; serial processing; serial programming; serial-parallel; server printer; service pack; service point; set point; shift pulse; sign position; sine potentiometer; single pass; single pole; single power; single precision; single probe; single processor; software package; solder pad; source program; space(r); speaker; spike; spindle; spool(er); spray paint; stack pointer; star program; static pad; static protection; station protector; statistical package; stochastic process; storage protection; stored program; string pitch; strobe pulse; structured programming; sub-program; summing point; suppressed packet; surface protector; surge protector; symbolic parameter; synchronized pulse; synchronizing pilot; system product; system programming

SPA   serial port arbitrator; Software Publishers Association

SPADE   single-channel-per-carrier, pulse-code-modulation, multiple-access, demand-assignment-equipment

SPAP   serial port arbitrator program

SPARC   scalable processor architecture

SPB   sectors per block; smart printer buffer

SPBI   special purpose bus interface

SPC   sequential power controller; serial-parallel circuit (*or* converter); serial port connection (*or* connector); silver plated copper; single phase clock; small peripheral controller; special purpose computer; statistical process control; stored program computer

SPD   series-parallel design

SPDIP   shrink plastic in-line package

SPDT   single-pole double-throw

SPE   synchronous payload envelope

SPEC   specification; spectrometer; spectrum; system performance and evaluation cooperative

SPEEDES   synchronous parallel environment for emulation and discrete event simulation

SPG   selectable PCM generator

SPGA   staggered pin grid array

SPHTS   self-propagating high-temperature synthesis

SPI   SCSI parallel interface; security parameters index; service provider interface; software priority interrupt

SPICE   simulation program with integrated circuit emphasis

SPID   service profile identification (*or* identifier)

SPIRES   Stanford public information retrieval system

SPL   spelling; structured (*or* system) programming language

SPLD   simple programmable logic device

SPLE   synchronous pay-load envelope

SPM   self-phase modulation; self-pulse modulation; sine potentio-meter; slanted package mounting; smart power management; special purpose machine; spurious pulse mode; system performance management (*or* monitor)

SPN   series-parallel network

SPOBC   shuttle portable on-board computer

SPOC	shuttle portable on-board computer
SPOOL	simultaneous peripheral operations on line
SPOT	shared product object tree
SPP	sequenced packet protocol; standard parallel port; super scalar (*or* pipelined) processor; synchronous preprocessor
SPPS	scalable power parallel system
SPR	serial-parallel register; single pulse repetition; special purpose register; statistical pattern recognition
SPREAD	system programming, research, engineering and development
SPS	serial printer switch; series-parallel-series; standby power system; switching power supply
SPSS	statistical package for social sciences
SPST	single-pole single-throw
SPT	sectors per track; serial printer
SPX	sequenced packet exchange
SPXIF	sequenced packet exchange installation flag
SPXMAV	sequenced packet exchange major version
SPXMIV	sequenced packet exchange minor version
SPXMRN	sequenced packet exchange major revision number
SPXPH	sequenced packet exchange packet header
SPXWD	sequenced packet exchange watch dog
SQ	scalar quantity; service quality; software quality; square; single quality
SQA	software quality assurance

SQE	single quality error
SQEHB	single quality error heart-beat
SQFP	small (*or* surface-mounted) quad flat package
SQL	structured query language; square loop
SQP	square pixel
SQR	square; square root; squareness ratio
SQRT	square root
SQW	square wave
SR	sampling rate; scanning rate; screen resolution; segment register; selenium rectifier; sensitive relay; sensitivity ratio; sequence register; series register; service request; service routine; shift register; silicon rectifier; silicon resistor; single ramp; single root; single route; slew rate; slotted ring; soft return; specific resistance; specific routine; stack register; standard refraction; step response; sticking relay; stripe recording; sub-routine; summary report; surface resistivity; swamping resistor; switch register; synchronous receiver; synchronous register
S/R	**SR**; send-receive(r); serial
Sr	Strontium
sr	Steradian
SRA	stack register addressing; sub-routine address
SRADC	single ramp analog-to-digital converter
SRAM	shadow (*or* static) random access memory
SRAPI	speech recognition application program interface
SRB	SCSI request block; source routing bridge

SRC	sample rate converter; shell request count; source
SRCI	sub-routine call instruction
SRCT	sub-routine call table
SRD	screen reader system
SR-DRAM	**SRDRAM**; self-refreshed dynamic random access memory
SREJ	selective reject
SRGB	sustained red-green-blue
SRIP	segment registers instruction pointer
SRL	sub-routine library (*or* linkage)
SRLI	sub-routine linkage instruction
SRM	security reference monitor
SRO	sequence read-out
SRP	script; self-relocating program; suggested retail price
SRPI	server-requester programming interface
SRQ	service request
SRS	sound retrieval system; stop-reset switch
SRT	speech recognition technology
SRTCS	serial real time communication system
SRV	server; service
SRWM	static read-write memory
SS	scale spun; second source; secondary storage; segment size; seizing signal; sequential sampling; serial storage; server station; server stub; set symbol; seven segment; shared storage; Shaffer stroke; short stack;

signalling system; silicon steel; single side; single stream; single strength; single switch; slide show; software simulator; solder short; solder sucker; solid state; sound synthesizer; sound system; source socket; source statement; source system; split screen; spread spectrum; spread-sheet; stable state; stack segment; static storage; static subroutine; steady state; stochastic simulation; sub-system; summary sheet; supervising system; support system; surge strip; switched system; symbolic set; symbolic string; synchronous speed; system simulation

SSA   serial storage architecture

SSAB   solid state accessory board

SSAP   source service access point

SSB   single shared bus; single side-band

SSB-AMSC   single side-band amplitude modulation suppressed carrier

SSC   silicon solar cell; single stream control; small signal current; solid state component; synchronous sequential circuit

SSCG   small signal current gain

SSCOP   service specific connection oriented protocol

SSCP   source (*or* system) service control point

SSD   seven segment display; single-sided disk; single step debugging; snap-shot debugging (*or* dump); soft-sectored disk; solid state disk; steady state deviation; synchronous serial data

SSDA   synchronous serial data adapter

SSEC   selective sequence electronic calculator

SSF	segment selector file; solicit successor frame
SSG	Shaffer stroke gate
SSGA	system suppport gate array
SSGE	semiconductor strain gauge element
SSHC	simultaneous sample-hold converter
SSI	scan string instruction; single system image; small scale integration
SSIC	solid state integrated circuit
SSL	secured-sockets layer
SSM	single stage model; single step mode; solid state memory; solid surface model
SSMA	second-shared memory address; spread spectrum multiple access
SSMAL	second-shared memory address length
SSN	system segment number
SSO	single step operation; steady state oscillation; system security officer
SSOP	shrink small outline package
SSP	solid state physics; system support program
SSPEC	system specification
SSPI	security service provider interface
SSPG	small signal power gain
SSR	software stack register; solid state relay; standard sub-routine; star shaped ring; static sub-routine
SSRP	simple server redundancy protocol

SSS	server session socket; snapshot storage scope
SST	salt spray test; spread spectrum technology; systems services technology
SS-TDMA	SSTDMA; satellite switched time division multiple access
SSTP	solder socket type pin
SSV	source-substrate voltage
SSW	step switch; system software
ST	satellite transmission; Schmitt trigger; seek time; semiconductor trap; sequence timer; serial transfer; serial transmission; server type; service technician; service type; set theory; set time; short term; signal tracing; signal transducer; silicon transistor; simple text; simplex transmission; skeleton table; skip test; slaved tracking; slot time; smart terminal; software tool; splice tray; spool time; stable trigger; stack; standard; star; star topology; start; state; static; station; stationary; stock trader; storage; storage tube; straight; strobe; stroke; stub testing; student; sub-task; switching time; symmetrical transistor; synchronous timing; synchronous transmission; syntax transducer; system test(er); system timing
ST³	STTT; sight to touch translator
St	stokes *((meter(metre) squared per second))*
st	stere *((cubic meter(metre)))*
STA	spanning tree algorithm
STAIRS	storage and information retrieval system
STALO	stable local oscillator
STAR	self-defining text archival

344

STAT	statement; statistics
STB	simply the best; spanning tree bridge; strobe
STC	sampling thermo-couple; scrambled television channel; signal tuned circuit
STCB	single throw circuit-breaker
STD	space time diagram; stand; standard; student
STDA	street-talk directory assistance
STDAUX	standard auxillary
STDBY	standby
STDERR	standard error
STDIN	standard input
STDM	statistical time division multiplexer (or multiplexing); synchronous time division multiplexer (or multiplexing)
STDOUT	standard output
STDPRN	standard printer
STDR	signal to distortion ratio; standard route
STE	segment table entry; special test equipment
STEP	standard for exchange of product
STG	saw-tooth generator
STIL	statistical interpretive language
STK	stack
STL	standard template library; synchronous transistor logic
STM	station manager

STMV	start top multi-vibrator
STN	server (*or* service) task number
STP	secured transfer protocol; shielded twisted pair; signal transfer point; standard temperature and pressure; synchronized transaction processing
STR	store task register; synchronous transmitter-receiver
STRESS	structural engineering system solver
STRUDL	structural design language
STS	software test set; static transfer switch; synchronous transport signal
STScI	Space Telescope Science Institute
STT	secured transaction technology; self-test technique
STTL	Schottky transistor-transistor logic
STTT	ST^3; sight to touch translator
STUF	stowage tactics for user flight
STW	saw-tooth wave
STX	start of text
STY	style
SU	set-up; source utility; start-up; statistical universe; step-up; symbolic unit; system unit
SUB	subject; subroutine; substitute; substitution; subtracter, subtraction
SUBB	subtraction borrow
SUD	set-up diagram; start-up disk
SUF	stack under flow

SUM	setup utility menu
SUN	**Sun**day
SUP	server utilization percentage; supervisor; supplement
SUPS	standby un-interruptible power supply
SUSA	stored up-stream address
SUT	set-up time; start-up time; step-up transformer
SUV	sun-burning ultra-violet
SV	segment value; semaphore value; sentinel value; single value; single variable; sophisticated vocabulary; statistics version; still video; storage volatility; string variable; sub-vector; super video; super voltage; supply voltage; surge voltage; symbolic variable; system value; system view
Sv	Sievert
SVC	service; switched virtual circuit (*or* connection)
SVD	simultaneous voice-data; starter voltage drop
SVF	simple vector format; still video format
SVGA	super video graphics adapter (*or* array) *(800x600 resolution)*
S-VHS	super very high speed
SVM	system virtual machine
SVN	string variable name; switched virtual network
SVP	surge voltage protector
SVR	server; shunt voltage regulator; supervisor
SW	sending window; sense wire; share-ware; side-way; sine wave; sinusoidal wave; sliding window; soft-ware;

	status word; stepping switch; storage switch; stroke weight; stroke width; switch
S/W	software
SWAC	standards western automatic calculator (*or* computer)
SWAIS	simple wide area information server
SWAP	shared wireless access protocol
SWARQ	stop and wait automatic-repeat request
SWC	sine wave carrier
SWCA	software cross assembler
SWF	serial work flow; sliding window flow
SWFC	sliding window flow control
SWH	software house
SWI	single word instruction; software interrupt
SWII	software interrupt instruction
SWISH	simple web indexing system for humans
SWL	software library
SWP	simple web printing; sliding window protocol; software package; square wave pulse; swap; sweep
SWR	standing wave ratio; status word register
SWS	silly window syndrome; software simulator
SWT	software tool; structured walk through
SWTE	Society of Wireless Telegraph Engineers
SX	single *speed*
SXGA	super extended graphics array *(1280x1024 resolution)*

SYL	syllabus
SYM	symbol; symmetrical; symmetry
SYN	synchronous; syndrome; synonym; syntax
SYNC	synchronization; synchronous
SYS	system
SYSADMIN	system administrator
SYSGEN	system generator
SYSIN	system input
SYSLIB	system library
SYSLOG	system log
SYSMOD	system modification
SYSOP	sysop; system operator
SYSOUT	system output
SYSREQ	system request
SZT	system zero tolerance

~T~

T	*period*; tag; tap; task; teaching; temperature; temporary, tension; tera; term; terminal; termination; terminator; tesla; test; text; ticket; time; toner; top; total; transfer; transient; transistor; trash
t	time; ton
TA	teaching assistant; terminal adapter; terminal area; test access; text area; three address; total access; total area; track access; transfer admittance; transfer algorithm; transient analyzer; transistor action; transistor amplifier; transit angle; trigger action; trustee assignment; tuned amplifier
Ta	Tantalum
TAB	table; tabulate; tabulation; tape automated bonding
TAC	twin axial cable
TACS	total access communications system
TAD	telephone answering device
TAI	*International Atomic Time*
TAN	tangent
TAO	track at once
TAP	telelocator alphanumeric protocol; telephony application program(ming); target application probe; test access port
TAPC	test access port control
TAPI	telephony application programming interface

tar   tape archive *(extension)*

TAS   telephone access server

TASI   time assignment speech interpolation

TASM   turbo assembler

TAT   track access time; turn-around time

TAVC   tri-axial video connector

TAXI   transparent asynchronous *transceiver* interface *(where
                  X→ transceiver)*

TB   Tera-byte; test bench; text book; text box; tight buffer;
                  token bus; tool bar; tool box; total blocks; total burst;
                  track ball

Tb   Terbium

TBA   to be announced

TBBS   the bread-board system

TBG   tone burst generator

TBGA   tape ball grid array

tbk   tool-book *(extension)*

TBM   taut-band meter (metre)

TBN   terminal based network

TBP   three bears problem

TBU   tape backup unit

Tbyte   Tera-byte

TC   tail circuit; tape cable; tape cartridge; tape conversion;
                  temperature compensation; terminal controller; test
                  card; test clock; test control; thermo-couple; thrashing
                  count; time constant; timing clock; timing counts;

tinned copper; toll connection; total cache; total capacitance; total changed; total changes; total counts; touch control; trace command; tracking converter; traffic collision; traffic control; traffic controller; transaction cycle; transceiver cable; transfer check; transfer circuit; transfer command; transfer current; transistor current; transitional coding; transmission control; transmission convergence; transmitter clock; transport control; triggering circuit; trigonometric conversion; trimmer capacitor; true complement; trunk cable; tuned circuit; tuning capacitor; twin check; two's complement

Tc	Technetium
TCAM	tele-communication access method
TCAS	traffic collision avoidance system
TCC	three card connector; time constant chart
TCCC	three card connector cage
TCFATS	total changed file allocation table sectors
TCG	transistor current gain
TCI	test clock input
TCIA	transfer coupled isolation amplifier
TCL	thermo-couple linearization; tool command language
TCM	Treillis-coded modulation
TCO	time charge occurrence; total cost of ownership
TCP	tape carrier package (*or* packaging); tape conversion program; transmission control protocol
TCP/IP	transmission (*or* transport) control protocol—Internet protocol

TCR   two's complement representation

TCS   terminal (*or* traffic) control system; transducer coupling system

TCSE   transducer coupling system efficiency

TCT   toll connecting trunk

TCW   total cache writes; transfer corona wire

TCXO   temperature compensated *crystal* oscillator

TD   tape disk; tape drive; target data; task data; telephone dialer; television distribution; terminal display; test data; text decoder; text delimiter; text description; thermal diffusion; time delay; time discriminator; time division; time domain; tone dialing; top down; total density; total directories; track density; transient distortion; transmit data; triple diffusion; tunnel diode

TDATS   transistor and diode automatic test system

TDC   tabular data control; tape drive controller; throttle duty cycle; time delay circuit; time domain concept

TDD   telecommunications device for the deaf; top down design

TDE   tape and disk eraser; terminal display editor

TDF   trace definition file; typeface definition file

TDFS   target data flow system

TDI   test data input; transport device interface

TDM   technical document management; terminal display mode; time division multiplexing; time domain measurement (*or* model); time duration modulation

TDMA   time division multiple (*or* multiplier) access

TDO	test data output
TDP	tag distribution protocol; tele-locator data protocol; three (*or* two) dimensions process; trap directed polling
TDR	test (*or* transmission) data register; time delay relay; time domain reflectometry; total data read
TDS	task data sheet; time delay (*or* division) switch; total directory slots; total dynamic space; transaction disk space
TDSR	transmitter data service request
TE	terminal emulation; terminal emulator; terminal equipment; termination expression; test engineer(ing); text encoder; thermo-electric; total emission; transmission error; transponder efficiency; truncation error; tunnel effect; type error
Te	Tellurium
TE/2	terminal emulator 2
TEB	thread environment block
TEC	text encoding converter; Tokyo Electronics Corporation
TECH	technical; technician; technique; technology
TED	test engineering diagnostics
TEE	thermo-electric effect
TEI	terminal end-point identifier
TELCO	telephone company
TELECOM	telecommunication
TELNET	telecommunication network

TEML   turbo editor macro language

TEMP   temperature; template; temporary

TER   thermal eclipse reading

TERM   terminal; termination; terminator; terminology

TET   target extension time; tetrode; text enhancement technology

TEXO   temperature-compensated *crystal* oscillator *(where X→ crystal)*

TF   tape format; text file; text format; thick film; thin film; transfer function; transversal filter; trap flag; trapped flux; type-face

TFC   thin film capacitor (*or* circuit)

TFD   thin film disk

TFDD   text file device driver

TFEL   thin film electro-luminescent

T-FET   TFET; tedrode field effect transistor

TFF   transistor flip-flop

TFGC   terminal forward gate current

TFI   true finder integration

TFIC   thin film integrated circuit

TFM   tagged font metric; tamed frequency modulation; thin film memory

TFME   thin film micro-electronics

TFMM   thin film magnetic module

TFO   terminal fan out; total files opened

TFP	thin film processing (*or* processor); turn-key front panel
TFR	thin film resistor
TFSC	transaction file size changes
TFSP	total file service packets
TFT	thin film technician (*or* technique *or* transistor); transaction files truncated; trivial file transfer
TFTP	trivial file transfer protocol
TG	tangent; temperature gradient; third generation; time gate; trap gate
TGA	thermo-gravimetric analysis
TGC	thin generation computer; transmission gate circuit
TGP	thermo-graphic printer
TGS	ticket granting server
TH	thermal heat; transport header; Trojan horse
Th	thorium
THD	third (*or* total) harmonic distortion; thread
THO	tape handling option
THOMAS	The US House of Representatives Open Multimedia Access System
THOR	Tandy high-performance optical recording; tape handling option routine
THR	Thursday; transmitter holding register
THS	thesaurus
THT	token holding time(r)

THU	Thursday
THUR	Thursday
THz	tera-hertz
TI	terminal impedance; terminal interface; test instrument; Texas Instrument; total input; transfer impedance; transmission impairment; trapped instruction
Ti	Titanum
TIA	Telecommunications Industry Association; thanks in advance; the Internet adapter; two input adder
TID	target identification
TIE	time interval error
TIES	time independent escape sequence
TIF	tagged image file
TIFF	tagged image file format
TIGA	Texas Instrument graphics adapter (*or* architecture)
TIGER	topologically integrated geographic encoding and referencing
TIIAP	Telecommunications and Information Infra-structure Assistance Program
TIL	technical information library
TIM	technical information memo (*or* menu)
TIMI	technology independent machine interface
TIMM	thermionic integrated micro-module
TIMS	text information management system
TIN	triangulated irregular network

TINA	telecommunication information networking architecture
TInet	The Institute network
TIP	terminal interface processor; transaction Internet protocol
TIR	ternary incremental representation; total internal reflection
TITOFET	tunneling-in tunneling-out field effect transistor
TJD	text job description
TJT	target job time
TK	test key; toggle key; track; turn-key
TKFP	turn-key front panel
TKS	turn-key system
TL	tape leader; taped line; telephone line; terminal lock; terminated line; test line; tie line; track label; transaction log; transducer loss; transistor logic; transmission line; transmission load; transport layer; trend line; tutorial light
Tl	Thallium
TLAB	translation look-aside buffer
TLB	telephone line bridge; translation look-aside buffer
TLC	telephone line controller; trend line chart; twist lock connector
TLD	terminal locking device; top level domain
TLF	timing library format
TLI	table lookup instruction; transport layer (*or* level) interface

TLLM	transmission line laser modelling
TLM	three layer model; transmission line modelling
TLP	tape load point; trouble location problem
TLS	terminal line sharing; transport level security
TLSI	terminal line sharing interface
TLU	table look-up
TLUI	table look-up instruction
TLX	telex
TM	task management; technical manual; terminal mode; test macro; test manual; test message; test monitor; text mode; thermo-meter; thread manager; time measurement; token management; trade-mark; transfer matrix; transfer mode; transient motion; transmission media; transmission mode; transport mode; trapping mode; tuning machine; tunnel mode
Tm	thulium
TME	telephone manager extension; time
TMF	thermo-mechanical fatigue
TMHC	too many hops count
TML	template
TMP	temporary
TMPX	trans-multiplexer
TMR	thermal microwave radiation
TMS	telemeter service; test (*or* text) mode select
TMUX	trans-multiplexer
TMW	terrestrial micro-wave; time measurement waveform

TN	task number; thermal noise; twisted nematic
TNC	terminal node controller
TNF	transfer non-flow
TNS	thermal noise source
TNV	Terranova network version
TNW	transit network
TNZ	transfer non-zero
TO	time origin; time-out; total output; transient oscillation; transistor oscillator
TOC	table of contents; time-out counts
TOD	time of day
TOE	time of execution
TOFDT	turn-off delay time
TOID	trustee object identification (*or* identifier)
TOL	time-out limit; tolerance
TON	tone(r)
TONC	time of next charge
TONDT	turn-on delay time
TOP	tagged object processor; technical and office protocol; topology; total other packets; turn-on power
TOPC	time of previous charge; turn-on power controller
TOPS	turn-on power switch
TOS	top octave synthesizer; top of stack

TP	target program; terminal point; test program; thermal printer; time period; token passing; trace program; transaction processing; transducer pulse; transport protocol; trigger pair; trustee path; twisted pair
TPC	twisted pair cable
tpc	tracks per centimeter
TPD	transducer pulse delay
TPDU	transport protocol data unit
TPE	twisted pair EtherNet
TPF	transactions processing facility
TPFG	tapped potentiometer function generator
TPG	time-pulse generator
TPI	ticks per instruction
tpi	tracks per inch
TPL	table producing language; third party lease; transaction processing language
TPLM	twisted pair local module
TPM	tape preventive maintenance; tapped potentio-meter; transactions per minute
TPORT	twisted-pair port transceiver
TPP	test program package; transistor power pack; transmission pre-processor
TPR	total packets routed (*or* routes); total per record
TPS	transactions per second; transaction processing system
TPT	torroid power transformer
TPW	twisted pair wiring

TQFP	thin quad flat package
TQM	total quality management
TR	task register; temperature rating; terminal ready; thermionic relay; token ring; trace; track; traffic; transfer; transfer rate; transfer ratio; transient; transient response; transistor; transmitter
T/R	**TR**; transmit-receive; transmitter-receiver
tr	time rise *(rise time)*
TRA	thermal run-away; token ring adapter
TRADIC	transistorized airborne digital calculator (*or* computer)
TRAN	transient; transistor; transition; translate; translation; translator; transmission; transmitter; transponder; transposition; transputer
TRC	token ring card (*or* controller)
TRF	tuned radio frequency
TRI	test reset input; trigger; trigistor; trigonometry; triple
TRIG	trigger; trigistor; trigonometry
TRL	transistor-resistor logic
TRM	terminal; traffic rate management; trustee rights mask
TRN	threaded read news; token ring network; train(er)
TRP	total received (*or* request *or* routed) packets
TRPC	total received packet counts
TRR	total read requests
TRS	Tandy Radio Shack
TR/SPM	TRSPM; transmitter-receiver, serial-parallel module

TRT   token rotational time; total read time

TRTP   total read transactions performed

TRUN   truncate; truncation

TS   tabulation stop; task state; task swapper; technical support; temporary storage; terminal server; thermal shock; three-state; time schedule; time series; time sharing; time slicing; time stamp; timing signal; timing slip; top secret; total surface; touch screen; transistor seconds; transmission system; trap setting; troubleshooting; turn-key system; two state

TSA   telephony service architecture; temporary storage area; total surface area; town send avalanche; transport service access

TSAP   telephony service application program; transport service access point

TSAPI   telephony service application program interface

TSB   termination status block

TSC   time schedule controller; time shared computer; town send criterion

TSD   terminal security device; time stamp disable; transformer step-down

TSF   tabulation sequential format

TSG   three (*or* triple) state gate

TSI   time slot interchanger

TSIC   time slot inter-changer

TSIDN   target server identification (*or* identifier) number

TSM   total server memory

TSMT	transmit
TSO	three-state output; time sharing option
TSOP	thin small outline package
TSP	technical support package; time-sharing poll(ing); transport service provider
TSPC	true single phase clock
TSR	terminate and stay resident
TSS	task state segment; telephone switching system; text string search; time sharing system; two stable states
TSSI	top secret sensitive information
TSSOP	thin shrink small outline package
TST	television signal transmission; test
TSTD	transponder suppressed time delay
TSTN	triple super-twisted nematic
TSU	transformer step-up; transmission system utilization; transport service user
TT	Tandem transistor; tape track; tape tracker; tape transport; test tube; tetrode transistor; total time; training time; transaction tracking; transceiver tester; transfer table; transfer time; transition time; translation table; transmission technology; transport time; transverse traverse; TrueType; truth table
TTA	transport-triggered architecture
TTAT	track-track access time
TTB	total time blocked
TTD	temporary text delay (*or* display); transducer translating device

TTET   transistor tetrode

TTF   test to failure; TrueType font

TTG   truth table generator

TTL   transistor-transistor logic

TTL-CG   transistor-transistor logic character generator

TTL-IO   transistor-transistor logic input-output

TTL-LC   transistor-transistor logic level clock

TTL-PDC   transistor-transistor logic parallel data connector

TTM   table-top mounting; transistor test meter; tri-state test mode

TTP   thermal-transfer printing; total transactions performed; total transmitted packets

TTPC   total transmitted packets count

TTRT   target token rotation time

TTS   text to speech; transaction tracking support (*or* system)

TTT   total transition time; track to track

TTTL   transistor-transistor-transistor logic

TTTS   track to track converter

TTU   total time used

TTW   teletypewriter

TTY   teletype

TTYC   teletype controller

TU   tape unit; test unit; total units; track unit; tube

TUBR	total unfilled backout requests
TUE	Tuesday
TUI	text-based user interface
TUMS	table update and management system
TUT	tuition; tutor; tutorial
TV	television; total view; trailer value
TVC	tri-axial video connector
TVI	television interference
TVN	transaction volume number
TVOL	television on-line
TVRO	television receive only
TVSOP	thin very small outline package
TW	technical writer; text wrap; transient wave; trap word; travelling wave; twin weave
TWAIN	technology without any interesting name
TWR	total write requests
TWRL	transistor width to ratio length
TWS	three (*or* two) wire system
TWT	total write transactions; travelling wave tube
TWTP	total write transactions performed
TWX	teletypewriter exchange
TX	*transmit(ter)*
TXD	*transmit data*
TXT	text; texture

TZ   track zero; time zone; trigger zone; total zone

TZD   track zero detector

~U~

U	unit; universal; university; uranium; user
u	unit *(of unified atomic mass)*
UA	un-numbered acknowledgement; user agent; user area
UAA	universally administered address
UAC	user access control
UADS	user attribute data set
UAE	unrecoverable application address
UAM	user authentication method
UART	universal asynchronous receiver-transmitter
UARTC	universal asynchronous receiver-transmitter controller
UARTS	universal asynchronous receiver-transmitter simulator
UAWG	universal ADSL working group
UB	unbalance(d)
UBC	unbalanced configuration; universal buffer controller
UBR	unspecified bit rate
UC	umbilical cord; under cut; upper case; used count
UCA	universal cable adapter
UCAID	University Corporation for Advanced Internet Development
UCB	unconditional branch
UCC	unconditional control

UCCT   unconditional control transfer

UCE   uncorrectable error; unsolicited commercial e-mail

UCJ   unconditional jump

UCL   universal communication language

UCPT   Union for the Coordination of the Production and Transport

UCR   under carpet ribbon

UCS   unacknowledged connectioness service; unicode conversion support; universal character set; user coordinate system

UCT   universal cable tester

UCVM   user coded virtual memory

UCWH   U contact wire harness

UD   un-delete; under-damped; undo; uni-directional; update;used directory; user developer; user dictionary; utility debug

UDA   universal data access

UDB   uni-directional bus; universal data buffer; used disk block

UDC   uni-directional current; universal decimal classification; up-down counter; user defined command

UDCM   up-down counter module

UDD   user data document

UDE   universal data exchange

UDEC   universal digital electronic computer

UDF	universal data file; universal disk format; user defined function
UDG	user defined gateway
UDMA	ultra-direct memory access
UDP	uni-directional pulse; user data (*or* diagram) protocol
UDT	uni-directional transfer; uniform data transfer; user data transfer; user definable type
UF	ultra-fiche; unformat; under flow; used file; user friendly
UFC	unformated capacity
UFS	UNIX file system
UFET	unipolar field effect transistor
UG	unity gain; user group
UGF	unity gain frequency
UH	ultra-high
UHCI	universal host controller interface
UHF	ultra-high frequency
UHL	universal hypertext link
UI	UNIX International; un-numbered information; user information; user interface; un-interrupt
UIAS	unbalanced instrumentation amplifier system
UIC	user identification code
UID	unique identifier; user identification (*or* identifier)
UIMS	user interface management system
UIPS	un-interruptible power supply

UJ	unconditional jump
UJT	uni-junction transistor
UK	unknown; United Kingdom *(Great Britain)*
UKE	unknown error
UKEC	unknown error count
UKN	unknown network
UKNC	unknown network count
UL	ultra-large; Underwriters Laboratories; unlisted; up-link; up-load; user library
ULA	uncommitted logic array
ULI	uni-lateral impedance
ULN	universal link negotiation
ULP	upper layer protocol
ULS	ultra-large scale
ULSI	ultra-large scale integration
UM	under modulation; user manual
UMA	unified memory architecture; upper memory area
UMB	upper memory block
UML	unified modelling language
UMP	unit magnetic pole; user micro-program; user microprogrammed processor
UMS	un-modulated signal
UMTS	universal mobile telecommunication system
UN	un-numbered; user network

UNA	un-numbered acknowledgement
UNC	universal naming convention
UNCOL	universal computed oriented language
UNI	un-numbered information; universal; university; user network interface
UNICOM	universal integrated communication
UNICOMS	universal integrated communication system
UNICOS	universal compiler system
UNICS	uniplexed information and computing service *or* UNIX *(where X→CS)*
UNII	unlicensed national information infra-structure
UNIV	universal; university
UNIVAC	universal automatic calculator (*or* computer)
UNIX	uniformity extension; **UNICS**→ uniplexed information and computing service *(where X→CS)*; universal interactive exchange; universal inter-exchange; united nightly in xerophagy
UNM	united network management
UNMA	united network management architecture
UNP	un-numbered poll; unpack
UNPK	unpack
UNSD	universal negotiation and statistical duplexing
UO	unary operation; unary operator
UOC	ultimate operating capability
UP	unpack; uni-processing; uni-processor; un-numbered poll; user program

UPC	uniform (*or* universal) product code
UPD	uni-polar device
UPG	upgrade
UPL	user program language
UPM	UNIX Programmer's Manual; user profile management
UPROMP	universal programmable read only memory programmer
UPS	un-interruptible power supply (*or* system); universal power supply; universal printer stand
UPT	uni-polar transistor
UQ	user questionnaire
UR	universal resource; utility routine
URAE	un-recoverable application address
URC	uniform resource characteristics; universal remote control
UREP	UNIX RSCS emulation protocol
URI	uniform (*or* universal) resource identifier
URL	uniform resource location (*or* locator)
URN	uniform resource name (*or* number)
US	ultra-short; ultra-strip; under-shoot; unit separator; United States (*of America*); unit string; united separator; universal serial; universal system; upper side; up-sizing; user selector
USA	United States of America (*or* U.S.A.)
USABC	United States Advanced Battery Consortium

USART	universal synchronous-asynchronous receiver-transmitter
USASI	United States of America Standards Institute
USB	universal serial bus; upper side-band
USBC	universal serial bus connector
USD	universal startup disk; user selected default
USENET	user network
USERID	user identification
USGE	unbonded strain gauge element
USI	unique security identifier
USNO	United States Naval Observatory
USO	universal service ordering
USOC	universal service ordering code
USP	under-size packet; un-structured program
USRA	universal synchronous receiver-amplifier
USRT	universal synchronous receiver-transmitter
USS	user supported software
USSA	User Supported Software Association
USTP	unshielded twisted pair
USTPC	unshielded twisted pair cable
UT	user terminal; uni-term; universal time; universal timer; universal transistor; up time
UTC	universal time coordinated *(coordinated universal time)*
UTD	uni-tunnel diode

UTI	universal text interchange (*or* interface)
UTM	universal tuning machine; universal Turing machine
UTP	unshielded twisted pair
UU	UNIX to UNIX (*decode* or *encode*); user to user
UUC	UNIX to UNIX copy
UUCP	UNIX to UNIX communication protocol; UNIX to UNIX copy program
UUD	UNIX to UNIX decoding
UUDB	unused disk block
UUE	UNIX to UNIX encoding
UUI	user to user information
UUID	universal unique identifier
UV	ultra-violet
UVA	UDF volume access
UVEL	ultra-violet erasing lamp
UV-EPROM	UVEPROM; ultra-violet erasable programmable read only memory
UVGA	ultimate video graphics adapter (*or* array) *(1024x768 resolution)*
UVR	user visible register
UVSG	ultra-violet safety goggles
UW	unwind
UXGA	ultimate extended graphics array *(1600x1200 resolution)*

~V~

V	value; vanadium; variable; vector; video; voice; volt(age)
VA	value analysis; variable address; vector algebra; video amplifier; virtual address; visual acuity; volt-ampere
VAB	voice answer back
VAC	vaccine; vacuum; volt-ampere characteristic
VAD	value added disk
VADD	value added disk driver
VADSL	very-high-rate asymmetric digital subscriber line
VAH	volt-ampere hour
VAIO	video audio integrated operation
VAL	validation; validity; value; voice application language
VAM	variable area meter; virtual access method; virtual address mode; volt-ampere meter
VAN	value added network
VAP	value added process
VAR	value added reseller (*or* retailer); variable; variance; variant; variation; varistor; volt-ampere reactive
VAS	value added service; virtual address space
VAST	variable array storage technology
VAT	voice altering technology
VAX	virtual address extension

VB	variable block; vertical blanking; very big; video blocking; video box; virtual block; Visual Basic; voice box
VBA	virtual block address; Visual Basic for application
VBE	VESA BIOS extension
VBF	variable block format
VBI	vertical blanking interval
VBL	vertical block line
vBNS	very-high-performance (*or* very-high-speed) backbone network service (*or* VBNS)
VBR	variable bit rate; vector base register
VBRUN	Visual Basic run-time
VBS	vertical blanking signal
VBX	Visual Basic extension
VC	validity check; variable capacitance; variable connector; vector computation; vernier capacitor; video camera; video card; video channel; video circuit; video connection; video control; virtual channel; virtual circuit; voice channel; voice coder; voice coil; voltage comparator; voltage converter; voltaic cell; volume control
VCA	voice coil actuator
VCC	virtual channel connection; voltage controlled clock
VCD	variable capacitance diode; video compact disc; video control device; virtual communication driver
VCF	visual carrier frequency
VCI	virtual channel (*or* circuit) identifier

VCIO	voltage-controlled input-output
VCL	virtual channel link; visual component library
VCM	voice coil motor
VCN	virtual circuit number
VCO	variable cycle operation; voltage controlled oscillator
VCOS	visual caching operating system
VCP	very critical point; video co-processor
VCPI	virtual control program interface
VCPUS	vertical central processing unit stand
VCR	video cassette recorder; voice control register
VCS	virtual circuit subnet; voltage controlled switch
VCSEL	vertical cavity surface emitting laser
VCSN	virtual circuit subnet
VCXO	voltage controlled *crystal* oscillator *(where X→crystal)*
VD	varactor diode; vector diagram; Veitch diagram; Venn diagram; video decoder; video disc; video display; virtual device; visual data; visual display; voltage doubler; voltage drop
VDA	video display adapter; visual data acquisition
VDC	voltage direct current
VDD	virtual device driver
VDDM	virtual device driver manager
VDE	vertical delta encoding; video display editor; visual development environment
VDFM	voice data facsmile *(or* FAX) modem

VDG   video display generator

VDI   virtual device interface; visual display interface

VDISK   virtual disk

VDM   virtual DOS machine

VDMA   virtual direct memory access

VDMAD   virtual direct memory access device

VDP   video display processor; video disc player

VDS   visual display station; volatile dynamic storage

vDSL   very-high-data-rate digital subscriber line (*or* VDSL)

VDSM   very deep sub-micron

VDT   video dial tone; visual display terminal

VDU   visual display unit

VE   variable expense; video editor; video encoder; video enhancer; virtual earth; virtual environment

VEC   vector

VEGA   Video-7 enhanced graphics adapter

VEL   velocity

VEM   virtual expanded memory

VEMM   virtual expanded memory manager

VEMMI   versatile multi-media interface

VER   verification; verifier; verify; version; vision electronic recording

VERA   verify read access

Veronica	**VERONICA**; **v**ery **e**asy **r**odent **o**riented **n**etwide **i**ndex to **c**omputerized **a**rchives
VERW	**ver**ify **w**rite access
VES	**v**ideo **e**diting **s**oftware; **v**ideo **e**ncoding **s**tandard
VESA	**V**ideo **E**lectronics **S**tandards **A**ssociation
VF	**v**ariable **f**ield; **v**ariable **f**ormat; **v**ariable **f**unction; **v**ector **f**eed; **v**ector **f**ield; **v**ector **f**unction; **v**ery **f**ast; **v**ideo **f**ormat; **v**irtual **f**ile; **v**irtual **f**loppy
vf	**VF**; **v**oice **f**requency
VFAT	**v**irtual **f**ile **a**llocation **t**able
vfB	**VFB**; **v**oice **f**requency **b**and
VFC	**v**ideo **f**eature **c**onnector
VFD	**v**acuum **f**luorescent **d**isplay; **v**ariable **f**requency **d**rive
VFG	**v**ariable **f**requency (*or* **f**unction) **g**enerator
VFL	**v**ariable **f**ield **l**ength
VFO	**v**ariable **f**requency **o**scillator
VFR	**v**ector **f**eed **r**ate
VG	**v**ector **g**raphic; **v**ery **g**ood; **v**ideo **g**raphics; **v**isual **g**raphics; **v**oice **g**rade; **v**oltage **g**ain; **v**oltage **g**enerator
VGA	**v**ideo **g**raphics **a**dapter (*or* **a**rray) *(640x480 resolution)*; **v**isual **g**raphics **a**dapter
VGC	**v**ideo **g**raphics **c**ontroller
VGL	**v**oice **g**rade **l**ine
VGTL	**v**oice **g**rade **t**ransmission **l**ine
VH	**v**ery **h**igh; **v**olume **h**ash

VHD	very high density; video high density
VHDL	VHSIC hardware description language
VHF	very high frequency
VHP	very high performance
VHS	very high speed; Video Home System
VHSIC	very high speed integrated circuit
VHSM	very high speed modem
VHX	video highway extreme; Video Highway Xtreme
VI	vector impedance; versatile interface; video image; video input; virtual image; visual interactive; visual interface; voluntary interrupt
VIA	versatile interface adapter; virtual interface architecture
VIC	video input card; volume is cached
VIDA	visual data acquisition
VIDAT	visual data
VIE	virtual information environment
VIF	virtual interface; virtual interrupt flag
VIG	video interface group
VIH	volume is hashed
VIM	video interface module; volume is mounted
VINES	virtual networking system
VIO	video input-output; virtual input-output
VIP	variable information processing; very important process; video information provider

VIPER	verifiable integrated processor for enhanced reliability
VIPS	voice interruption priority system
VIR	virus; virtual; volume is removable
VIS	vector interrupt system; video *(or* voice) information system; visual instruction set
VISS	VHS index search system
VITAL	VHDL initiative towards ASCII libraries
VJ	voltage jump
VL	variable length; very large; very long; video link; virtual library; visual librarian; voltage level; volume label
VLAN	virtual local area network
VLB	VL-BUS; very large block; VESA local bus
VLD	variable length decoder
VLF	very large filter; very low frequency
VLI	variable length instruction; very long instruction
VLINK	visited link
VLIW	very long instruction word
VLM	virtual loadable module
VLP	very large page; virtual library page
VLR	variable length record; very long range *(or* record)
VLS	very large scale
VLSI	very large scale integrated *(or* integration)
VLSIPS	very large scale immobilized polymer synthesis
VLT	variable list table; video lottery terminal

VM	valid memory; vector modulator; vector multiplication; verification mode; video mode; virtual machine; virtual memory; voice mail; volt-meter; voltage memory; voltage multiplier
VMA	valid (*or* virtual) memory address
VMB	virtual machine boot
VMC	variable master clock
VME	Versa Modular Eurocard; virtual memory environment; virtual mode extension
VML	vector markup language
VMM	virtual machine manager; virtual memory machine (*or* manager); virtual multi-meter
VMOS	vertical metal oxide semiconductor
VMP	virtual memory pointer; virtual modem protocol
VMS	versatile memory support; video mode selection; virtual machine (*or* memory) system; voice message system
VMT	virtual memory technique
VN	virtual network; virtual number; volume name; volume number
VNA	virtual network architecture; von Neuman architecture
VNBN	von Neuman bottle-neck
VNC	von Neuman computer
VNT	video networking technology
VO	voice; voice output
VOB	video object

VOC	vocal; voice over carrier
VOCODER	voice coder
VOD	video on demand; voice over data
VODLM	voice over data local multiplexer
VOIP	voice over Internet protocol
VOL	volatile; volume; volume label
VOM	volt-ohm meter (metre); volt-ohm milli-ammeter
VOMAM	volt-ohm milli-ampere meter (metre)
VOP	velocity of propagation
VOR	VHF omni-directional range
VOS	verbal (*or* voice) operating system
VOX	*Latin:* voice
VP	vector potential; vector power; vector processing; vector processor; vector programming; velocity of propagation; vertical parity; vertical polarization; vice president; view port; virtual page; virtual path; virtual printer; visual programming; voice processing; voltaic pile
VPC	vertical parity check; virtual path connection
VPD	virtual printer device; virtual private data
VPDN	virtual private data network
VPDS	virtual private data service
VPE	vapor phase epitaxial; visual programming environment
VPI	vectored priority interrupt; virtual path identifier
VPL	virtual programming language

VPM	video port manager
VPN	virtual page number; virtual private network
VPR	variable point representation
VPS	vacuum plasma spraying; voice processing system
VPT	virtual print technology
VQ	vector quantity
VR	variable resistor; vector ratio; vertical resolution; video recorder; viewing ratio; virtual reality; virtual reliability; voltage reduced; voltage regulator; voltage restricted; voltage restriction
VRAM	video random access memory
V-RAM	variable random access memory
VRC	vertical redundancy check(ing)
VRCP	voice recognition call processing
VRD	voice recognition device; voltage regulator diode
VRE	voltage reduced (*or* regulated *or* restricted) extended
VRFY	verify
VR/L	voltage regulation/load
VRM	virtual reality model; voltage regulator module
VRML	virtual reality markup (*or* modelling) language
VROOMM	virtual real-time object oriented memory manager
VRP	variable resistance pickup
VRPT	variable reluctance pressure transducer
VRR	visual radio range

VRT	voltage reduction (*or* regulation) technology; variable resistance transducer
VS	variable symbol; vertical scanning; vertical scroll; vertical socket; vertical storage; very sensitive; very short; very small; video screen; video select; video server; video signal; virtual storage; virus scan(ning); voltage spike; voltage stabilizer; voltage standard; voltage supply
VSA	very small aperture
VSAM	virtual storage access method
VSAT	very small aperture terminal
VSB	vestigial side-band
VSBT	vestigial side-band transmission
VSC	virus-scan configuration
VSD	voltage supply drain
VSE	virtual storage extended
VSF	vertical scanning frequency
VSG	video sequence generator
VSI	virtual socket interface
VSIO	virtual serial input-output
VSM	virtual shared memory; virtual storage management; visual system management
VSN	volume serial number
VSO	Versa-Modular-Eurocard Standards Organization
VSOS	virtual storage operating system
VSP	virtual software processor

VSPTAP   virtual software processor target application probe

VSR   vertical scanning rate

VSS   virtual storage system

VSU   video start-up

VSW   very short wave; voice sound wave

VSWR   voltage standing wave ratio

VSYNC   vertical synchronization

VT   vacuum tube; vertical; vertical tabulation; video tape; video terminal; virtual terminal; voice technology

VTA   virtual telecommunication access

VTAM   virtual telecommunication (*or* terminal) access method

VTC   vacuum tube computer; vertical tabulation character; virtual tele-communication

VTD   volume tracking driver

VTFC   voltage to frequency converter

VTN   virtual terminal network

VTNS   virtual telecommunication network service

VTOC   visual table of contents

VTP   video tape player

VTR   video tape recorder; vector transfer ratio

VTSRS   voice type speech recognition system

VTT   valid transmission time(r)

VTVM   vacuum tube volt-meter

VUB	virtual un-bundling
VUI	video user interface
VUP	VAX unit of performance
V&V	verification *and* validation
VVT	voice view technology
VWB	visual work-bench
VWL	variable word length
VXD	virtual extended (*or* extension) driver

W	wait; watch; water; watt; wave; week; weight; wet; white; wide; width; wire; wolfram(ium) *(tungsten)*; work; wrist; write
w/	with
W3	WWW; World Wide Web
W4	WWWW; what works with what
WA	wave amplitude; wave analyzer; word area; write addressing; writing analyzer
W3A	world wide web applet
WAAS	wide area augmentation service
WAB	wide area bridge
WABI	Windows application binary interface
WAC	write address counter; write around cache
WACK	wait acknowledgement
WAF	word address format
WAI	web application interface
WAIS	wide area information search (*or* server *or* service)
WAITS	wide area information transfer system
WAMS	wide area measurement system
WAN	wide area network
WAP	wireless application protocol

WAS   Wheatstone automatic system

WAT   West Africa Time

WATS   wide area telecommunication (*or* telephone) service

WAV   wave; wide area view

WB   warm boot; wave band; web sharing; white balance; write-back

Wb   weber

WBC   wide-band coder; write-back cache

WBEM   web-based enterprise management

WBF   wide-band frequency

WBFM   wide-band frequency modulation

WBFSK   wide-band frequency shift key(ing)

WBM   Windows bit-maps

WBT   wide-band transmission

WBTL   wide-band transmission line

WC   wave carrier; wave-length converter; wild card; wire-cutter; word comparator; word count; worst case; write-compute

W3C   WWWC; World Wide Web Consortium

WCC   worst case circuit

WCCA   worst case circuit analysis

WCD   worst case design

W-CDMA   WCDMA; wide-band code division multiple access

WCN   worst case noise

WCNP	worst case noise pattern
WCR	word count register
WCS	World Coordinate System; writable control store (*or* system); writing control store
WCT	word comparator time
WD	watch-dog; Western Digital; Winchester disk; winding drive; work distribution
WDC	Western Digital Corporation; work distribution center
WDD	Winchester disk drive; write deleted data
WDDC	watch-dog destroyed connection
WDF	wave distribution function
WDIO	watch-dog is on
WDL	Windows driver library
WDM	wave-length division multiplexing
WDMA	wave-length division multiple access
WDMAP	wave-length division multiple access protocol
WDP	watch-dog program
W-DRAM	WDRAM; Windows dynamic random access memory
WDT	Winchester disk track
WDTF	Winchester disk track format
WE	wall energy; Western Electric; write enable; write error
WebNFS	web network file system
WEC	write error count

WED	Wednesday; word error display
WELD	web-based electronic design
WER	word error rate
WF	wave-form; wave function; write forward
WFA	wave-form analyzer
WFG	wave-form generator
WFM	wave-form monitor; wired for management
WFT	Wiltalk File Transfer
WFW	Windows for Workgroups
WG	wave guide; wave generator; wire gauge; word generator; work group
WGC	work group concentration
WGN	white Gaussian noise
WGNP	white Gaussian noise process
WGS	work group system
WH	watt-hour; wiring harness; wiring hub; write head
WHAM	waveform hold and modify
WHC	work-station host connection
WHR	web-sites to hosts ratio
WHT	Walsh-Hadamard transform; white
WI	waste instruction; wire in; write in
WIM	wireless instant messaging
WINE	Windows emulator
WINF	wireless information networks forum

WINS	Windows Internet naming service
WINSOCK	Windows sockets
WISE	Windows information system environment
WISP	wireless Internet service provider
WIT	web interactive talk
WK	week; work
WKB	work-book
WKS	weeks
WKT	Weiner-Khintchine theorem
WL	waiting list; wave length; wire line; wire-less; word length; word line; write lock
WLAN	wireless local area network
WLC	wave-length converter; wire line carrier
WLIC	wall-less ionization chamber
WLL	wireless local loop
WLT	wire-less transmission
WM	watt-meter; width modulation; word mark; write multiple
WMAN	wireless metropolitan area network
WMC	write multiple command
WMF	Windows meta-file
WML	wireless markup language
WMO	write micro-operation
WMP	width modulation pulse

WN	white noise
WNIC	wide-area network interface co-processor
WNIM	wide-area network interface module
WO	wear-out; work output; wire-out; write-out
w/o	without
WOF	wear-out failure
WOL	wake-up on LAN
WOQ	work output queue
WORM	write once read many
WOROM	WO/ROM; write only read only memory
WOS	Windows operating system; word organized storage; work-station operating system
WOSA	Windows operating service (*or* system) architecture
WP	wafer package; wall paper; wall plate; wired program; wiring pencil; word pattern; word processing; word processor; WordPerfect; write policy; write protect; write pulse
WPBM	writer per bit minute
WPC	wired program computer
WPD	Windows printer description
WPHD	write-protect hard disk (*or* drive)
WPM	Windows pixel-maps; words per minute; WordPerfect macro
WPOS	work-place operating system
WPS	Windows printing system; work-place shell

WPVM	Windows parallel virtual machine
WR	whisker resistance; working register; write; write-read; writing rate
WRAM	Windows random access memory
WRI	write
WRK	Windows resource kit
WRMS	web reception monitoring service
WRU	who are you *(news-group)*
WS	waiting state; Wall Street; wave shape; word size; WordStar; work station; work space; working storage; wrist strap; writing speed
W/S	WS; workmanship standard
W3S	WSSS; work station session socket
WSAPI	web site application program interface
WSAS	Wheatstone automatic system
WSB	Wheatstone bridge; write sector buffer
WSE	web sharing extension
WSH	washer; Windows scripting host
WSI	wafer scale integration
WSL	white stripe laser
WSLP	white stripe laser problem
WSM	wasted server memory
WSS	wedge servo-system
WSSS	W3S; work station session socket

WST	Wheatstone transmitter
WSWS	word section word select
WT	waiting time; wave theory; Williams tube; World Time; write through
WTJ	waiting time jitter
WTL	wide-band transmission line
WTS	word terminal synchronous
WTV	web television
WUT	warm-up time
WV	write verify
WVP	web video phone
WVS	write verify sector
WW	wire wrap; word wrap; world wide
WWB	wire wrapped board
WWIS	world wide information system
WWM	wire wrapped module
WWN	world wide network
WWP	wire wrapped panel
WWS	wire wrapped socket
WWSB	wire wrapped socket board
WWT	wire wrapped tool
WWW	W3; World Wide Web
WWWA	world wide web applets
WWWC	W3C; World Wide Web Consortium

WWWVL   World Wide Web Virtual Library

WWWW   what works with what (*or* W4); world wide web worm

WXGA   wide extended graphics array

WYSBYGI   what you see before you get it

WYSIWYG   what you see is what you get

X	exchange; *reactance*; *speed*; *times*; *trans-* X-ray
XA	extended address(ing); extended architecture; extended attribute
XAE	extended arithmetic element
XAPIA	X.400 Application Program Interface Association
X2B	hexadecimal *to* binary
XC	external copy
X_C	*reactance* of capacitvie *(capacitance reactance)*
X2C	hexadecimal *to* character
XCHG	exchange
XCK	extender card kit
XCMD	external command
XCOPY	extended copy
XD	external data; external delay; external device
X2D	hexadecimal *to* decimal
XDC	external device code
XDF	extended density format
XDR	external data representation
XDS	Xerox data system
xDSL	*all types of* digital subscriber line *(where x→ all types of)*
Xe	Xenon

XEC	execute; executed; execution
XEM	external event module
XFCN	external function
XGA	extended graphics array *(1024x768 resolution)*
XI	external icon; external interrupt
XID	exchange identification *(or identifier)*
XIO	execute input-output
XIOS	extended input-output system
XIP	execute in place; execute instruction pointer
XL	Excel; external label; extra large; extra long
X_L	*reactance* of *inductive* *(inductive reactance)*
XLAT	*translate (where X→ trans)*
XLL	extensible link language
XM	extended memory; external modem; extra memory
XMI	XML meta-data interchange
XMIT	*transmit (where X→ trans)*
XML	extensible *(or* extensive) markup language
XMM	extended memory manager
XMS	extended memory specification
XMT	*transmit (where X→ trans)*
XMTR	*transmitter (where X→ trans)*
XN	execution node
XNOR	exclusive NOR *(gate)*

XNS	Xerox network system
XOFF	*trans*mitter **off** *(where X→ trans)*
XON	*trans*mitter **on** *(where X→ trans)*
XOR	exclusive **OR** *(gate)*
XP	experience
XPRM	Xerox print resources manager
XQL	extensible query language
XQLM	extensible query language manager
XR	extension register; X-ray
XREF	*cross* reference *(where X→ crosss)*
XRS	external reference synchronization
XRT	extension for real-time
XSL	extensible style language
XSM	extended storage module
XSMD	extended storage module driver
XT	extended technology; extension
XTAL	external crystal *(where X→ crys)*
XTCLK	external transmit clock
XTND	extend(ed)
XTP	express transfer protocol
Xu	x unit
XV	external voice
XVT	extensible virtual tool-kit; external voltage

~Y~

Y	*admittance*; *luminance*; year; yellow; yes; yolk; yotta; yttrium
y	yellow; yocto
YAHOO	yet another hierarchically officious oracle
YAM	yet another modem
YAP	yield analysis pattern
YB	year book; yellow book
Yb	ytterbium
YC	Y-circuit
YEL	yellow
Y2K	year *2000 (where 2K →2000)*
YIG	yttrium-iron-garnet
Y/N	yes/no
YP	yellow page
YTC	yield-to-call
YTD	year-to-date
YUV	*luminance* ultra-violet

~Z~

Z	*impedance*; zetta; zero; zone
z	zepto
ZA	zero add; zero adjust
ZAA	zero and add
ZAI	zero address instruction
ZAK	zero administration kit
ZAM	zero address machine
ZAS	zero access storage
ZAW	zero administration for Windows
ZB	zero beat; zero bit; zone bit
ZBD	zener break-down
ZBID	zero bit insertion-deletion
ZBR	zero (*or* zone) bit recording
ZC	zener current; zero capacity; zero compression; zero crossing; zero cut
ZCAV	Z-CAV; zoned constant angular velocity
ZCC	*impedance* control circuit; zero cut crystal
ZCD	zero crossing detector
ZCDC	zero crossing detector circuit
ZCI	zata code indexing
ZCR	zero crossing rate

ZD	zener diode; zero delay; zero dispersion; zero detection; zone digit
ZDC	zener diode coupling
ZDL	zero delay line (*or* lockout *or* loop)
ZDP	zero dispersion point
ZDR	zener diode regulator
ZDS	Zenith Data Systems
ZDW	zero dispersion wave-length
ZDWL	zero dispersion wave-length
ZE	zero; zero emission; zero error; zoo event
ZER	zero; zero error reference
ZF	zero field; zero fill; zero force
ZFE	zero forcing equalizer
ZG	zero gradient
ZGS	zero gradient synchrotron
ZGV	zero gate voltage
ZGVDC	zero gate voltage drain current
ZI	zero input; zero insertion
ZIF	zero insertion force
ZIP	zipped; zipper; zipping; zig-zag in-line package; zone information protocol; zone improvement plan
ZL	zero level; zero load; zone level; zone levelling
ZLA	zero level addressing
ZM	zero maintenance

Zn	*Zincum* (*Latin:* zinc)
ZO	zero-ohms; zero output
ZOA	zero-ohms adjustment
ZP	zero page; zero paging; zero phase; zero potential; zero power; zero pulse; zero pulsing
ZPA	zero page addressing
ZPL	zero power level
ZPR	zero power reactor (*or* resistance)
ZPV	zoomed port video
ZR	zener; zero rate
Zr	Zirconium
ZRE	zero rate error
ZS	zero sensitive; zero slope; zero stability; zero suppression
ZSL	zero slot LAN
ZT	zero tension; zero time; zero tolerance; zero transmission; Zulu Time
ZTL	zero transmission level
ZTLRP	zero transmission level reference point
ZV	zener voltage; zero variance; zero voltage
ZW	zero wait
ZWC	zero word count
ZWS	zero wait state
ZZ	zig-zag

ZZL   zig-zag line

ZZLC   zig-zag line chart

APPENDIX A:
TABLE OF OVERSEAS OPERATING VOLTAGES

Territory	VOLTS (AC)
• Australia; Kuwait; Malta; New Zealand; Northern Ireland; Papua New Guinea; Oman; Qatar; United Kingdom.	240
• Israel; Pakistan; Singapore.	230
• India, South Africa.	220 - 250
• Austria; Belgium; Denmark; Finaland; France; Germany; Greece; Italy; Luxembourg; Netherlands; Norway; Spain; Sweden; Switzerland.	220 - 230
• Bahrain; Chile; China; Czechoslovakia; Egypt; Geenland; Hungary; Iceland; Iran; Jordan; Liechtenstein; Napal; Paraguay; Poland; Romania; Russia and the Commonwealth of Independent States; United Arab Emirates; Yemen; Yugoslavia.	220
• Açores; Angola; Brasil *(north)*; Cabo Verde; São Tomé e Príncipe; Cabinda; Goa, Damão, Diu; Guinea Bissau; Macau; Madeira; Moçambique; Portugal; Timor Leste.	220
• Algeria; Indonesia; Libanon; Libya; Peru; S.Korea; Vietnam.	220 *or* 100
• Hong Kong.	200
• Brasil *(south)*; Columbia; Mexico; Saudi Arabia.	127
• Bermuda; Canada; Puerto Rico; United States; Venezuela.	120
• Ecuador; Jamaica; Phillipines; Taiwan.	110
• Japan.	100

IMPORTANT NOTES:

1) In some countries, you may have dual voltages. Upon arrival to a destination, if you are not sure which voltages you have, check with your electricity supply company before plugging in your computer or any other electrical equipment.

2) If your computer has a dual power selector switch, to operate your computer set, it is advisable that for any voltages between 100VAC and 130VAC, set the voltage switch to 115VAC; and between 200VAC and 270VAC, set it to 230VAC. If you are not sure what to do, check with your authorized computer dealer or a qualified electrician, before making any changes.

APPENDIX B:
SI ELECTRICAL CHARACTERISTICS SYMBOLS

Quantity	Symbol	Basic Unit
Admittance	Y	siemens (S)
Angle (plane)	rad	radian (rad)
Angle (solid)	sr	steradian (sr)
Capacitance	C	farad (F)
Celsius (temperature)	°C	Celsius (°C)
Charge	Q or q	coulomb (C)
Conductance	G or g	siemens (S)
Current	I or I	ampere (A)
Force	N	newton (N)
Frequency	f	hertz (Hz)
Illuminance	lx	lux (lx)
Impedance	Z	ohm (Ω)
Inductance	L	henry (H)
Luminous flux	lm	lumen (lm)
magnetic flux	Wb	weber (Wb)
Period	T	second (s)
Power	P	watt (W)
Reactance	X	ohm (Ω)
Resistance	R or r	ohm (Ω)
Susceptance	B	siemens (S)
Voltage	V or v	volt (V)

Note: Capital letters **I, Q, V** are generally used for a peak, rms, or DC value; small letters **i, q, v** are used for instantaneous values. Small **r** and **g** are used for internal values.

APPENDIX C:
SCIENTIFIC USAGE OF GREEK ALPHABET

Capital letter	Small letter	Name	Usage
A	α	alpha	α for alpha particles; angles; transistor characteristics.
B	β	beta	β for angles; beta ray; transistor characteristics.
Γ	γ	gamma	γ for gamma ray; gamma mass; photon; surface tension.
Δ	δ	delta	Δ and δ for small change in value; Δ for prism diopter.
E	ε	epsilon	ε for base of natural logarithm; electric field intensity; electromotive force; permittivity
Z	ζ	zeta	-
H	η	eta	η for efficiency; viscosity (dynamic)
Θ	θ	theta	Θ and θ for phase angle.
I	ι	iota	-
K	κ	kappa	κ for kaon.
Λ	λ	lamda	λ for wave-length; volume; Λ for lambda particle.
M	μ	mu	μ for amplification factor; magnetic momentum; mass absorption coefficient; micro-; micron; modulus; muon; permeability; population mean; viscosity. amplification factor.
N	ν	nu	ν for degrees of freedom; frequency; viscosity (kinematic); neutrino; reluctivity.
Ξ	ξ	xi	Ξ for xi particle.
O	o	omicron	-
Π	π	pi	π is 3.1416... for ratio of circumference to diameter of a circle; osmotic pressure; Π for product symbol.
P	ρ	rho	ρ for correlation coefficient; density; resistivity; rho particle.

Σ	σ	sigma	σ for 1/1000 of a second; conductivity; cross-section; standard deviation; surface tension; Σ for sigma particle; sigmoid; sigmoidoscopy; summation.
T	τ	tau	τ mean life; time constant; torque; transmittance.
Y	υ	upsilon	-
Φ	φ	phi	Φ and φ for angles; electric potential; file; luminous flux; magnetic flux.
X	χ	chi	-
Ψ		ψ	psi
Ω		ω	omega

APPENDIX D:
COMMON DECIMAL SI PREFIX SYMBOLS

The following prefixes are used to indicate decimal multiples and submultiples of SI units.

Prefix	Symbol	Factor
yotta	Y	10^{24}
zetta	Z	10^{21}
exa	E	10^{18}
peta	P	10^{15}
tera	T	10^{12}
giga	G	10^{9}
mega	M	10^{6}
kilo	k	10^{3}
hecto	h	10^{2}
deka (*or* deca)	da	10^{1}
unit		$10^{0} = 1$
deci	d	10^{-1}
centi	c	10^{-2}
milli	m	10^{-3}
micro	μ	10^{-6}
nano	n	10^{-9}
pico	p	10^{-12}
femto	f	10^{-15}
atto	a	10^{-18}
zepto	z	10^{-21}
yocto	y	10^{-18}

APPENDIX E:
LATIN/ROMAN NUMERICAL SYMBOLS

Latin	Roman	Latin	Roman
0			
1	I	30	XXX
2	II	40	XL
3	III	50	L
4	IV	60	LX
5	V	70	LXX
6	VI	80	LXXX
7	VII	90	XC
8	VIII	100	C
9	IX	200	CC
10	X	300	CCC
11	XI	400	CD
12	XII	500	D
13	XIII	600	DC
14	XIV	700	DCC
15	XV	800	DCCC
16	XVI	900	CM
17	XVII	1000	M
18	XVIII	2000	$\overline{\text{M}}$M
19	XIX	5000	$\overline{\text{V}}$ *(see note)*
20	XX	10000	$\overline{\text{X}}$ *(see note)*
21	XXI	100000	$\overline{\text{C}}$ *(see note)*
22	XXII	1000000	$\overline{\text{M}}$ *(see note)*

Note: A line placed over a Roman letter increases its value by one thousand times.

APPENDIX F:
E-MAIL AND NEWSGROUP SMILEY FACES

In E-mail and Newsgroup "emoticons " *or "* Smiley Faces" are
used rather than words to express feelings. They are created using the
alphanumeric
of the keyboard.

Note: Put your left ear on your left shoulder to see the emoticons!

O:-)	Angel	[:]	Robot
(:-)	Bald	(:-$	Sick
|-O	Bored	(:-(	Sad
~:O	Baby	:-!	Smoker
:-}	Bearded person	:-)	Smile
:*)	Clown	:-X	Sealed-lips
:-#	Censored	:-]	Smirk
:-X	Close-mouthed	:-D	Talkative
:/)	Disgusting	:-?	Tasty
X-(	Dead; Died	:-T	Tight-lipped
:-)))	Fat	;-&	Tongued-tied
[ ]	Hug	:-(	Unhappy
:-**	Kisses	8-)	Wears Glasses
>:->	Leer	;-)	Wink; Winking
:-D	Laughing	`-)	Wink; Winking
:-||	Mad	*and*	
+<:-|	Nun; Monk	(^Y^)	Announcement
:-O	Open-mouthed	<g>	Grin
@--->---	Rose	<jk>	just kidding
>---		(-_-)	Secret Smile

John S. DeSousa, B.S.E.E., M.S.E.E.

ALPHABETICAL COMMENTS ABBREVIATIONS:

AFAIK	as far as I know
AKA	also known as
BRB	be right back
BTW	by the way
CFV	call for votes
FAQs	frequently asked questions
FOAF	friend of a friend
IMHO	in my humble (*or* honest) opinion
LOL	laughing out loud
Netiquette	network etiquette
OTOH	on the other hand
RFD	request for discussion
ROFL	rolling on floor, laughing
ROTF	rolling on the floor
TIA	thanks in advance
TLA	three letter acronym

APPENDIX G:
E-MAIL COUNTRY CODE
TO LOCATE ORIGIN OF AN E-MAIL

The two-letter abbreviations assigned to country names and which are used in addresses on the Internet are shown below. This list should be useful when checking the original destination of the E-mail received.

Part I: Listings By Country Code:

aa	Aruba	bo	Bolivia
ad	Andorra	br	Brasil (Brazil)
ae	United Arab Emirates	bs	Bahamas
af	Afghanistan	bt	Bhutan
ag	Antigua and Barbuda	bv	Bouvet Island
ai	Anguilla	bw	Botswana
al	Albania	by	Belarus
am	Armenia	bz	Belize
an	Antilles	ca	Canada
ao	Angola	cb	Cambodia *(unofficial code)*
ar	Argentina	cc	Cocos Islands
as	American Somoa	cd	Congo, Democratic Republic
at	Austria	cf	Central African Republic
au	Australia	cg	Congo
aw	Aruba	ch	Switzerland
az	Azerbaijan	ci	Cote D'Ivoire (Ivory Coast)
ba	Bosnia-Herzegovina	ck	Cook Islands
bb	Barbados	cl	Chile
bd	Bangladesh	cm	Cameroon
be	Belgium	cn	China
bf	Burkina Faso	co	Colombia
bg	Bulgaria	cr	Costa Rica
bh	Bahrain	cu	Cuba
bi	Burundi	cv	Cabo Verde (Cape
bj	Benin		Verde)
bm	Bermuda	cx	Christmas Island
bn	Brunei Darussalam	cy	Cyprus

423

cz	Czech Republic	gs	S.Georgia &
de	Germany		S.Sandwich islands
dj	Djibouti	gt	Guatemala
dk	Denmark	gu	Guam
dm	Dominica	gw	Guinea-Bissau
do	Dominican Republic	gy	Guyana
dz	Algeria	hk	Hong Kong
ec	Ecuador	hm	Heard & McDonald
ee	Estonia		Islands
eg	Egypt	hn	Honduras
eh	Western Sahara	hr	Croatia-Hrvatska
er	Eritrea	ht	Haiti
es	Spain	hu	Hungary
et	Ethiopia	id	Indonesia
fi	Finland	ie	Ireland
fj	Fiji	il	Israel
fk	Falkland Islands	in	India
	(Malvinas)	io	Indian Ocean Territory
fm	Micromedia-Federated		(British)
	States	iq	Iraq
fo	Faroe Islands	ir	Iran
fr	France	is	Iceland
fx	France, Metropolitan	it	Italy
ga	Gabon	jm	Jamaica
gb	Great Britian	jo	Jordan
	(England)	jp	Japan
gd	Grenada	ke	Kenya
ge	Georgia	kg	Krygyzstan
gf	Guiana-French	kh	Cambodia (official
gh	Ghana		code)
gi	Gibraltar	ki	Kiribati
gl	Greenland	km	Comoros
gm	Gambia	kn	Saint Kitts & Nevis
gn	Guinea	kp	Korea-North
gp	Guadeloupe	kr	Korea-South
gq	Guinea-Equatorial	kw	Kuwait
gr	Greece	ky	Cayman Islands
		kz	Kazakhstan

la	Laos	np	Nepal
lb	Lebanon	nr	Nauru
lc	Saint Lucia	nt	Neutral Zone
li	Liechtenstein	nu	Niue
lk	Sri Lanka	nz	New Zealand
ls	Lesotho	om	Oman
lt	Lithuania	pa	Panama
lu	Luxembourg	pe	Peru
lv	Latvia	pf	Polynesia-French
ly	Libya	pg	Papua New Guinea
ma	Morocco	ph	Phillipines
mc	Monaco	pk	Pakistan
md	Moldova	pl	Poland
mg	Madagascar	pm	St. Pierre & Miquelon
mh	Marshall Islands	pn	Pitcairn
mk	Macedonia	pr	PuertoRico
ml	Mali	pt	Portugal
mm	Myanmar	pw	Palau
mn	Mongolia	py	Paraguay
mo	Macau	qa	Qatar
mp	Mariana Islands-Northern	re	Reunion
mq	Martinique	ro	Romania
mr	Mauritania	ru	Russia-Russian
ms	Montserrat		Federation
mt	Malta	rw	Rwanda
mu	Mauritius	sa	Saudi Arabia
mv	Maldives	sb	Solomon Islands
mw	Malawi	sc	Seychelles
mx	Mexico	sd	Sudan
my	Malaysia	se	Sweden
mz	Moçambique (Mozambique)	sg	Singapore
na	Namibia	sh	St. Helena
nc	New Caledonia	si	Slovenia
ne	Niger	sj	Svalbard & Jan Mayen Islands
nf	Norfolk Island	sk	Slovakia
ng	Nigeria	sl	Sierra Leone
ni	Nicaragua	sm	San Marino
nl	Netherlands (Holland)	sn	Senegal
no	Norway	so	Somalia

sr	Suriname	va	Vatican
st	São Tomé e Príncipe	vc	St. Vincent & the Grenadines
su	Soviet Union *(former)*	ve	Venezuela
sv	El Salvador	vg	Virgin Islands (British)
sy	Syria	vi	Virgin Islands (US)
sz	Swaziland	vn	Vietnam
ta	Tunisia	vu	Vanautu
tc	Turks & Caicos Islands	wf	Wallis & Futuna Islands
td	Chad	ws	Samoa
tf	French Southern Territories	ye	Yemen
tg	Togo	yt	Mayotte
th	Thailand	yu	Yugoslavia
tj	Tajikistan	za	South Africa
tk	Tokelau	zm	Zambia
tm	Turkmenistan	zr	Zaire Congo Democratic Republic
tn	Tunisia	zw	Zimbabwe
to	Tonga		
tp	Timor Leste (East Timor)		
tr	Turkey		
tt	Trinidad & Tobago		
tv	Tuvalu		
tw	Taiwan		
tz	Tanzania		
ua	Ukraine		
ug	Uganda		
uk	United Kingdom (England)		
um	US Minor Outlying Islands		
us	United States		
uy	Uruguay		
uz	Uzbekistan		

Part II: Listings By Country Name:

Afghanistan	**af**	Cambodia (*unofficial code*)	**cb**
Albania	**al**	Cameroon	**cm**
Algeria	**dz**	Canada	**ca**
American Somoa	**as**	Cayman Islands	**ky**
Andorra	**ad**	Central African Republic	**cf**
Angola	**ao**	Chad	**td**
Anguilla	**ai**	Chile	**cl**
Antigua and Barbuda	**ag**	China	**cn**
Antilles	**an**	Christmas Island	**cx**
Argentina	**ar**	Cocos Islands	**cc**
Armenia	**am**	Colombia	**co**
Aruba	**aa**	Comoros	**km**
Aruba	**aw**	Congo	**cg**
Australia	**au**	Congo, Democratic Republic	**cd**
Austria	**at**	Cook Islands	**ck**
Azerbaijan	**az**	Costa Rica	**cr**
Bahamas	**bs**	Cote D'Ivoire (Ivory Coast)	**ci**
Bahrain	**bh**	Croatia-Hrvatska	**hr**
Bangladesh	**bd**	Cuba	**cu**
Barbados	**bb**	Cyprus	**cy**
Belarus	**by**	Czech Republic	**cz**
Belgium	**be**	Denmark	**dk**
Belize	**bz**	Djibouti	**dj**
Benin	**bj**	Dominica	**dm**
Bermuda	**bm**	Dominican Republic	**do**
Bhutan	**bt**	Ecuador	**ec**
Bolivia	**bo**	Egypt	**eg**
Bosnia-Herzegovina	**ba**	El Salvador	**sv**
Botswana	**bw**	Eritrea	**er**
Bouvet Island	**bv**	Estonia	**ee**
Brasil (Brazil)	**br**	Ethiopia	**et**
Brunei Darussalam	**bn**	Falkland Islands (Malvinas)	**fk**
Bulgaria	**bg**	Faroe Islands	**fo**
Burkina Faso	**bf**	Fiji	**fj**
Burundi	**bi**	Finland	**fi**
Cabo Verde (Cape Verde)	**cv**	France	**fr**
Cambodia (*official code*)	**kh**	France, Metropolitan	**fx**

French Southern Territories	**tf**	Korea-North	**kp**
Gabon	**ga**	Korea-South	**kr**
Gambia	**gm**	Krygyzstan	**kg**
Georgia	**ge**	Kuwait	**kw**
Germany	**de**	Laos	**la**
Ghana	**gh**	Latvia	**lv**
Gibraltar	**gi**	Lebanon	**lb**
Great Britian (England)	**gb**	Lesotho	**ls**
Greece	**gr**	Libya	**ly**
Greenland	**gl**	Liechtenstein	**li**
Grenada	**gd**	Lithuania	**lt**
Guadeloupe	**gp**	Luxembourg	**lu**
Guam	**gu**	Macau	**mo**
Guatemala	**gt**	Macedonia	**mk**
Guiana-French	**gf**	Madagascar	**mg**
Guinea	**gn**	Malawi	**mw**
Guinea-Bissau	**gw**	Malaysia	**my**
Guinea-Equatorial	**gq**	Maldives	**mv**
Guyana	**gy**	Mali	**ml**
Haiti	**ht**	Malta	**mt**
Heard & McDonald Islands	**hm**	Mariana Islands-Northern	**mp**
Honduras	**hn**	Marshall Islands	**mh**
Hong Kong	**hk**	Martinique	**mq**
Hungary	**hu**	Mauritania	**mr**
Iceland	**is**	Mauritius	**mu**
India	**in**	Mayotte	**yt**
Indian Ocean Territory (British)	**io**	Mexico	**mx**
Indonesia	**id**	Micromedia-Federated States	**fm**
Iran	**ir**	Moçambique (Mozambique)	**mz**
Iraq	**iq**	Moldova	**md**
Ireland	**ie**	Monaco	**mc**
Israel	**il**	Mongolia	**mn**
Italy	**it**	Montserrat	**ms**
Jamaica	**jm**	Morocco	**ma**
Japan	**jp**	Myanmar	**mm**
Jordan	**jo**	Namibia	**na**
Kazakhstan	**kz**	Nauru	**nr**
Kenya	**ke**	Nepal	**np**
Kiribati	**ki**	Netherlands (Holland)	**nl**

Neutral Zone	**nt**	Slovakia	**sk**
New Caledonia	**nc**	Slovenia	**si**
New Zealand	**nz**	Solomon Islands	**sb**
Nicaragua	**ni**	Somalia	**so**
Niger	**ne**	South Africa	**za**
Nigeria	**ng**	Soviet Union *(former)*	**su**
Niue	**nu**	Spain	**es**
Norfolk Island	**nf**	Sri Lanka	**lk**
Norway	**no**	St. Helena	**sh**
Oman	**om**	St. Pierre & Miquelon	**pm**
Pakistan	**pk**	St. Vincent & the Grenadines	**vc**
Palau	**pw**	Sudan	**sd**
Panama	**pa**	Suriname	**sr**
Papua New Guinea	**pg**	Svalbard & Jan Mayen Islands	**sj**
Paraguay	**py**	Swaziland	**sz**
Peru	**pe**	Sweden	**se**
Phillipines	**ph**	Switzerland	**ch**
Pitcairn	**pn**	Syria	**sy**
Poland	**pl**	Taiwan	**tw**
Polynesia-French	**pf**	Tajikistan	**tj**
Portugal	**pt**	Tanzania	**tz**
PuertoRico	**pr**	Thailand	**th**
Qatar	**qa**	Timor Leste (East Timor)	**tp**
Reunion	**re**	Togo	**tg**
Romania	**ro**	Tokelau	**tk**
Russia-Russian	**ru**	Tonga	**to**
Federation		Trinidad & Tobago	**tt**
Rwanda	**rw**	Tunisia	**ta**
S.Georgia & S.Sandwich islands	**gs**	Tunisia	**tn**
Saint Kitts & Nevis	**kn**	Turkey	**tr**
Saint Lucia	**lc**	Turkmenistan	**tm**
Samoa	**ws**	Turks & Caicos	**tc**
San Marino	**sm**	Islands	
São Tomé e Príncipe	**st**	Tuvalu	**tv**
Saudi Arabia	**sa**	Uganda	**ug**
Senegal	**sn**	Ukraine	**ua**
Seychelles	**sc**	United Arab Emirates	**ae**
Sierra Leone	**sl**		
Singapore	**sg**		

United Kingdom (England)	**uk**
United States	**us**
Uruguay	**uy**
US Minor Outlying Islands	**um**
Uzbekistan	**uz**
Vanautu	**vu**
Vatican	**va**
Venezuela	**ve**
Vietnam	**vn**
Virgin Islands (British)	**vg**
Virgin Islands (US)	**vi**
Wallis & Futuna Islands	**wf**
Western Sahara	**eh**
Yemen	**ye**
Yugoslavia	**yu**
Zaire → Congo Democratic Republic	**zr**
Zambia	**zm**
Zimbabwe	**zw**

Internet Domains:

COM	= Commercial	**INT**	= International	**ORG**	= Organization
EDU	= Education	**MIL**	= Military		
GOV	= Government	**NET**	= Network		

APPENDIX H:
SI WEIGHTS AND MEASURES

LENGTH

unit	symbol	equivalent
centimeter	cm	0.393 inch
decameter (dekameter)	dam	32.81 feet = 393.7 inches
decimeter	dm	3.937 inches
dekameter (decameter)	dam	32.81 feet = 393.7 inches
hectometer	hm	109.36 yards = 328.08 feet
kilometer	km	0.621 miles
meter	m	39.37 inches = 3.28 feet
millimeter	mm	0.039 inch
myriameter	mym	6.21 miles

AREA/LAND

unit	symbol	equivalent
are (100 square metres)	a	119.6 square yards
centiare (1 square metre)	cent.; sq. m	1549.9 square inches
hectameter (100 ares; hectare)	ha; sq. hec	2.471 acres
hectare (100 ares; hectametre)	ha; sq. hec	2.471 acres
square centimeter	cm^2; sq. cm	0.15499 square inch
square decimeter	dm^2; sq. dm	15.499 square inches

square dekameter	dam^2; sq. dek	393.7 square inches
square kilometer	km^2 ; sq. km	0.3861 square mile = 247.1 acres
square meter	m^2; sq. m	1549.9 square inches = 1.196 yard
square millimeter	mm^2; sq. mm	0.00155 square inch

VOLUME/CAPACITY

unit	symbol	equivalent
centiliter	cl; cL	0.6 cubic inch = 0.338 fluid ounce
cubic centimeter	c.c.; cm^3	0.06102 cubic inch = 3.53 cubic feet
cubic decimeter	c.d.	61.023 cubic inches = 0.0353 cubic foot
cubic decameter	Dm^3	353.14 cubic feet = 13.08 cubic yards
cubic meter	c.m.; m^3	35.314 cubic feet = 1.308 cubic yards
deciliter	dl; dL	6.102 cubic inches = 0.18 pint (d); 0.21 pint (l)
dekaliter (decaliter)	dal; daL	0.35 cubic foot = 2.64 gallons = 1.14 pecks
hectoliter	hl; hL	3.53 cubic feet = 26.418 gallons = 2.84 bushels (l)
kiloliter	kl; kL	1.307 cubic yards = 264.18 gallons = 35.315 cubic feet
liter	l; L	61.02 cubic inches = 0.908 quart (l); 1.057 quarts (d)
milliliter	ml; mL	0.061 cubic inch = 0.27 fluid dram
stere	st	35.314 cubic feet = 1.308 cubic yards

Note: (d) = dry; (l) = liquid

MASS AND WEIGHT

unit	symbol	Grams	equivalent
1 centigram	cg	0.01	0.1543235 grain = 0.000353 ounce
1 decagram (dekagram)	dag	10	154.3235 grain = 0.3527 ounce
1 decigram	dg	0.1	1.543235 grain
1 dekagram (decagram)	dag	10	154.3235 grain = 0.3527 ounce
1 gram	g; gm	1	15.43235 grain = 0.0352 ounce
1 hectogram	hg	100	15432.23 grain =3.574 ounces
1 kilogram	kg	1000	15432.35 grain = 2.2046 pounds
1 metric ton	Mt; t	1000000	1.1 tons = 2204.6 pounds
1 milligram	mg	0.001	0.01543235 grain
1 myriagram	myg	10000	22.046 pounds
1 quintal	q	100000	220.46 pounds

UNITS OF ENERGY

unit	equivalent
1 Calorie	1 kilocalorie = 1000 calories = 4184 Joules
1 Calorie	4.26649×10^7 gram-centimeters = 3085.96 foot-pounds
1 Joule	0.2386 Calorie = 0.2386 kilocalorie
1 gram/centimeter	980.665 dynes/centimeter
1 foot-pound	13558200 ergs = 13825.5 grams-centimeters

UNITS OF TIME

second (s); minute (m); hour (h); day (d)

1 millisecond = 1/1000 of a second = 0.001 second
1 second = 1/60 of a minute = 0.001667 minute
1 minute = 1/60 of an hour = 0.001667 hour
1 hour = 1/24 of a day = 0.041667 day

UNITS OF TEMPERATURE

Celsius (°C); Fahrenheit (°F); Kelvin (°K); Rankine (°R)

$$°C = (°F-32) \times 5/9 = 0.5556 \times (°F-32)$$
$$°F = (°C \times 9/5) + 32 = 1.8 \times °C + 32$$
$$°K = °C + 273.15$$
$$°R = 459.67 + °F$$

Note: Celsius Degrees are equivalent to Centigrade Degrees.

Quick Reference

1 CUP	=	8 ounces					
1 PINT	=	2 cups	=	16 ounces			
1 QUART	=	2 pints	=	4 cups	=	32 ounces	
1 GALLON	=	4 quarts	=	8 pints	=	16 cups	= 96 ounces

APPENDIX I:
US SPELLED WORDS *VERSUS*
INTERNATIONAL ENGLISH

Some of the following words which are used in this book, show their spelling in International English versus US. Both spelling types are seen used in USA.

US	International	US	International
analog	analogue	kilometer	kilometre
analyze	analyse	leveling	levelling
analyzer	analyser	license	licence
catalog	catalogue	linearization	linearisation
centigram	centigramme	liter	litre
centiliter	centilitre	metalization	metalisation
centimeter	centimetre	meter	metre
center	centre	milligram	milligramme
color	colour	milliliter	millilitre
decagram	decagramme	millimeter	millimetre
decameter	decametre	miniaturization	miniaturisation
decigram	decigramme	modeling	modelling
deciliter	decilitre	myriagram	myriagramme
decimeter	decimetre	optimized	optimised
defense	defence	optimization	optimisation
dekagram	dekagramme	organization	organisation
dekaliter	dekalitre	packetized	packatised
dekameter	dekametre	packetize	packetise
dialog	dialogue	packetizing	packetising
diameter	diametre	parameterization	parameterisation
fiber	fibre	program	programme
gram	gramme	quantization	quantisation
hectogram	hectogramme	quantizing	quantising
hectoliter	hectolitre	standardization	standardisation
hectometer	hectometre	traveling	travelling
kilogram	kilogramme	tunneling	tunnelling
kiloliter	kilolitre	vapor	vapour

APPENDIX J:
INSPIRATION AND MOTIVATION WORDS

1. If everything is under control, you are going too slow.

2. Do not set your goals by what other people deem important. Only you know what is best for you!

3. Do not dismiss your dreams. To be without dreams is to be without hope; to be without hope is to be without purpose.

4. Do not be afraid to encounter risks. It is by taking chances that we learn how to be brave.

5. Success usually comes to those who are too busy to be looking for it.

6. Take a chance! All life is a chance. The person who goes the furthest is generally the one who is willing to do and dare.

7. A failure establishes only this, that our determination to succeed was not strong enough.

8. My philosophy is that not only are you responsible for your life, but doing the best at this moment puts you in the best place for the next moment.

9. The difference between the impossible and the possible lies in a person's determination.

10. Be absolutely clear about who you are and what you stand for. Refuse to compromise!

11. Determination is the wake-up call to the human will.

12. It is not how much we do, but how much love we put in the doing. It is not how much we give, but how much love we put in the giving.

13. Patience, persistence and perspiration make an unbeatable combination for success.

14. Patience can never be imposed on you from outside. It is your own inner Wealth, Wisdom, Peace and Victory.

15. There is no beauty but the beauty of action!

16. Success is never wondering what **if!**.

17. The difference between the impossible and the possible lies in a person's determination.

18. Success is not measured by what you accomplish but by the opposition you have encountered, and the courage with which you have maintained the struggle against overwhelming odds.

19. Creativity means believing you have greatness. Nothing happens until you make it happen.

20. People rarely succeed unless they have fun in what they are doing.

21. The first and most important step toward success is the feeling that we can succeed.

22. All our dreams can come true - if we have the courage to pursue them.

23. I attribute my success to this - I never gave or took any excuse.

24. Failure will never overtake me if my determination to succeed is strong enough.

25. I am only one, but still I am one. I cannot do everything, but still I can do something; and because I cannot do everything I will not refuse to do the something that I can do.

26. Always bear in mind that your own resolution to succeed is more important than other.

27. There are defeats more than triumphant and victories.

28. It is possible to fail in many ways. While to succeed is possible only in one way.

29. Real success is finding your lifework in the work that you love.

30. Try not to become a person of only success but rather to become a person of value with success!

31. **Natural Talent + Opportunity = Success.**

32. You are on the road to success when you realize that failure is only a detour.

33. You have not failed until you quit trying.

34. Failure is <u>Not</u> my Destiny.

35. I cannot give you the formula for success, but I can give you the formula for failure which is: Try to please everybody.

www.ingramcontent.com/pod-product-compliance
Lightning Source LLC
Chambersburg PA
CBHW051220050326
40689CB00007B/744